Sacraments
Signs of Our Faith

Principal **Consultants**

Dennis J. Bozanich, MBA

Michael Carotta, EdD

Rev. Leonard Wenke, MDiv

Principal **Reviewers**

Mary Lee Becker, MPM

Robert J. Kealey, EdD

M. Annette Mandley-Turner, MS

Harcourt
Religion Publishers

Nihil Obstat
Rev. Richard L. Schaefer
Censor Deputatus

Imprimatur
✠ Most Rev. Jerome Hanus, OSB
Archbishop of Dubuque
January 31, 2001
Feast of Saint John Bosco, Patron of Youth and Catholic Publishers

The nihil obstat and imprimatur are official declarations that a book or pamphlet is free of doctrinal or moral error. No implication is contained herein that those who granted the nihil obstat and imprimatur agree with the contents, opinions, or statements expressed.

Our Mission
The primary mission of Harcourt Religion Publishers is to provide the Catholic and Christian educational markets with the highest quality catechetical print and media resources. The content of these resources reflects the best insights of current theology, methodology, and pedagogical research. These resources are practical and easy to use, designed to meet expressed market needs, and written to reflect the teachings of the Catholic Church.

Photography Credits
AP Wide World Photos: Paul Sakuma: 98; **Art Resource:** Erich Lessing: 66; Museo Pio Christiano, Vatican Museums, Vatican State: 87; **Timothy Boone:** 5; **The Crosiers:** Gene Plaisted: 6, 7, 12, 16, 44, 61, 88; **Digital Imaging Group:** Erik Snowbeck: 16, 36, 45, 65, 78; **Jack Holtel:** 4, 10, 17, 25, 26, 28, 29, 40, 54, 88, 99; **Image Bank:** Ken Huang: 78; Vicky Kasala: 34; Tom Stewart: 70; Paul J. Sutton: 62; Mari Taglienti: 96; **Wolfgang Kaehler:** 89; **Liaison International:** James D. Wilson: 21; **The Merton Legacy Trust:** Sibylle Akers: 38; **National Catholic Youth Conference,** St. Louis, Missouri 1999/National Federation for Catholic Youth Ministry, Inc., Washington, DC: 19; **Nicholas Studios:** Nick Falzerano: 64, 95; **PictureQuest:** PhotoEdit/Michael Newman: 42; Stock Boston/Spencer Grant: 76; Stock Boston/Lawrence Migdale: 67; Woodfin Camp & Associates/Anthony Howarth: 57; **PhotoEdit:** Robert Brenner: 46; Myrleen Ferguson Cate: 8, 61, 84; Tom Freeman: 58; Tony Freeman: 34, 39, 46, 48, 98; Spencer Grant: 75; Micheal Newman: 25, 35, 47, 96; Jonathan Nourok: 17, 74; Alan Oddie: 24, James Shaffer: 69; David Young-Wolfe: 34, 78, 82, 96, 101; **Photo Researchers:** Jeff Greenberg: 38; Renee Lynn: 6; Lawrence Migdale: 22; **Stock Boston:** Dorothy Littell Greco: 85; **The Stock Market:** Ronnie Kaufman: 50, 72; Dilip Mehta: 8; Gabe Palmer: 102; David Woods: 72; **Stone:** Z & B Baran: 74; Myrleen Ferguson Cate: 49; Stewart Cohen: 77; Walter Hodges: 15; Kevin Horan: 80; Philip & Karen Smith: 32; James Strachan: 94; Zigy Kaluzny: 90; **Superstock:** 36, 56: **Jim Whitmer Photography:** Jim Whitmer: 14, 48; **W. P. Wittman Photography:** Bill Wittman: 5, 47, 68, 86

Cover Photos
AGI Photographic Imaging; Cleo Photography; Jack Holtel

Feature Icons
Catholics Believe: Jack Holtel; **Opening the Word:** PictureQuest; **Our Christian Journey:** PictureQuest: Chuck Fishman/Contact Press Images

Location and Props
Dayton Church Supply; St. Christopher Catholic School, Vandalia, OH; St. Peter Catholic School, Huber Heights, OH

Printed in the United States of America

ISBN 0-15-900542-6
10 9 8 7 6 5

LIVING Our FAITH
Sacraments
Signs of Our Faith

What We Believe About Adolescent Religious Education and *Living Our Faith*

Foundational Concepts of *Living Our Faith*

We believe that formation in faith is a lifelong journey, undertaken in community and guided by the Spirit.

We believe that young adolescents can make a unique contribution to the Church community and to the world.

We believe that the family is the primary community in which faith, Christian values, and life skills are shared and nurtured. The whole Church community, beginning at the parish level, is a partner with the family in helping form young adolescent Catholics.

Program Philosophy

We believe that the young person is the starting point of adolescent catechesis— that he or she has a story to tell, hopes and aspirations to be encouraged, and experiences to share.

> So *Living Our Faith* meets young adolescents where they are, with materials that honor their experiences and invite them to grow in their faith.

We believe that a vital goal of young adolescent faith formation is the development of young people's relationship with God and their development into confident and competent members of their families, Church communities, and society.

> So *Living Our Faith* incorporates a unique Christian skills dimension into text lessons and family materials, providing young people (and the adults with whom they share their lives) the opportunity to acquire, develop, and practice important skills of religious experience, gospel living, moral decision making, forecasting, and emotional management. These skills have been proven to add to young people's ability to apply what they know and believe and to give them confidence and competence in all areas of their lives.

We believe that all catechesis—but especially the catechesis of young adolescents— must be marked by a profound attention to relationships and by an understanding of the unique nature and needs of adolescents.

> So *Living Our Faith* encourages young people to exercise peer ministry, to take the initiative in leading class discussions and prayer, and to become involved in mentoring relationships (both as learners and as mentors themselves) within the faith community. A key dimension of *Living Our Faith* is the relational nature of the Leader's Guide, which provides direction for classroom teachers and catechists to become involved in a truly interactive journey with young people.

We believe that the faith formation of young people does not occur in isolation but both affects and is affected by the family experience.

So *Living Our Faith* materials help young people make the connection between religious education and the home. Leader's Guides help teachers and catechists maintain open communication with the families of the young adolescents. And *Living Our Faith* includes a special Family Resource that encourages adult family members to reinforce Christian life skills with their young adolescents.

We believe that young adolescents should evaluate their culture from a Christian standpoint, make responsible critical decisions, and act to make a difference in the world.

So *Living Our Faith* provides young people with the tools to evaluate the messages they receive from their peers, the media, and the larger culture and to measure those messages against Christian values. *Living Our Faith* also capitalizes on the energy and idealism of young people by offering practical opportunities for outreach, service, and witness for justice.

We believe that young people deserve to hear the good news of Jesus Christ in its fullness, shared with authenticity, and that they are capable of understanding and integrating the key content of the Christian message.

So *Living Our Faith* texts are based on the foundational themes of our Catholic faith and present fundamental teachings in ways designed to engage and challenge the young adolescent. Lessons integrate doctrine, worship, morality, prayer, community, and active participation in the Church's life and mission as outlined in the *Catechism of the Catholic Church, Renewing the Vision,* and the *General Directory for Catechesis.*

We believe that young adolescents benefit from access to our rich Catholic heritage of Scripture, ritual, and tradition, as well as to the cultural and spiritual diversity of the universal Church.

So *Living Our Faith* incorporates opportunities for young people to become more familiar with Scripture and how it can inform their lives, to explore and make the treasures of Christian ritual and spirituality their own, and to recognize the gifts of wonder, respect, and solidarity in the diversity of the Church and the world.

Skills for Christian Living

Young adolescents are faced with many new responsibilities and choices. To give them the tools they need to make wise decisions, *Living Our Faith* incorporates a unique program-wide skills dimension. Over the course of the program, the students are introduced to five different skill areas: Religious Experience, Moral Decision Making, Emotional Management, Gospel Living (or Justice and Service), and Forecasting. Within each of these skill areas, specific Skills for Christian Living help the students understand and apply the behaviors they will need to live a healthy and virtuous life.

Religious Experience skills help improve our ability to communicate with God. They strengthen the *vertical*, or religious, dimension of spirituality. The six skills of Religious Experience are *How to Pray, Recognizing God's Presence, Keeping the Lord's Day, Applying the Bible Message, Using Religious Imagination,* and *Celebrating.*

Moral Decision Making skills help improve our ability to relate to one another. They strengthen the *horizontal* direction of spirituality. The six skills of Moral Decision Making are *Social Analysis, Forming a Conscience, Being Accountable, Examining Conscience, Confronting,* and *Discerning What Is Right.*

Emotional Management skills strengthen the *internal* dimension of spirituality by helping us deal with strong feelings that have a direct impact on our moral life. The six skills of Emotional Management are *Staying Hopeful, Handling Anger, Lamenting, Expressing Affection, Dealing with Anxiety,* and *Letting Go.*

Gospel Living skills touch on all three dimensions of spirituality. The six skills of Gospel Living are *Practicing Empathy, Reconciling, Giving Thanks, Offering Solidarity, Honoring the Body,* and *Resolving Conflict.*

Forecasting skills help us anticipate situations and take initiative for the next step. These skills help us move out of a passive and reactionary mode and into a more active and productive mode. The skills touch on all three dimensions of spirituality. The six skills of Forecasting are *Goal Setting, Keeping Promises, Identifying Consequences, Choosing Good Friends, Making Changes,* and *Reverencing the Ordinary.*

The Family Resource

Families should be an integral partner in the students' skill development. To help foster this interaction, a supplementary book titled *Living Our Faith: Nurturing the Spiritual Growth of Your Adolescent* has been created for parents and guardians to use with their children.

The Challenge of Young Adolescents: Evangelization, Catechesis, and Discipleship

Dennis J. Bozanich, MBA

Few experiences in life are as humbling as hearing from your thirteen-year-old, "Dad, that was back then; things are different now. *Please,* catch up." It really doesn't matter whether you are talking about the price of sports equipment, the appropriateness of certain entertainment choices, or the resurrection of Jesus. All of us who are actively engaged in a relationship with a young adolescent have experienced the challenge of offering them anything "old-fashioned" enough to be put into a book. I have some good news for you: We don't have to allow faith development to be simply a "back then" process. It can and should be something that is truly alive.

The challenge in catechizing early adolescents today is that we need to stop being teachers and become missionaries. The first thing good missionaries do when encountering a new culture is to learn as much as they can about the language, art, symbols, history, personalities, and needs of that particular group. Good missionaries build a *relationship* with the people, never judging or criticizing. Only after a trusting relationship is built will an effective missionary offer the people the good news.

This process of evangelization with young people also involves a clear proclamation of our own commitment to Jesus and an invitation to experience the conversion and discipleship of a relationship with Jesus. We should not take for granted that the sacraments are a guarantor of conversion. The "new evangelization" proclaimed by Pope John Paul II for the third Christian millennium is specifically for those who have been baptized but have not been converted to a trusting relationship with God. Many young people need us for just this reason.

Following conversion, we must nurture the spirit of the young adolescent through catechesis. As teachers and catechists, we must offer young people the opportunity to see faith as more than a simple recipe to be followed. To build a trusting relationship with God means embarking on a journey of questions and answers. As we learn new life skills, we discover the answers to many of our original questions. But at the same time, we uncover new, and sometimes more difficult, questions. We need to help foster this sense of discovery in young people, while recognizing that our own journey continues.

Finally, our efforts are not complete until we can help incorporate young people into the mysteries of the Christian life. This emphasis on discipleship is critical for young adolescents today because most truly learn only by "doing." As adults we can communicate to young people that they will be learning, growing, and adding skills as new moments in their relationships with God occur. Our classrooms or meeting spaces may need to stretch to become practice facilities for these young disciples.

I sincerely hope that nothing offered here is too overwhelming for you. It is meant to challenge you. Today, start in some small but concrete way to address the challenges of our young adolescents. Tomorrow, pick another small but concrete way, and the next day do the same thing. Together we will be signs of the reign of God.

Dennis Bozanich has served as Associate Director for Youth and Young Adult Ministries for the Diocese of San Jose, the Director of Young Adult Outreach and Adult Faith Formation for the Diocese of Santa Rosa, and the Director for the Office of Youth and Young Adult Ministries for the Diocese of Phoenix. He also served on the parish and diocesan level in the Archdiocese of Los Angeles and on the Board of Directors for the National Federation for Catholic Youth Ministry, Inc. He is the proud father of three young adolescents.

Teaching Skills for Spiritual Growth

Michael Carotta, EdD

The key to solid adolescent catechesis today is a two-handed approach that develops religious knowledge and invests a great deal of effort promoting specific behaviors. This approach embraces the spirituality of today's young adolescents more fully than past efforts, which often focused only on imparting knowledge.

So how do we begin? We can start by reclaiming some of the time-honored Christian practices that model the teachings of Jesus and help us experience his presence. Honoring the body, visiting the sick, keeping the Lord's Day, prayer, and fasting are just a few examples of Christian practices.

Think about which aspects of adolescent life would be called to light just by discussing one Christian practice, such as honoring the body. You would find that catechesis around this one Christian practice would open up discussions related to sexual activity, smoking, substance abuse, eating disorders, sleep deprivation, overextended scheduling, body piercing, music, movies, alcohol, clothing, hygiene, exercise, and nutrition.

While adolescent catechesis that includes a focus on Christian practices produces rich, relevant discussions, we must not stop there. We can teach young people about such behaviors, but we need to help them learn how to do these things more consistently.

For example, we can teach adolescents about the value of the Christian practice of prayer. We can even share how the practice of prayer has helped us in our own lives, thus helping them develop a positive attitude toward prayer. We can show them what Jesus taught—and what the Church teaches—about prayer, thereby increasing their knowledge.

However, we need to go one step further and teach them *how to pray.*

When we encourage these Christian practices, we help young adolescents develop a three-dimensional spirituality—one that includes a vertical dimension, a horizontal dimension, and an internal dimension. Skills that help us improve the way we relate to God enhance our vertical, or religious, spirituality. Skills that improve the way we treat other people affect our horizontal, or moral, spirituality. Finally, skills that help us handle the things that hurt inside enrich our internal, or emotional, spirituality.

In *Living Our Faith* thirty different skills are introduced and reinforced that together help adolescents build a three-dimensional spirituality. Skills related to religious experience will help young people improve their communication with God. Skills related to gospel living and moral living will help them practice discipleship and morality. Forecasting skills will introduce them to how they can anticipate situations and take initiatives to avoid unwanted consequences. Skills related to emotional management will show them how they can deal with a variety of strong feelings that can have a direct effect on their moral life.

This added focus on the skills involved in Christian practice is new. You are not expected to be an expert. And these skills will not automatically change young people's lives. But they can help take you and your students to a place of new conversations, specific behaviors, and greater expectations regarding what it means to live as Jesus did.

Dr. Michael Carotta has worked with adolescents for more than twenty-five years as a teacher, administrator, catechist, diocesan consultant, researcher, author, and volunteer. He spent four years with at-risk youth as the Director of Religious Education at Girls and Boys Town in Omaha, Nebraska. He was also the first layperson to serve as Executive Director of the NCEA's Department of Religious Education in Washington, D.C. He and his wife, Cathy, have three children and live in Louisville, Kentucky.

The Parish Community—Its Role in Catechesis

Rev. Leonard Wenke, MDiv

The parish is the community in which the average person and his or her family experience the Church—all its history, aspirations, and pretensions. This community is where we experience the rhythms of life through birth, marriage, illness, death, and so much more. The impressions made at these times are often lasting impressions that shape what we think "the Church" is all about.

The role of the parish in faith development is essential, so much so that the *General Directory for Catechesis* reminds us that "Catechesis is the responsibility of the entire Christian community" (*General Directory for Catechesis*, 1997). In familiar words, *It takes an entire village to raise a child.* Each parish must foster a common responsibility within the community for catechesis. It must provide for planning, promote formation of catechists, and seek to work cooperatively by promoting freedom and trust.

The parish must always remember that "Family catechesis . . . precedes, accompanies and enriches all other forms of catechesis" (*On Catechesis in Our Time*, 1979). Parents are witnesses of Christian life, and they are the ones most often present during the times of religious awakening in their children. For this reason the community must give special attention to the role and formation of parents.

Parishioners' days are filled with things to do and places to go. Their lives are jam-packed, and they are almost always running late. Beneath all of this activity, something else is going on, a deep longing or sense of unfulfillment. Catechesis must find its place within this world of activity and develop a process that invites, forms, and instructs.

Parish leaders are called to help one another (and the parish community) discover who God is and what the reign of God is all about. A gracious God unconditionally loves us. God's love restores every human to his or her personal dignity. Discovering that God's loving presence is at the core of our being and in our daily lives is our principal task. The praxis Jesus calls us to is a liberating, saving reality.

If the reign of God and the praxis of Jesus truly guide our ministry, we must always remember that catechesis is not about indoctrinating or controlling but about formation. It is "faith seeking understanding." It is freeing people from their fears and alienation and facilitating their personal encounter with God so they can live to the full in the liberating joy of the kingdom.

The process used for the catechumenate in our parishes should serve as an inspiration. This process demands that parishes sometimes rethink their approach and models for catechesis. An effective process should include love, community building and creative hospitality, storytelling or personal witness, sharing of the tradition, engaging and reflective worship, and opportunities for an apprenticeship as disciples. Time is a key ingredient. There are no short cuts or quick recipes. Neither will lots of unconnected activity likely help. Even programs such as *Living Our Faith* can go only so far. We must be creative and adapt our curriculum to the unique circumstances of our parish.

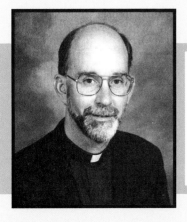

Father Len Wenke is presently pastor of Saint Anthony Church in Cincinnati, Ohio. Father Wenke served as faculty member and chaplain at Carroll High School in Dayton, Ohio, from 1979 to 1982; was Archdiocesan Director of Youth Ministry from 1982 to 1991; and executive director for the National Federation for Catholic Youth Ministry, Inc., from 1991 to 1997. He has regularly led workshops and days of reflection on issues related to youth ministry.

Living Our Faith Program Themes

The six themes that comprise *Living Our Faith* can be customized to fit many different schedules and grade levels. Each theme is self-contained, allowing you the flexibility to select how and when you teach specific information. Together the titles create a dynamic religious education series for young adolescents.

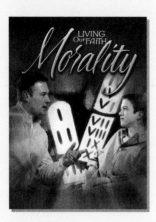
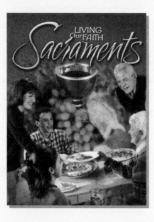
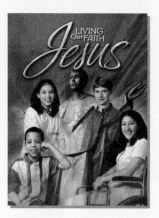

Morality
Challenges and Choices

Morality invites the students to reflect on their values, self-image, and relationships. As the subtitle suggests, each day brings new opportunities to live out our faith. The decisions we make determine who we are and who we will become.

Morality: Challenges and Choices helps the students understand that, as Catholics, we have been called to

- make responsible and respectful choices.
- develop and maintain a positive self-image.
- open ourselves to God's will as we begin to explore our future vocation.
- learn from Scripture, from the Church, and from one another.
- respect our sexuality as a gift from God.
- share the loving message of the gospel with others.

Sacraments
Signs of Our Faith

How do we practice and express our faith? What does it mean to be Catholic? In *Sacraments* the students will explore how the Church celebrates the seven sacraments and how we experience the effects of the sacraments in our daily lives.

Sacraments: Signs of Our Faith helps the students understand that as people of faith we celebrate

- through rituals and rites.
- the grace of God and the power of the Holy Spirit.
- the saving mystery of Jesus' suffering, death, and resurrection.
- Baptism, Confirmation, and Eucharist, which are the Sacraments of Christian Initiation.
- Reconciliation and the Anointing of the Sick, which are the Sacraments of Healing.
- Matrimony and Holy Orders, which are the Sacraments of Service.

Jesus
Word Made Flesh

Jesus Christ is the center of our faith. His words teach us, his faith guides us, and his sacrifice brought us forgiveness of sins and eternal life. In *Jesus* the students will discover how Jesus Christ—as Teacher, Healer, Prophet, and Savior—continues to inspire our lives.

Jesus: Word Made Flesh helps the students understand the importance of

- Scripture, through which we learn about the Father, Son, and Holy Spirit.
- Mary as the mother of Jesus and the Mother of God.
- accepting and sharing the gospel message.
- living virtuously as Jesus taught us.
- Christ's saving action, the Paschal mystery.
- a vital and ever-present prayer life.

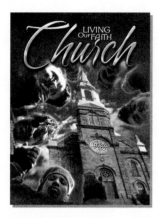

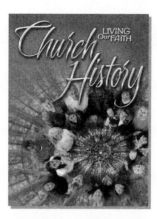

Church
A Community of Faith

We are a community of believers and a community of faith. Together we share in the history and tradition of Christ's Body. *Church* highlights the various ways we express and celebrate our Catholic faith.

Church: A Community of Faith helps the students understand that our Church is

- one, holy, catholic, and apostolic.
- rooted in the words and actions of Jesus and the apostles.
- led by the magisterium and nourished by the family, the domestic Church.
- expressed through our faithful words and actions.
- a celebration of a worldwide community that includes the entire communion of saints.
- part of salvation history that will continue until Christ returns.

Church History
Our Christian Story

Church History tells the story of our Church from the events of the Old Testament to the role of the Church in today's society. Like our personal histories, the history of the Church is filled with hope and despair, kindness and cruelty, crisis and reconciliation.

Church History: Our Christian Story helps the students understand that the history of the Church includes

- a foundation in the lives of the apostles.
- persecution by those who do not understand or who are threatened by Jesus' message.
- leadership in matters of faith and culture.
- challenges to the Church's beliefs and practices.
- prayerful review and reflection of the Church's message.
- evangelization of the gospel message throughout the world.

God
Revelation and Relationship

How do you imagine God? Each of us has a slightly different view of him, which is part of our personal faith. Regardless of *how* we experience God, though, we are each called to recognize his power and celebrate his love for us.

God: Revelation and Relationship helps the students understand that God is

- the Father, Son, and Holy Spirit.
- a mystery of faith.
- the Creator of all things, seen and unseen.
- revealed to us through salvation history, through Scripture, and fully in Jesus.
- present to us through the actions of the Holy Spirit.
- available to us through prayer, both private and communal.

Program Features

Living Our Faith is designed to engage and challenge young adolescents. A variety of interactive features help the students understand and explore the content of the chapter.

Features

What Do You Think? is a personal pre-assessment activity completed by the students as they begin the chapter.

Opening the Word provides thematically relevant Scripture passages along with reflection questions. Those passages that are part of the Lectionary cycle are noted for the students.

Catholics Believe includes a summary statement from the *Catechism of the Catholic Church*. Space is also provided for the students to reflect on how the statement affects their faith journey.

Our Christian Journey contains information about specific people, places, or events important to the history of the Church.

Media Message asks the students to review the media they enjoy in a way that helps illuminate the chapter.

Rite Response includes background to specific Catholic rites and practices.

Our Global Community presents a unique cultural event, group, or custom relevant to the chapter theme.

Focus On highlights specific information discussed in the text.

Wrap Up summarizes the key points from the material covered in the chapter and allows the students to write any questions they have.

Around the Group presents a discussion-starting question that extends the material presented in the chapter.

Briefly asks the students how the chapter has called them to reconsider their reactions and responses to the chapter theme.

Special Features

Student Leader Connection—This optional activity is unique to *Living Our Faith*. It gives the students the opportunity to share their talents and insights through individual presentations and by leading group discussions. (See page L15 for more information.)

Faith Partnerships—Through one-on-one partnerships this optional activity encourages the students to discover more about their faith and the faith of their peers. (See page L15 for more information.)

Reflecting on Your Faith—This feature allows you, the teacher or catechist, to join in the same personal faith journey experienced by the students. You will be asked to reflect on questions that help explore and develop your personal faith.

Liturgical Lessons—To help the students understand the importance of the liturgical year, *Living Our Faith* includes activity lessons based on the various Church Seasons. (See page R1 for more information.)

Using the Leader's Guide

Preparing to Teach

Preceding each chapter are two teacher Planning Pages. These pages help you prepare for and structure your lesson.

Before you teach each chapter,
- take time to review the Planning Pages.
- read through the lesson pages.
- make notes on the steps you will follow and the optional activities you will use.
- gather any necessary materials.
- preview additional resources.

Planning Chart

The planning chart provides an easy-to-follow outline of the chapter. Chapter content is broken down into four sections—*Open, Search, Reflect,* and *Live.* A Pacing Guide provides suggested times for covering this material, but you are free to adapt the pace to your own needs. Also included in the planning chart are a list of the chapter's objectives and a materials list.

Catechism in Context

This section of the Planning Pages provides a brief reflection on the doctrinal content of the chapter, keyed to the Catechism paragraph referenced in the chapter's *Catholics Believe* feature. You are encouraged to read the particular paragraph from the *Catechism of the Catholic Church* to add to your own understanding.

One-Minute Retreat

This section offers you a way to prepare yourself spiritually to teach the chapter.

A thought-provoking quotation focuses on the chapter theme. A reflection question helps you look at the chapter theme as it is lived out in your own experience. Finally a brief prayer invites God to be with you as you teach.

Library Links

This section of the Planning Pages offers annotated suggestions for additional resources tied to the chapter theme, including

*Books for Adolescents—These may be used by the students for independent reading. They are available in libraries, through publisher's catalogs, or in bookstores.

*Books for Adults—These resources add to your understanding of the chapter topic. Adult resources may also be shared with the students' families. Like the books for adolescents, these books are available in libraries, through publishers' catalogs, or in bookstores.

Multimedia—This section lists videotapes, audiotapes, and CD-ROMs relevant to the chapter's theme. They are available from catalogs or diocesan or parish media centers.

***Note:** *Youth Update* and *Catholic Update* are single-topic newsletters published by St. Anthony Messenger Press. They may be ordered at bulk rates from the publisher.

Feature Preparation

This section helps you prepare for the Student Leadership activities, the Faith Partnerships, and the skill lesson features of the chapter.

Teaching a Chapter

Lesson Pages

The lesson pages of this Leader's Guide take you through a chapter in an easy-to-follow process. Each lesson page contains a core lesson plan and a Resource Center area with optional activities and background information.

The Core Lesson Plan

Each chapter's core lesson plan is divided into four developmental steps:

Sections:

> *Open*—This section lays the groundwork for the chapter.
>
> *Search*—This section explores the chapter theme, especially through Scripture, the Catechism, Church history, and personal reactions and responses.
>
> *Reflect*—This section helps the students review the information presented in the *Search* section through personal reflection, group discussion, and activities.
>
> *Live*—This section presents the chapter's skill lesson.

Features of the Core Lesson Plan:

> Key Points from the Previous Chapter—A review of the material covered during the previous session
>
> Gathering—Suggestions for bringing the students together to share the lesson
>
> Prayer—Reminder to share the opening prayer and the closing prayer
>
> Working with the Text and Pictures—Strategies for working with the concepts and images presented on the page
>
> Working with the Activity—Strategies for working with the various text features (for example, *Opening the Word* and *Media Message*)
>
> Working with the Skill—Strategies for working with the skill pages

The Resource Center

This section contains background features, teaching tips, and optional activities to extend and enrich the core lesson material.

Features of the Resource Center:

> Prayer Environment—Suggestions for creating and maintaining a prayer space
>
> Vocabulary—Definitions of key vocabulary terms presented in the pupil text
>
> Background (including Scripture Background and Art Background)—Additional information on key material that will be helpful for students
>
> Links to other subject areas—Suggestions for linking the discussion to subjects such as science, social studies, liturgy, and family
>
> Teaching Tip—Suggestions for managing lessons, clarifying content, handling sensitive topics, and answering questions
>
> Multiple Learning Styles—Strategies for adapting teaching situations to the various learning styles and pedagogical needs of the students
>
> Extension Activity—Activities that can be used to extend and enhance the lesson
>
> Skill Note—Opportunities for you to discuss the skill that is part of the chapter (See page L15 for more information.)
>
> Faith Partnerships—Suggestions for guiding the discussion of the chapter's Faith Partners

Teaching the Skills

Each Skill for Christian Living has been divided into two lessons. In the first lesson (presented in the odd-numbered chapters) the students are asked to learn about and evaluate their use of the skill. The second lesson (presented in the even-numbered chapters) allows the students to practice and extend their knowledge of the skill. Each skill lesson provides several opportunities for the students to practice the skill. As you present the lesson, remind the students that they should look for ways to incorporate the skill into their daily lives.

Using the Skill Notes (S)

Skill Notes have been provided within the Resource Center of each chapter and are marked with the Skill Note icon. To help you locate the appropriate student text, a corresponding icon has been placed on the reduced student page. Refer to the various Skill Notes as you teach the skill lesson to illustrate the different ways we can experience and use the Skills for Christian Living.

Using the Student Leader Feature

The optional Student Leader activity invites individual students to play an important (but supervised) role as a group leader. Because each learning situation is different, it is up to you to determine how best to use the Student Leader. He or she can research additional information relating to the chapter, lead group discussions, or present small reports on people or events mentioned in the chapter.

Typically one Student Leader is assigned per chapter, though you can modify this depending on your situation. Student Leader Prep pages have been included to provide possible chapter-specific activities. (See page R1 of this book.) The Student Leader Connection, an abbreviated version of the Prep pages, appears on the left-hand Resource Center page throughout the chapter as a prompt and a reminder should you choose to incorporate this activity.

Note: Often the role of a Student Leader will require him or her to prepare materials for the group ahead of time. Therefore, it is recommended that you meet with the student before the appointed session to review his or her role and assignment.

Creating Faith Partnerships

An optional feature of *Living Our Faith,* Faith Partnerships are pairs of students who meet periodically throughout the chapter to discuss how the content is reflected in their personal faith experiences. Faith Partnerships provide an important opportunity for the students to share their thoughts outside of the large-group format. Faith Partners are assigned by the teacher or catechist and remain together for two consecutive chapters. If you choose to incorporate this feature, Faith Partner Introductions have been provided at the beginning of the odd-numbered chapters and Faith Partnership prompts are provided in the Resource Center of each chapter.

Using the Check Mark ✓

Time is often limited, especially in a parish group setting. To help you focus your lesson, a check mark has been used to call out the essential questions, statements, activities, and features.

Assessment Pages

To allow for an objective test of the chapter material, assessment pages have been provided beginning on page R9.

Symbols *and* Signs

KEY CONTENT SUMMARY

Signs are the manifestation of the reality of God with us; symbols are directed at our hearts for transformation. The sacraments mark us as members of the Catholic Church. The sacraments have their origins in Christ. The celebration of the sacraments is done by and for the Church. We celebrate our faith through rituals and rites. Sacramentals are sacred signs of God's presence in our everyday lives.

PLANNING THE CHAPTER

OPEN	PACING	CONTENT	OBJECTIVES	MATERIALS
	Suggested Time: **Parish 10 min.** **School 25 min.** Your Time: ___ min.	pp. 4–5	• Recognize that we use words, symbols, and actions in our celebrations of faith.	• note paper and pens (optional) • candle, matches, Bible (optional) • symbol representing chapter theme (optional) • music for prayer (optional)

SEARCH				
	Suggested Time: **Parish 25 min.** **School 70 min.** Your Time: ___ min.	pp. 6–9	• Identify the sacraments and examine how they have their origins in Christ. • Explore how the sacraments are "by the Church" and "for the Church."	• sacramentals (optional) • Bibles • sacramentary or other rites book (optional)

REFLECT				
	Suggested Time: **Parish 10 min.** **School 30 min.** Your Time: ___ min.	pp. 10–11	• Reflect on the importance of the sacraments in our lives.	• art supplies (optional) • newspapers and scissors (optional) • Bible (optional) • Catholic bookstore catalog (optional)

LIVE				
	Suggested Time: **Parish 15 min.** **School 35 min.** Your Time: ___ min.	pp. 12–13	• Apply our knowledge of the sacraments to strengthen and express our faith.	• examples of religious art (optional) • Student Leader Prep Page for Chapter 2 (p. R4) (optional) • music for prayer (optional) • copies of Assessment Page for Chapter 1 (p. R9) (optional)

CATECHISM IN CONTEXT

See *Catechism of the Catholic Church, #1127.*

Christ is at the center of all the sacraments. When we celebrate the sacraments with him, Jesus acts to confer on us the grace that each sacrament signifies. As believers, we know that the grace of the sacraments comes to us as a gift. By sharing in the sacraments, we participate in the mission of the Church throughout our earthly lives and prepare ourselves for the fulfillment of faith that is eternal life. When we are kind to our families, sensitive to the needs of our friends, and compassionate and just toward those who are poor and displaced, we demonstrate the transforming power of sacramental grace. The sacraments have their origin in Christ and are entrusted to the Church. They are efficacious signs of God's covenant with us.

ONE-MINUTE RETREAT

READ

"The symbol . . . opens the believer's inner eye, the eye of the heart, to the realization that [one] must come to be centered in God because that, in fact, is where [one's] center is."
—Thomas Merton

REFLECT

What symbol reminds me of God's presence?

PRAY

Lord, source of every blessing, may the symbols that surround me proclaim your presence. May these sacred signs strengthen my faith, transform my heart, and fill my life with blessing. Give me the courage to be a witness for my faith—a living sign of your presence.

LIBRARY LINKS

BOOKS
FOR ADOLESCENTS

50 Ways to Tap the Power of the Sacraments, by Bert Ghezzi (Our Sunday Visitor, 1995).

Brief reflections on the sacraments and suggestions for putting them into practice.

The Catholic Source Book, by Rev. Peter Klein (Harcourt Religion Publishers, 2000).

Contains a wealth of information on Catholic beliefs and practices—including symbols, sacraments, and sacramentals—tied to the *Catechism of the Catholic Church.*

Why Do Catholics . . . ? A Guide to Catholic Belief and Practice, by Sister Charlene Altemose MSC (Harcourt Religion Publishers, 1990).

Informative explanations of Catholic teachings, rituals, and celebrations.

FOR ADULTS

Living Our Faith: Nurturing the Spiritual Growth of Your Adolescent, by Michael Carotta (Harcourt Religion Publishers, 2002).

Written to complement the *Living Our Faith* series, this book encourages adult family members to develop the Skills for Christian Living in their own lives to reinforce these skills in the lives of their adolescents.

Sacraments: A New Understanding for a New Generation, by Raymond Noll (Twenty-Third Publications, 1999).

A resource book on the theology, history, and pastoral practice of the sacraments.

Sometimes We Dance, Sometimes We Wrestle: Embracing the Spiritual Growth of Adolescents, by Michael Carotta (Harcourt Religion Publishers, 2002).

Explores ways any faithful adult can participate in the spiritual growth of adolescents.

MULTIMEDIA

Of Sacraments and Symbols (video) (produced by Franciscan Communications; St. Anthony Messenger Press).

An introduction to symbolism and a classic exploration of the images and symbols associated with the sacraments.

Together in Faith (video) (produced by Salt River Production Group; Harcourt Religion Publishers).

Reviews the customs, beliefs, and practices of the Catholic faith, including symbols and sacramentals.

FEATURE PREPARATION

STUDENT LEADER CONNECTION

The Student Leader activities are optional. For those who wish to incorporate a Student Leader into their lesson presentation, Student Leader Prep Pages have been provided at the back of this book. For your convenience each chapter's Prep Page has been summarized within that chapter's Resource Center. Prior to the session, you may wish to meet with the Student Leader to distribute the Prep Page and discuss how he or she might be most valuable. The Prep Page for Chapter 1 is located on page R4.

FAITH PARTNERSHIPS

The Faith Partnership activities are optional. For those who wish to incorporate Faith Partnerships into their lesson presentation, several opportunities for Faith Partner discussions are marked throughout the chapter. You may wish to review these and consider other opportunities as you prepare the lesson.

SKILL NOTES

The skill for this chapter is Using Religious Imagination. As you teach the skill lesson on pages 12 and 13, you may wish to refer to the Skill Notes marked throughout the chapter. These notes will help you identify terms and ideas related to the skill.

A check mark indicates the chapter's essential questions, statements, activities, and features. If time is limited, such as in a parish group setting, this icon will help you direct the students through the lesson.

Symbols and Signs

✓ GATHERING

Have each student write his or her name in the center of a sheet of notebook paper. In each corner of their papers, have the students put words or symbols describing themselves (likes, dislikes). Have the students introduce one another to the group using this information.

✓ PRAYER

Invite the students to bow their heads. Pray aloud the opening prayer. You may wish to play instrumental music softly in the background. If fire regulations permit, you may wish to light a candle at this time.

Lord,

show us your

love and help

us recognize

you in the signs

you give us.

Teach us your

ways, support

us when we feel

lost and lonely,

and help us

work to be

better people.

Amen.

4

RESOURCE Center

PRAYER ENVIRONMENT

You may wish to create in the room a sacred space that serves as a focal point during prayer times. A small table with space for a candle and an open Bible may be sufficient. You might further enhance the space by adding some sacramentals representing the theme of each chapter.

TEACHING TIP

Allowing time for research Several activities provide suggestions for further research. When possible, allow time for the students to use the school or parish library or the Internet to find information. For information that cannot be gathered during class time, you may wish to set aside time at the beginning of the next session so the students can share their research results. You may also wish to create a gradable take-home assignment based on the research.

FAITH PARTNER INTRODUCTION

If you haven't done so already, assign each student a Faith Partner. Have the Faith Partners use the information from the gathering exercise to introduce one another to the class.

Student Leader Connection

Consider having the Student Leader do the following:

• Pray aloud the opening prayer.

• Read aloud the text on page 5 and help the group brainstorm examples of self-expression.

• Record responses to the discussion.

What Do You Think?

List the kinds of things that make you who you are. Include anything you might use to identify yourself to another person, such as your gender, color of skin, height, body frame, skills, desires, or groups to which you belong.

_____

_____

_____

If someone were to describe you as a person of faith, what words or symbols would he or she use?

_____

_____

Who We Are

We are members of many groups. Some groups are beyond our choice, such as our family and our cultural or ethnic group. (S) The way we style our hair, the music we listen to, the friends we choose, and the schools we attend are ways we identify ourselves. But what about our faith?

Though we are members of many groups and communities, it is our membership in the Body of Christ that should have the greatest impact on our lives.

So how do we identify ourselves as Catholic? As members of the Catholic Church, what objects and actions do we use?

WORKING WITH THE ACTIVITY

What Do You Think?

✓ • Allow time for the students to record their thoughts in the space provided.

• See *Reflecting on Your Faith* below.

✓ • *What Do You Think?* is intended as a personal pre-assessment. The students should not be asked to share their responses.

WORKING WITH THE TEXT AND PICTURES

✓ • Read the text on this page, and review the pictures on pages 4 and 5.

✓ • Brainstorm with the students examples of the objects, actions, gestures, and behaviors that people use to express who they are. *(Possible answers include hairstyles, clothing, and music.)*

• Discuss the images. **What can a candle symbolize?** *(Possible response: It can be a sign of light, knowledge, or love.)* **What does a group of Catholics gathered in Church symbolize?** *(a community of believers, a family of faith, the people of God)*

✓ • See *Skill Note* below.

EXTENSION ACTIVITY

Handling pressures Encourage the students to talk about the pressures they face in expressing their own identities. You may wish to have the students role-play examples of these pressures. Ask the students to examine the point of view of the parents, teachers, catechists, and others who may be pressuring them.

(S) SKILL NOTE ✓

Use the text on this page to introduce the idea of religious imagination by having the students recognize how people express the religious side of their personalities. Refer to pages 12 and 13 for more information.

TEACHING TIP

Brainstorming Brainstorming stimulates creative thought. The quantity of ideas is more important than the quality. A brainstorming session should never run longer than a few minutes, and no discussion or evaluation should occur while ideas are being suggested and recorded. Use one or two words to record each idea as it is contributed. To keep things flowing, ask two volunteers to record responses on the board or on chart paper. At the end of the session, ask the students to review the list and choose the most appropriate and useful ideas for the current discussion.

WORKING WITH THE TEXT AND PICTURES

✓ • Read the text and review the pictures on pages 6 and 7.

✓ • Use *Vocabulary* below to help the students understand the terms *sign* and *symbol*.

✓ • At this age the students are aware of religious signs and symbols. ***What signs of God's presence can you name?*** *(Accept all reasonable responses.)* Make sure the students are aware of the use of sacramentals, such as the palm and ashes depicted on pages 6 and 7. If possible, show the students several sacramentals, such as a religious medal, a statue of Mary, a crucifix, and holy water.

• Emphasize that this book discusses the sacraments, about which the students will be learning in detail. For this first chapter, invite volunteers to share their thoughts about the sacraments.

WORKING WITH THE ACTIVITY

Opening the Word

• Ask a volunteer to read aloud *Opening the Word*.

✓ • Allow the students sufficient time to read the additional Scripture passages and respond to the question. *(Answers will vary.)*

✓ • See *Scripture Background* below.

Signs and **Symbols** of Faith

What is your favorite sports team? What is your favorite brand of clothes? Chances are that both are identified by a sign or a symbol. We use signs and symbols every day to express ourselves and to understand others. A **sign** is an object or event that represents or explains something else. It is used to communicate information. A friendly wave is a sign for hello. A big golden arch is the sign of a certain fast-food restaurant. A **symbol** is like a sign, but it has special emotional or spiritual significance. There is something more powerful, more effective, more objectively meaningful about a symbol.

Signs and symbols are especially important in our faith lives. Religious signs and symbols can help us deepen our understanding of God and remind us of what it means to live as followers of Jesus. One of the most important signs of God's presence is the world around us—God's creation. Through creation we experience God's glory and his power.

For what can be known about God is plain to them, because God has shown it to them. Ever since the creation of the world his eternal power and divine nature, invisible though they are, have been understood and seen through the things he has made. Romans 1:19–20

Read *Romans 1:19–32* as well as *Exodus 33:18–23, 1 Kings 19:11–13,* and *Luke 24:13–35.* What do these passages tell us about how we experience God?

_____

_____

_____

_____

6 SYMBOLS AND SIGNS

VOCABULARY ✓

A *sign* points to or explains something else. It communicates information.

A *symbol* is a sign that has effective emotional or spiritual meaning. Symbols are ways through which we express profound insights about God, ourselves, and our world.

SCRIPTURE BACKGROUND ✓

Romans 1:19–20 explains that God reveals himself to us through creation. Everything in his creation tells us something about God and our relationship with him.

TEACHING TIP

Leading a discussion   Students at this age are more apt to join in a discussion focused on concrete examples than one based on abstract ideas or feelings. Involve the students in the discussion by suggesting some real-life experiences and signs that remind them of God's presence. Then invite them to suggest their own distinctions between signs and symbols.

Student Leader Connection

Consider having the Student Leader do the following:

• Collect examples of sacramentals and share them with the group.

• Read aloud one or more of the additional Scripture passages in *Opening the Word*.

• Research and present information on one of the items on the time line from *Our Christian Journey*.

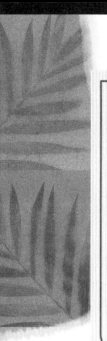

OUR CHRISTIAN JOURNEY

A New Approach to the Sacraments Augustine was a bishop who lived in the North African town of Hippo. He is best known for explaining Church beliefs, especially in his most famous works, **Confessions** and **The City of God.** Through his writings, Augustine helped deepen our understanding of the sacraments, which he described as sacred signs. He emphasized that God freely and lovingly acts in our lives, and that the sacraments help us recognize and celebrate his presence. Augustine discussed Baptism and Eucharist in particular. In the Sacrament of Baptism, he wrote, we are not changed overnight. Instead, our Baptism begins a lifelong opportunity to become more generous and loving people. Augustine viewed the celebration of the Eucharist in a similar way. He explained that the Sacrament of the Eucharist helps us become new people in Christ. Saint Augustine's feast day is August 28.

For further information:
Read a biography of Augustine, or research his writings in an encyclopedia.

300 **450**

320
BEGINNING OF INDIA'S GOLDEN AGE

354–430
SAINT AUGUSTINE'S LIFE

379–395
REIGN OF THEODOSIUS THE GREAT, THE LAST EMPEROR OF A UNITED ROMAN EMPIRE

410
GERMANIC TROOPS CONQUER ROME

(S) Catholics have certain symbols or sacred signs called sacramentals that make us aware of God's presence in our lives. One of the symbols we use is the crucifix. It speaks to our hearts about Jesus' saving actions and his love for us. Blessings, holy water, candles, the rosary, statues, palm leaves, and ashes are other examples of sacramentals. Sacramentals are usually used with prayer and sometimes with an action, such as the Sign of the Cross or the sprinkling of holy water. Does your family use sacramentals? If you keep a statue of a saint in a special place, or if you pray a blessing before or after meals, you use sacramentals. Perhaps you received a rosary for your First Communion or for your birthday. If so, then you have a sacramental.

Signs and symbols are also a part of our group celebrations within the Church. We often use signs and symbols to help us celebrate Catholic rites. A rite is an established procedure for celebrating specific ceremonies in the Church. Among the most important of our Catholic rites are the seven sacraments—Baptism, Eucharist, Confirmation, Reconciliation, Anointing of the Sick, Matrimony, and Holy Orders. Through our celebration of the sacraments, Jesus joins with the assembled community in liturgical actions that are signs and sources of God's grace, or God's life and loving relationship with us.

WORKING WITH THE TEXT AND PICTURES

- Review the text and pictures on this page.
- Use *Vocabulary* below to help the students understand the highlighted terms.
- Discuss how the sacraments originate in Jesus' words and actions. ***What Scripture stories remind you of the sacraments?*** *(Possible answers: the Gospel stories of healing and nourishment, the baptism of Jesus, and the Last Supper.)*
- Invite volunteers to share their knowledge of the sacraments. List and describe the seven sacraments. *(Accept all reasonable answers explaining Baptism, Confirmation, Eucharist, Reconciliation, Anointing of the Sick, Matrimony, and Holy Orders.)*
- Point out that when we celebrate the sacraments, God enters our lives in a special way. Sacramental grace draws us closer to him.
- See *Skill Note* below.

WORKING WITH THE ACTIVITY

Our Christian Journey

- Ask a volunteer to read aloud *Our Christian Journey.*
- Discuss with the students who Saint Augustine was *(a bishop in North Africa)* and why he is important. *(He answered many of our questions about the sacraments.)*
- Discuss the time line and explain its purpose. You may wish to use a world map to point out where the events on the time line occurred.
- See *Background* below.

VOCABULARY ✓

Sacramentals are sacred signs that bear a resemblance to the sacraments. They make us aware of God's presence in our everyday lives. Some examples of sacramentals are religious medals, statues, prayer cards, scapulars, holy water, crucifixes, blessings, candles, and rosaries.

Rites are established procedures for celebrating specific ceremonies in the Church. A rite has fixed words and actions that are followed each time the rite is celebrated.

The *sacraments* are celebrations in which Jesus joins with the assembled community in liturgical actions that are efficacious signs and sources of God's grace. The sacraments (seven distinct celebrations of Christ's Church) make God present with us.

Grace is God's life in us. It is the freely given and undeserved help God gives us to respond to the call of holiness. Grace is our loving relationship with God.

(S) SKILL NOTE ✓

Use the text on this page to discuss religious imagination further. Point out that Catholics use this skill to recognize signs and symbols of God's presence in their lives.

BACKGROUND

Time line By about 380 most of India had become a single empire, and Hinduism, one of the world's largest religions, had spread throughout the subcontinent.

Brilliant and well-educated, Augustine defended Christianity against the Roman Empire's philosophical and theological challenges. His clarification of Christian thought continues to influence Catholicism today.

Theodosius the Great helped Christianity flourish in the eastern part of the Roman Empire; he convened the First Council of Constantinople in 381.

The fall of the city of Rome signaled the end of the power of the Roman Empire.

WORKING WITH THE TEXT AND PICTURES

✓ • Read *The Mission of Jesus Christ* and *The Church as Sacrament* on pages 8 and 9.

• Christ as the head of the Church and the Church as his Body is an important image for Christians. ***How does this image symbolize our relationship with Christ?*** *(He leads us; we do Christ's work on earth.)*

• Read aloud *Ephesians 1:22–23* to familiarize the students with this important Scripture passage.

✓ • Discuss how the sacraments are by and for the Church. Ask the students to explain this in their own words. ***How are the sacraments for the Church?*** *(We are drawn closer to God; we are nourished and strengthened.)* ***How are the sacraments by the Church?*** *(The Church is a sign of Christ's presence in the world. We share God's love with everyone throughout the world.)*

• You may wish to prepare a chart that lists and briefly explains each sacrament. Refer to this chart and have the students volunteer additional information.

• Review the definition of *sacrament* found on page 7.

WORKING WITH THE ACTIVITY
Catholics Believe

• Ask a volunteer to read aloud *Catholics Believe.*

✓ • Allow time for the students to write their responses to the question. *(Answers will vary.)*

• See *Reflecting on Your Faith* below.

• Encourage the students to share with the group their thoughts about the paraphrased Catechism statement and their responses to the question that follows.

The Mission of Jesus Christ

The seven sacraments, which have their origin in Christ's words and actions, are his gifts to his Church. In the Gospels we read stories about how Jesus healed people who were sick (see *Luke 4:38–40*), how he forgave people (see *Matthew 9:2–8*), and how he broke bread with his disciples (see *Mark 14:22–25*). Each of these stories reminds us of how Jesus cares for us and how he wants us to live. In our celebration of the sacraments, we participate in the saving actions of Jesus.

After Jesus returned to his Father, the Holy Spirit was sent to help the followers of Jesus continue his work and to strengthen their faith. The first Christians spread the good news of Jesus and God's kingdom. They prayed and worshiped together as Jesus taught them, and they celebrated their faith with the sacred signs and symbols that we call sacraments. The early Church kept Jesus' message and work alive. Through the centuries Christians have continued to share the good news and celebrate the sacraments.

The Church as Sacrament

The writer of the Letter to the Ephesians in the New Testament explains how Christians are united in the Lord by describing Christ as the head of the Church and the Church as his Body. (See *Ephesians 1:22–23*.) This image helps us understand how the Church is united with Christ. As members of his Body, we are called to help one another grow closer to God our Father. The Body of Christ needs to be nourished and cared for. In the sacraments Christ meets us in community and touches our lives so that we are strengthened to live as he did.

In the sacraments, Christ works in our lives. See Catechism, #1127.
How can Christ change your life through the sacraments?

_____

_____

_____

Share your responses and thoughts with your Faith Partner.

8 SYMBOLS AND SIGNS

REFLECTING ON YOUR FAITH
Reflect on your own experiences of the sacraments. How has Christ entered your life and changed it?

FAITH PARTNERSHIPS
Invite the Faith Partners to discuss how their attitudes and behavior would be affected if the sacraments were not part of their lives.

TEACHING TIP
Charting the Sacraments   Create three columns with these headings: *Sacraments of Initiation, Sacraments of Healing,* and *Sacraments of Service.* Under *Sacraments of Initiation,* list Baptism—we become members of the Church; Eucharist—we receive the Body and Blood of Jesus; and Confirmation—the Holy Spirit strengthens us with the gifts of the Holy Spirit. Under

Sacraments of Healing, list Reconciliation—God forgives us and gives us his grace; and Anointing of the Sick—we are strengthened in times of sickness, frailty, and death. Under *Sacraments of Service,* list Matrimony—a man and a woman make a lasting covenant with God and with each other; and Holy Orders—a man becomes part of the ordained ministry.

Student Leader Connection

Consider having the Student Leader do the following:

• **Help make a chart to list and describe each sacrament.**

• **Help moderate the group discussion on the symbolism of the Body of Christ.**

• **Read aloud *Ephesians 1:22–23*.**

A World Family
Did you know that there are more than a billion members of the Catholic Church worldwide? Wherever they live, Catholics pray together and celebrate the sacraments in their own languages, including Urdu (India), Sinhalese (Sri Lanka), Kikuyu (Kenya), Yoruba (Nigeria), Arabic (Lebanon), and Vietnamese (Vietnam).

Through the sacraments the Holy Spirit makes us a holy people. We form a community of love to strengthen and support one another and do our part to transform the world. We can look forward to a life with God forever in the fullness of his kingdom.

As we participate in our faith community, we may hear people say that the sacraments are "by the Church" and "for the Church." In saying that the sacraments are "by the Church," we mean that the Church itself, the Body of Christ, is a sacrament through which Jesus and the Holy Spirit work to bring to the world God's gifts of grace, forgiveness, and eternal life. At the same time, these seven signs, and particularly the Eucharist, are said to be "for the Church." This means that the sacraments are special opportunities to draw closer to the mystery of our unique relationship with the loving God—one in three Persons, who created us, saved us, and continues to inspire and help us.

We
Celebrate

When we celebrate the sacraments, God is blessed and adored. God the Father sends the Spirit to bring us into communion with Christ. Our lives can be changed if we are open to the power of God's grace.

How do you think God's grace can change your life? Think about the kind of person you are. What gifts and talents do you have? What aspects of your life do you struggle with and wish you could improve? Experiencing God's life and love will help you appreciate how special you are in God's eyes. Through the sacraments, especially the Eucharist and Reconciliation, you will experience God's everlasting love. This experience will help change how you view your life and how you view others. If you are tempted to do things that are harmful to yourself or others, such as drinking or smoking, God's grace in the sacraments can give you the strength you need to avoid these actions. If you aren't getting along with family members, the sacraments can help you reconcile with them. Encountering God in the sacraments changes how you see things and ultimately changes how you want to live as a person in the right relationship with God.

SEARCH 9

WORKING WITH THE TEXT AND PICTURES

✓ • Read *We Celebrate* and review the picture on the page.

• Ask the students to review what they have learned about sacraments and sacramentals. ***How are sacraments and sacramentals different from one another?*** *(Sacraments are signs that accomplish what they signify; for example, the Sacrament of Reconciliation doesn't just remind us of God's forgiveness—through this sacrament our sins actually are forgiven. Sacramentals are signs that remind us of God.)*

✓ • Invite the students to think of examples of how God's grace encountered in the sacraments might affect a person's life. ***How can grace affect our lives?*** *(Answers will vary but should express the idea that the grace of the sacraments helps a person do what is right and good.)*

WORKING WITH THE ACTIVITY
Our Global Community

• Ask a volunteer to read aloud *Our Global Community.*

• Invite the students to name other countries in which there are Catholics and other languages in which Mass and the sacraments are celebrated.

✓ • Encourage the students to share anything they may know about Catholic life and practice in other parts of the world.

MULTIPLE LEARNING STYLES
Hands-on activities Organize the students into seven groups and assign each group one of the sacraments. Make adjustments according to group size. Give group members several minutes to brainstorm what they know about their sacrament. Have each group prepare a skit, charade, or game about the sacrament. Have the groups take turns presenting their work to the large group. Hands-on activities make abstract ideas more real and therefore more understandable to the students.

LINK TO LITURGY
Borrow a copy of the sacramentary or another book used in celebrating the sacraments. Show this book to the students, pointing out that the words and rituals are described so that the sacraments will be celebrated properly. Invite the students to recall details of the sacraments, such as those of the Eucharist, that they have observed.

EXTENSION ACTIVITY
Creating an acrostic Write the word *sacrament* in large letters on the board or on chart paper. Invite the students to use the letters in the word to suggest other words about the Catholic faith. For example, the letter *s* could be used in the name *Jesus,* the letter *a* in the word *faith,* and so on. This activity will help the students make connections between many of the ideas important to living as Christians.

10 CHAPTER 1

WORKING WITH THE TEXT AND PICTURES

✓ • Read the text on this page, and review the picture on pages 10 and 11.

• Emphasize that in our celebrations of the sacraments we encounter God and he enters our lives. **What does the Holy Spirit do for us in the sacraments?** *(The Holy Spirit strengthens us, forgives us, heals us, and helps us grow as members of the Body of Christ.)*

• Point out the photograph. **When could your parish use such a banner, and why?** *(Accept all reasonable responses expressing the idea that Catholics do not celebrate the sacraments by themselves but as part of a community.)*

✓ • Explain that our faith makes us signs of God's presence to one another. **What do we mean when we say we can be a sacrament to others?** *(We mean that by living our faith we are a sign of God's presence in the Church and one way others experience God's love.)*

WORKING WITH THE ACTIVITY

Wrap Up

• Have a volunteer read aloud the summary statements.

✓ • Allow time for the students to consider their remaining questions and write them in their books.

• Discuss any remaining questions the students may have. You may wish to have the students write their questions on separate sheets of paper so that you can collect them and respond during the next session.

A Life in Christ

We celebrate the sacraments together as the Body of Christ, offering our prayers of thanks and praise. But we don't celebrate these rituals to gain God's favor. We celebrate them to become one with him and with one another. The sacraments are God's gifts to us. Christ has given them in love to his Church.

When we celebrate the sacraments, the Holy Spirit acts through signs and symbols to change our hearts and make it possible for us to become more loving and more generous. These signs and symbols are not merely reminders of God's love; through them the Holy Spirit helps us live our lives as Christians—strengthening us, forgiving our sins, healing us, and enabling us to grow as members of the Body of Christ.

With your Faith Partner, discuss or make a poster showing how you can be a sacrament to others.

FaiTH PaRTNeRSHiP

WRAP UP

• As Catholics we have certain signs and symbols that identify who we are and that bring us closer together with God and one another.

• The sacraments are Christ's gifts to his Church.

• The sacraments mark us as members of the Catholic Church.

• When we celebrate the sacraments, the Holy Spirit transforms our lives through God's love.

What questions do you have about this chapter?

_____

_____

_____

10 SYMBOLS AND SIGNS

RESOURCE Center

FAITH PARTNERSHIPS

Have the Faith Partners create a poster showing how someone could be a sacrament to others. Distribute art supplies such as sheets of chart paper and markers. Have the partners work together to review the chapter, discuss their ideas, and express these ideas creatively in a poster.

EXTENSION ACTIVITY

Finding signs of God's presence   Distribute newspapers and scissors to the group. Challenge the students to look through the newspapers to find evidence of grace in our world today. The students might look for stories with happy endings, stories about achievements and technological advances that are being used to help others, and stories about efforts to bring justice to our world. Ask volunteers to read aloud and explain their selections to the group.

Student Leader Connection

Consider having the Student Leader do the following:

• Read aloud the *Wrap Up* summary statements.

• Record on the board or on chart paper the results of the *Around the Group* discussion.

• Collect newspapers and lead the *Extension Activity* to find signs of God's presence in our world.

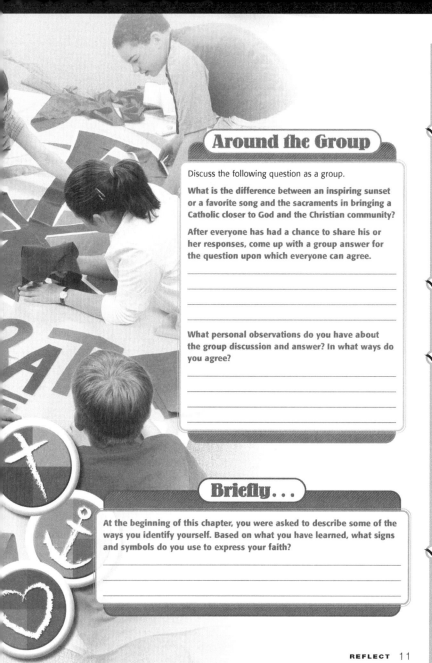

Around the Group

Discuss the following question as a group.

What is the difference between an inspiring sunset or a favorite song and the sacraments in bringing a Catholic closer to God and the Christian community?

After everyone has had a chance to share his or her responses, come up with a group answer for the question upon which everyone can agree.

_____

_____

_____

_____

What personal observations do you have about the group discussion and answer? In what ways do you agree?

_____

_____

_____

_____

Briefly . . .

At the beginning of this chapter, you were asked to describe some of the ways you identify yourself. Based on what you have learned, what signs and symbols do you use to express your faith?

_____

_____

_____

REFLECT 11

WORKING WITH THE ACTIVITIES

Around the Group

✓ • Present the question to the group, and allow time for discussion. You may need to moderate to keep the students focused on the question.

• Encourage the group members to listen to the opinions and perspectives of others.

• If necessary, remind the students that, unlike other signs of God's presence, sacraments are not just reminders of God—they always effectively make him present in our lives.

✓ • If the group has agreed on an answer, direct the students to write it in their books. If they could not agree, direct them to list in their books the issues that were left unresolved and explain why.

✓ • Encourage the students to note in their books their personal observations about the discussion and any final thoughts they have.

• See *Reflecting on Your Faith* below.

Briefly . . .

• Encourage the students to consider how their opinions may have changed since they responded to *What Do You Think?* on page 5.

• Introduce the reflection question by asking the students to think about what they believe and how they express their beliefs.

✓ • Allow time for the students to write their responses in their books.

• See *Reflecting on Your Faith* below.

REFLECTING ON YOUR FAITH

Around the Group: How did the students come to an understanding of the special place the sacraments have in our lives? How do you see the sacraments in your own life?

Briefly: Basing your response on your work with the students on this chapter, how do you think you might express your faith to the students so that you can encourage and nurture their faith?

TEACHING TIP

Respecting symbols of faith   Help the students understand the significance of the symbols they have drawn in response to the question in *Briefly* by asking them to suggest ways that they might use or wear the symbols. You may wish to ask the students what they think of wearing religious symbols as "jewelry" or how they are affected by the use of Christian art and logos on bumper stickers, business cards, billboards, and so on. Offer the students examples of ways to use Christian signs and symbols as daily reminders of their faith. You may find a catalog from a Catholic bookstore useful for this purpose.

WORKING WITH THE SKILL

✔ • Begin the discussion by pointing out that we all have imagination. *What does it mean to use your imagination? (Possible answers: the ability to think of what might happen, what something looks like or might look like, what someone might say.)* Explain to the students that using religious imagination is a skill that can help us live as Christians.

✔ • Ask a volunteer to read aloud *Expressions of Faith. When do you use your religious imagination? (Possible responses should include using faith to recognize God in creation and the Bible and praying with sacramentals.)*

• Ask a volunteer to read aloud *John 15:1.* Explain that we use our imaginations to understand what Jesus meant by this image of the vine. Invite the students to close their eyes and imagine a grapevine with large flat leaves, clusters of grapes, and curving, twisting vine stems. *Why do you think Jesus used this symbol? (Accept all reasonable responses.)*

✔ • See *Scripture Background* below.

✔ • Ask a volunteer to read aloud the text and reflection statement for *Think About It.* Give the students time to write their responses.

• See *Reflecting on Your Faith* below.

• Discuss the students' answers. Invite the students to talk about how their experiences give meaning to these symbols. Some students may have specific stories to share.

SKILLS FOR Christian Living

Using Religious Imagination

Expressions of Faith-

Signs and symbols express who we are as individuals and groups. Religious imagination means using language, symbols, and gestures to offer ourselves to God and to recognize how God reveals himself and comes to dwell with us. Religious imagination is a skill that Catholics use often. We use it when we see God in our relationships, recognize signs of God in creation, read the Bible, celebrate the sacraments, and pray with sacramentals in our homes and at church.

Think About It-

Scripture is filled with examples of religious imagination. In fact, Jesus often taught his message by using nontraditional images to explain concepts or traditions that people might otherwise not understand. Jesus uses the image of the vine and branches to symbolize our relationship to him. In *Luke 14:15–24* Jesus uses the image of a great banquet as a way to convey how God welcomes us all into his kingdom.

Choose one of the following Catholic symbols that you experience in your life and explain what it might symbolize: a candle, holy water, music, the sign of peace, ashes, chrism, the Advent wreath, the crucifix, a statue of a saint.

_____
_____
_____
_____
_____
_____
_____
_____

12 **SYMBOLS AND SIGNS**

SCRIPTURE BACKGROUND ✔

Explain that the Old Testament prophets frequently used the vine as an image because it is a symbol of life and indicates the abundance and gifts of the Lord. The vine is almost always described as a grapevine, a common plant grown in Palestine. The fruit of the vine was used to make wine. In this quote from the Gospel according to John, Jesus uses the image of the vine to refer to himself as the source of life. You may wish to point out that this passage is part of the readings for the Fifth Sunday of Easter, Cycle B. Refer to page 108 of this book for more information about the liturgical year.

RESOURCE Center

REFLECTING ON YOUR FAITH
Select one of the symbols in *Think About It,* and consider what it means to you.

Student Leader Connection

Consider having the Student Leader do the following:

• Read aloud *Expressions of Faith.*

• Gather examples of religious art to show the group.

• Organize a small group to plan a prayer service.

Special Note: Remember to meet briefly with the Student Leader for Chapter 2. You may wish to provide him or her with the Student Leader Prep Page for Chapter 2, found on page R4.

Skill Steps

The skill of Using Religious Imagination is like a muscle. We have it, but we don't always use it. However, the more often we use it, the better we become. This in turn will help strengthen our faith.

A religion teacher once asked a group of students to describe one of their favorite Catholic symbols. One student said, "Incense." When the teacher asked why, the student replied, "Because it reminds me that you pray best after you get burned." For this student, incense is a symbol that reminds him or her that we don't pray with words as much as with our hearts.

Exercise your religious imagination by choosing two Catholic gestures from the list. Describe what each signifies for you.

kneeling during Mass
making the Sign of the Cross
burning incense in church

dipping your finger in holy water
covering the cross on Good Friday
wearing a cross as jewelry

Explain your choices.

_____

_____

Check It Out

Place a check mark next to the sentences that apply to you.

○ I experience God's presence in everyday situations.
○ I use my religious imagination when I pray.
○ I see the opportunity to use my religious imagination at home.
○ I experience my Catholic faith through people and relationships as well as objects.

How many did you check? Based on your response, what things do you need to work on?

_____

Closing Prayer

Lord, you reveal yourself to us in so many ways. The majestic heights of the mountains, the pounding surf of the ocean, the fragile beauty of a bird's feather, the poetry of the psalms, and the prayers and rituals of your Church all help us experience your love for us. Thank you for continually giving us signs of your presence. Thank you for loving us so much that you are always willing to act in our lives.

WORKING WITH THE SKILL

- Ask a volunteer to read aloud *Skill Steps*. **How can we develop the skill of Using Religious Imagination?** *(Possible answers: by opening ourselves to art and music, paying attention to experiences of closeness to God and others, being aware of the beauty of nature, becoming sensitive to the needs of others, paying attention to the quiet inner promptings we experience.)*
- See *Link to Art* below.
- Invite the students to suggest other examples of religious imagination. Encourage them to think about the music, people, gestures, and celebrations that can capture our imaginations.
- Allow time for the students to complete *Check It Out.* If appropriate, ask volunteers to share their responses.
- See *Reflecting on Your Faith* below.

CLOSING PRAYER

- Gather together to pray the closing prayer. You may wish to use the following music from the *Give Your Gifts* series: "Joyfully Singing" *(The Songs)*, "He Came Down/We Are Marching (Siyahumba)" *(The Basics)*, or "Heaven Will Sing" *(More Songs)* (GIA Publications, Inc.; distributed by Harcourt Religion Publishers).
- If time permits, direct the students to create their own closing reflections or prayers. You may wish to ask a few volunteers to read aloud what they have created or to plan a prayer service.

LINK TO ART

Take the students on a tour of the parish church, or use pictures of religious art to show the group how Christians use religious imagination to express their faith and nurture the faith of others. Direct the students' attention to stained-glass windows, statues, architecture, and other artistic expressions. Ask the students what kind of religious art they find most interesting or which objects of religious art they like best.

REFLECTING ON YOUR FAITH

Consider your own responses to the *Check It Out* statements. How can you strengthen your religious imagination?

TEACHING TIP

Research follow-up You may wish to take time to review any research the students have been asked to complete. If the students need additional time to complete their research, set aside a few minutes at the beginning of the next session to allow them to share the information they have gathered.

MULTIPLE LEARNING STYLES

Closing prayer You may wish to have the students create their closing prayers in the style of a formal prayer or reflection; a poem or song; or a prayer service with readings, psalm response, and music. Remind the students that the tone of their responses can be different from that of the example but should remain respectful.

ASSESSMENT

The Assessment Page for Chapter 1 can be found on page R9.

LINK TO FAMILY

If you wish to recommend to parents or guardians the Family Resource, *Living Our Faith: Nurturing the Spiritual Growth of Your Adolescent,* the corresponding pages for this skill are 46–50. (See page R3 of this book for a sample Family Letter.)

Moments
of Grace

KEY CONTENT SUMMARY

Grace flows from our relationship with God. The sacraments are signs of God's grace. The Paschal mystery is celebrated in each sacrament and throughout the liturgical year. The sacraments allow us to better understand our relationship with God.

PLANNING THE CHAPTER

OPEN	PACING	CONTENT	OBJECTIVES	MATERIALS
	Suggested Time: Parish **10 min.** School **25 min.** Your Time: ____ min.	pp. 14–15	• Recognize that loving relationships are signs of God's grace.	• candle, matches (optional) • symbol representing chapter theme (optional) • art supplies (optional)
SEARCH				
	Suggested Time: Parish **25 min.** School **70 min.** Your Time: ____ min.	pp. 16–19	• Identify and examine the presence of the Paschal mystery in the sacraments and through the liturgical year. • Explore how the sacraments are realized through the grace of God and the power of the Holy Spirit.	• recording of "Amazing Grace" or copies of the parish hymnal containing the lyrics (optional) • Bibles • liturgical calendar (optional) • art supplies (optional)
REFLECT				
	Suggested Time: Parish **10 min.** School **30 min.** Your Time: ____ min.	pp. 20–21	• Reflect on how the sacraments allow us to better understand our relationship with God.	• art supplies (optional)
LIVE				
	Suggested Time: Parish **15 min.** School **35 min.** Your Time: ____ min.	pp. 22–23	• Apply the experiences of God's grace to our lives.	• Student Leader Prep Page for Chapter 3 (p. R5) (optional) • music for prayer (optional) • *Living Our Faith Prayer Services* (optional) • copies of Assessment Page for Chapter 2 (p. R10) (optional)

CATECHISM IN CONTEXT

See Catechism of the Catholic Church, #1997.

Grace is the signature of the Trinity and the legacy of the Church; it is the free and undeserved gift of God that enables us to respond to his call and meet our responsibilities in leading Christian lives.

In accepting God's grace, we learn to care for others, to practice social justice, and to respect our environment. As members of the Body of Christ, we try every day to live and act in keeping with God's will for us.

Grace, the gift of the Holy Spirit, brings us to wholeness in Christian formation. One who recognized this truth was Joan of Arc, the great French heroine and saint. When asked whether she knew herself to be in God's grace, Joan replied, "If I am not, may it please God to put me in it; if I am, may it please God to keep me there."

ONE-MINUTE RETREAT

READ

"Perhaps the challenge of the gospel lies precisely in the invitation to accept a gift for which we can give nothing in return. For the gift is the life breath of God himself, the Spirit who is poured out on us through Jesus Christ." —Henri Nouwen

REFLECT

What does it mean for me to be an undeserving recipient of God's grace and love?

PRAY

Loving God, thank you for the free and undeserved gift of your love. May my embrace of the Paschal mystery enable me to better understand my relationship with you. Through the power of the Holy Spirit, guide me in your grace to respond to the call to live a life of holiness.

LIBRARY LINKS

BOOKS
FOR ADOLESCENTS

"Being Catholic: What Does It Mean?" by Brett C. Hoover CSP (*Youth Update*; St. Anthony Messenger Press).

Helps young Catholics explore their Catholic identity, the meaning of the sacraments, and the importance of community.

I Know Things Now: Stories by Teenagers, ed. by Carl Koch (St. Mary's Press, 1996).

First-person accounts of life-changing spiritual turning points.

A Wrinkle in Time, by Madeline L'Engle (Bantam Doubleday Dell Books for Young Readers, 1998).

The classic parable about the power of love to transform the world.

FOR ADULTS

Sacrament: The Language of God's Giving, by David Noel Power (Crossroad Publishing Co., 1999).

A fresh look at the meaning of grace and the sacramental encounter with God.

The Sacraments: How Catholics Pray, by Thomas Richstatter OFM (St. Anthony Messenger Press, 1995).

A popularly written overview of the sacraments, with prayers and reflection questions.

Signatures of Grace: Catholic Writers on the Sacraments, ed. by Thomas Grady and Paula Huston (Dutton/Plume, 2000).

An anthology of some of the best contemporary writing on the sacramental experience.

MULTIMEDIA

All Life Is a Holy Festival (audiocassette) (Ave Maria Press).

Popular lecturer Joyce Rupp helps listeners cultivate an awareness of the sacred and find God's presence in creation.

Creativity: Touching the Divine (video) (USCC).

Discusses the potential for encountering God through creativity in the fine arts and daily living.

FEATURE PREPARATION

STUDENT LEADER CONNECTION

The Student Leader Prep Page for this chapter is located on page R4. You may wish to provide this information to the Student Leader as an introduction and resource for the chapter.

FAITH PARTNERSHIPS

Chapter 2 has the same Faith Partners as Chapter 1. Several opportunities for Faith Partner discussions have been marked throughout the chapter. You may wish to consider other opportunities as you prepare the lesson.

SKILL NOTES

The skill for this chapter is Using Religious Imagination. You may wish to build on what the students have learned in the previous chapter as you teach this chapter. A few Skill Notes have been called out to help you. The skill lesson for this chapter can be found on pages 22 and 23.

A check mark indicates the chapter's essential questions, statements, activities, and features. If time is limited, such as in a parish group setting, this icon will help you direct the students through the lesson.

KEY POINTS FROM CHAPTER 1

You may wish to review these points with the students before you begin the new chapter:

- Signs are the manifestation of the reality of God with us; symbols are directed at our hearts for transformation.
- The sacraments mark us as members of the Catholic Church.
- The sacraments have their origins in Christ.
- The celebration of the sacraments is done by and for the Church.
- We celebrate our faith through rituals and rites.
- Sacramentals are sacred signs of God's presence in our everyday lives.
- Using Religious Imagination is a Skill for Christian Living.

✓ **GATHERING**

Ask volunteers to share a time when they felt the closest to God.

✓ **PRAYER**

Have the students close their eyes and spend a few moments in silence. Ask a volunteer to pray the prayer aloud. If fire regulations permit, you may wish to light a candle at this time.

Moments of Grace

Almighty God, throughout the ages you have cared for your people, leading and guiding us, patiently supporting us when we are troubled, lonely, uncertain, or frightened. We know you are always with us. Thank you for your love.

14

PRAYER ENVIRONMENT

If you have created a prayer space for the room, you may wish to display sacramentals and specific symbols associated with the sacraments to represent the theme of this chapter.

TEACHING TIP

Handling sensitive issues   Some students may be reluctant to discuss their personal experiences of closeness to God. Remind the students that these experiences are not to be communicated to others outside the group. The students may always choose to pass when asked to share their personal experiences.

RESOURCE Center

Student Leader Connection

Consider having the Student Leader do the following:

- Pray aloud the opening prayer.
- Read aloud or review *Getting a Helping Hand.*
- Help moderate the group discussion about experiences of help and support.
- Help moderate a group discussion on the characteristics of people who can be counted on to be supportive.

What Do You Think?

Draw a symbol or create an image that represents a situation when someone helped you and another symbol or image that represents a situation when you helped someone.

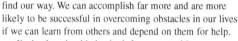

Getting a Helping Hand

There are times when each of us needs help and guidance. Family members, friends, teachers, and coaches may be sources of strength and wisdom for us. We may depend on another's humor, kindness, patience, or experience to help us find our way. We can accomplish far more and are more likely to be successful in overcoming obstacles in our lives if we can learn from others and depend on them for help.

Each of us should also look for opportunities to return the favor. We have talents and characteristics that others admire and need, and we can share them with those around us. By depending on one another, we can learn to deal with the problems we face every day. Loving relationships are built on giving and receiving.

OPEN 15

WORKING WITH THE ACTIVITY

What Do You Think?

✓ • Allow time for the students to record their thoughts in the space provided.

• See *Reflecting on Your Faith* below.

✓ • *What Do You Think?* is intended as a personal pre-assessment. The students should not be asked to share their responses.

WORKING WITH THE TEXT AND PICTURES

✓ • Read the text on this page, and review the pictures on pages 14 and 15.

• Have the group discuss ways that teens experience help from others and extend help to others. *When do people your age get help from others? Extend help to others?* *(Answers will vary.)*

✓ • Discuss with the students qualities that are supportive. *What are the qualities you rely on most in others? (Possible responses: humor, kindness, patience, wisdom, experience.)*

• Refer the students to the photographs. Have volunteers identify how each photograph shows people supporting and helping one another.

✓ • Make the point that all relationships are built on giving and receiving support.

REFLECTING ON YOUR FAITH
Think about the support you have received from others. When have you most appreciated such help?

MULTIPLE LEARNING STYLES

Picturing experiences Some students may find it easier to express their experiences of support by drawing about specific events in their lives. Have drawing supplies on hand to offer the students the option of drawing such events.

TEACHING TIP

Being a good helper Emphasize that a good helper is one who has only the best interests of others at heart. Such a helper does not seek favors in return for the help offered, but gives freely of whatever time and effort may be required. Point out, too, that a good helper is always reliable and does not promise what he or she cannot deliver. You may wish to point out that receivers of help also have responsibilities. Receivers should accept help graciously and gratefully and avoid taking advantage of their helpers.

WORKING WITH THE TEXT AND PICTURES

- ✓ • Read *The Grace of God* and review the pictures on pages 16 and 17.

- ✓ • Invite the students to reflect on God's grace. **What effect does grace have in our lives?** *(It brings us joy, honesty, peace, and generosity.)*

- • Grace is the loving relationship that God shares with us. Point out the examples in the text. **What are other examples of God's grace in our lives? How does the pictured group of young people suggest ways that our relationship with God affects our relationships with others?** *(Answers will vary.)*

- ✓ • Discuss the pictured crucifix and other signs and symbols the students use to express their faith. **What signs and symbols are important for our faith?** *(Possible answers may include the Bible, the sacraments, and sacramentals such as the cross, statues of Mary and the saints.)*

WORKING WITH THE ACTIVITY

Our Christian Journey

- • Ask a volunteer to read aloud *Our Christian Journey*.

- • Talk with the students about the hymn "Amazing Grace." If possible, play a recording of it or distribute copies of the parish hymnal containing the hymn's lyrics and have the students sing it.

- ✓ • Discuss how music can express ideas and emotions. **What did John Newton express in "Amazing Grace"?** *(He expressed how much he relied on God's grace because he had experienced its strengthening power.)*

- • See *Background* below.

- ✓ • See *Skill Note* below.

God's Amazing Grace

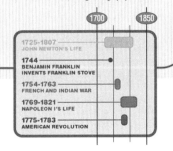

The well-known hymn "Amazing Grace" was written by John Newton between 1760 and 1770 to express the wonderful gift of God's grace. A former captain of an English slave ship, Newton displayed no faith in God until he prayed during a terrible storm in 1748. Surviving the storm, Newton turned away from his former life and became a minister in the Church of England, preaching and writing hymns. Newton turned from a life of ignoring God to a life of experiencing God's grace and proclaiming it. Here is a verse from "Amazing Grace" that describes Newton's experience: Ⓢ

  Through many dangers, toils and snares,
  I have already come;
  'Tis grace hath brought me safe thus far,
  And grace will lead me home.

For more information: Find the music and lyrics to "Amazing Grace." You may also wish to research the life of John Newton, using a biography of his life.

 1700   1850

1725-1807
JOHN NEWTON'S LIFE

1744
BENJAMIN FRANKLIN
INVENTS FRANKLIN STOVE

1754-1763
FRENCH AND INDIAN WAR

1769-1821
NAPOLEON I'S LIFE

1775-1783
AMERICAN REVOLUTION

The Grace of God

Grace can have a profound effect on our lives. Have you ever faced a difficult challenge and wondered where the strength to do the right thing came from? This may have been God's grace at work in your life. Grace is God's free gift of himself that helps us overcome the challenges we face every day. For example, you have the opportunity to cheat on a test. Do you do it? Someone at school tries to draw you into a fight. Do you allow yourself to be drawn in, or do you walk away? When we accept God's grace in our lives, we respond to God's love, change our hearts, and are able to make morally right choices. You know that cheating on the test is wrong, so you choose not to do it. You know that the best thing for everyone involved is for you to control your anger and walk away from the fight, so you do. Through grace, God helps us value virtue and goodness.

16   MOMENTS OF GRACE

BACKGROUND

Time line   Benjamin Franklin (1706–1790), a brilliant statesman, writer, inventor, and scientist, was a signer of the Declaration of Independence.

During the French and Indian War, French and British colonists, as well as Native Americans from various tribes, battled for control of the colonial territories in areas that are today the United States and Canada.

Declared emperor in 1804, Napoleon I helped France emerge from the chaos of the French Revolution. He attempted to unify Europe and conquer Russia but was defeated by the British in 1815.

The American Revolution was fought against Britain by its colonies in North America. The British were defeated, and their thirteen colonies won independence.

Ⓢ SKILL NOTE ✓

Point out the use of religious imagination in the song "Amazing Grace"—lost, found; blind, see; and so on. Refer to pages 22 and 23 for more information.

Student Leader Connection

Consider having the Student Leader do the following:

- • **Read aloud selected text.**
- • **Find a recording of "Amazing Grace" or distribute copies of a parish hymnal.**
- • **Record the results of the discussion about the importance of the Paschal mystery.**
- • **Read aloud** *Opening the Word*.
- • **Research and present information on one of the items on the time line from** *Our Christian Journey*.

Counting
on Christ

We experience the effects of grace in our lives all the time, even though we may not recognize them. Have you ever had an experience when someone did an unexpected favor for you? Maybe you were losing a board or video game and someone gave you an extra turn just so you could catch up. Maybe someone called you when you were feeling lonely and asked you to go to a movie. Generosity, joy, and honesty from people around us point to God's grace at work in our lives. Through God's grace we are strengthened to live responsibly and wisely.

Share with your Faith Partner an experience of grace.

FaITH
ParTNeRSHiP

Our faith in Jesus Christ is the source of our lives as Christians. We believe that Jesus suffered, died, and was raised from the dead so that we might be saved from the power of sin and everlasting death. Catholics call this saving mystery the **Paschal mystery.** The sacraments unite us with Christ's Paschal mystery, and we celebrate God's saving actions in the world. In each of the sacraments, we die to our old selves. Then we rise to new life in God's grace, guided by the Holy Spirit to love and serve as Jesus did.

Opening the Word

Easter Tuesday

When she had said this, she turned around and saw Jesus standing there, but she did not know that it was Jesus. Jesus said to her, "Woman, why are you weeping? Whom are you looking for?" John 20:14–15

Read *John 20:11–18* as well as *Acts 2:22–36* and *Colossians 1:15–20*. What do these passages tell us about the Paschal mystery?

_____
_____
_____
_____

WORKING WITH THE TEXT AND PICTURES

• Read *Counting on Christ* and review the pictures on pages 17 and 18.

• Explain that Jesus is the center of our lives. *Why is Jesus important to Christians? (He saved us from the power of sin and everlasting death. He loves us and guides us. He makes it possible for us to share in divine life.)*

• Use *Vocabulary* below to help the students understand the term *Paschal mystery.*

• Point out to the students how important the Paschal mystery is. Emphasize that it is through the sacraments that we are united in Christ so that the Church can continue his work in the world. *Why do we celebrate the sacraments? (because God's grace in the sacraments helps us deepen our relationship with him and live as people of God)*

• See *Reflecting on Your Faith* below.

WORKING WITH THE ACTIVITY
Opening the Word

• Ask a volunteer to read aloud *Opening the Word.*

• Allow the students sufficient time to read the additional Scripture passages and respond to the question. *(Possible answers may include that we must learn to recognize the presence of Jesus in our lives.)*

• See *Scripture Background* below.

VOCABULARY
The term *Paschal mystery* means the saving mystery of Jesus' passion, death, resurrection, and ascension. The word *pasch* means "Passover." Passover is the name of the Jewish feast that celebrates God's saving act in the life of the Jewish people—their deliverance from slavery in Egypt. As Christians we sometimes refer to Easter as the Pasch because this is the feast day on which we celebrate Christ's passage from death to new life.

SCRIPTURE BACKGROUND
John 20:14–15 depicts Mary's meeting Jesus in the garden and not recognizing him. This personal encounter between Mary and Jesus reminds us of the personal encounter we have with Jesus in the sacraments. We can ask ourselves whether or not we will recognize him in our lives. You may wish to point out that this passage is part of the readings for Easter Tuesday, Cycles A, B, and C. Refer to page 108 of this book for more information about the liturgical year.

FAITH PARTNERSHIPS
Allow time for the Faith Partners to meet and discuss their experiences of grace. Remind the students that their experiences, while significant, will not necessarily be moments of high drama.

REFLECTING ON YOUR FAITH
In what significant ways have you come to know Jesus? How do you experience the Paschal mystery?

EXTENSION ACTIVITY
Making a symbol Have the students work in small groups to use their religious imagination to come up with a symbol for the Paschal mystery and to illustrate the symbol. You may wish to suggest a few symbols, such as a cross with a shroud, a butterfly, or the seasons of the year.

WORKING WITH THE ACTIVITY
Catholics Believe
- Ask a volunteer to read aloud *Catholics Believe.*
✓ - Allow time for the students to write their reflections on the question. *(Answers will vary.)*
- See *Reflecting on Your Faith* below.
- Encourage the students to share with the group their thoughts about the paraphrased Catechism statement and their responses to the question that follows.

WORKING WITH THE TEXT AND PICTURES
✓ - Read *The Liturgical Year,* and review the pictures on pages 18 and 19.
✓ - Use *Vocabulary* below to help the students understand the term *liturgical year.*
✓ - The liturgical year helps us commemorate and celebrate events in Jesus' life. **When do we celebrate Jesus' birth?** *(Christmas, December 25)* **When do we celebrate Jesus' resurrection?** *(Easter Sunday)* **What other feasts and holy days do we celebrate?** *(Answers will vary.)*
- Emphasize that color symbolizes the meaning of a holy day or season. **What color is used for Christmas? For Lent? For Easter? For Pentecost?** *(white or gold for Christmas and Easter, purple for Lent, red for Pentecost)*
- Discuss the photographs. **How does each picture relate to the liturgical year?** *(Possible responses: The adolescents are actively participating in a celebration or worship service marked in the liturgical calendar; vestments indicate the special colors used for each holy day and season.)*
✓ - See *Skill Note* below.

In the sacraments we are united with Christ and become members of his Body, the Church, which continues his work in the world. Our sins are forgiven, and the Holy Spirit strengthens us so that we can live our faith and witness to the saving power we have experienced in our lives. The sacraments help us deepen our faith and live as disciples of Jesus.

The writer of the Acts of the Apostles gives us many examples of the early Christians experiencing the Holy Spirit. Peter, for example, was a frightened man, unsure of himself and his faith in Jesus; the night before the crucifixion, he denied knowing Jesus. But the Spirit strengthened and guided Peter, and soon Peter was bravely teaching others about Jesus. (See *Acts 2:14–42.*) Through our participation in the sacraments, the Spirit strengthens us, too.

The Liturgical Year

Through the seasons and holy days of the **liturgical year,** the Church celebrates Jesus' passion, death, resurrection, and ascension—the Paschal mystery.

The liturgical year is different from the ⓢ calendar year with which we are familiar.

The liturgical year begins with the Season of Advent, the first Sunday of which occurs in late November or early December. During Advent we recall the first coming of the Son of God into human history, and we prepare for the coming of Christ, in our hearts, in history, and at the end of time. Some families use an Advent calendar to mark the days before Christmas, or they might have a Jesse tree that recalls the many holy people who prepared the way for Jesus. Churches usually use an Advent wreath, something you may also have in your home. Lighting the candles of the wreath and praying and singing together help us prepare for Christmas. The liturgical color for Advent is violet.

The color for Christmas is white. (Any time white is used, gold may be used.) On Christmas we celebrate the Incarnation, the Son of God becoming one of us.

Catholics Believe

Grace is participation in the life of God. See Catechism, #1997.
How does participating in the life of God change you?
_____
_____
_____
_____

18 **MOMENTS OF GRACE**

RESOURCE Center

VOCABULARY ✓
The *liturgical year* is the annual cycle of Church seasons comprising the Church year. The liturgical year, which is different from the traditional calendar, celebrates Christ's life, death, resurrection, and ascension.

ⓢ SKILL NOTE ✓
Discussion of the liturgical year can enhance the students' understanding of how Catholics use religious imagination to celebrate their faith. See pages 22 and 23 for more information.

EXTENSION ACTIVITY
Celebrating with a faith calendar Distribute art supplies such as paper, markers, scissors, and glue. Have the students create calendars that show how they celebrate their faith throughout the year. In addition to the liturgical seasons and significant holy days, the students may include other days important to them, such as birthdays and wedding anniversaries.

REFLECTING ON YOUR FAITH
In what ways has participating in the life of God helped you become a better person?

Student Leader Connection
Consider having the Student Leader do the following:
- Select two or three feasts or liturgical seasons to research, and report the findings to the group.
- Record the results of the group discussion on the liturgical year.
- Use a television show with which the group is familiar to discuss *Media Message.*

Media Message

THE FAITHFUL MEDIA? Church is not the only place we hear about religion and our spiritual lives. We can also get messages about God and spirituality in the media: through the movies and television shows we watch, the songs we listen to, the magazines we read, the video games we play, and the Internet sites we visit. The messages may be about reincarnation, supernatural powers, angels, and beliefs about how God acts or doesn't act in our lives.

How has the media affected your understanding of your relationship with God? How do you decide what is hurtful and what is helpful?

_____
_____
_____
_____
_____
_____

Lent is the season of prayer and sacrifice that begins with Ash Wednesday and lasts about forty days. Lent has always been a time of repentance through prayer, fasting, and almsgiving. During Lent we may spend more time in private prayer or participate in the Stations of the Cross or communal penance services. In remembering Jesus' willing sacrifice for us, we may decide to give up eating a favorite food. And we can try to be more generous, perhaps devoting time to helping with community projects. In Lent we prepare for Easter by examining our lives and finding ways to follow Jesus more closely by preparing for or renewing our conversion and Baptism. The liturgical color for Lent is purple.

Easter is the high point of the liturgical year because it celebrates Jesus' resurrection from the dead. The week beginning with Palm Sunday is called Holy Week. Lent ends on Holy Thursday evening, and the Easter Triduum begins. The Triduum, or three holy days, includes the observance of Holy Thursday (white), Good Friday (red), and the Easter Vigil on Holy Saturday (white).

In many wonderful ways our Church celebrations, especially during the Easter Season, express our joy in experiencing new life in Christ. As at Christmas, we use the color white during the Easter Season. This season lasts about seven weeks (fifty days) until Pentecost. At Pentecost, we celebrate the gift of the Holy Spirit sent to the followers of Jesus gathered in the upper room in Jerusalem.

The liturgical color for Pentecost is red, a color that is also used during the celebration of the Sacrament of Confirmation because of that sacrament's connection with the Holy Spirit.

The majority of the liturgical year is called Ordinary Time. In this case the term *ordinary* means "ordered" (like "ordinal numbers") or "numbered" rather than "common." Ordinary Time is the time during the Church year that is not part of the Advent, Christmas, Lent, or Easter Seasons. During Ordinary Time the Church community reflects on what it means to walk in the footsteps of Jesus—to be his disciples. The liturgical color for Ordinary Time is green.

During the liturgical year we celebrate and commemorate Jesus' life and grow in discipleship. The liturgical year is the framework for the members of the Body of Christ to come together for prayer and liturgical celebrations.

WORKING WITH THE TEXT AND PICTURES

- Review the text and picture on the page.
- Discuss the seasons of the Church year with the students. *What are some of the ways you and your family prepare for Christmas? For Easter? How do you celebrate these feasts?* *(Accept all reasonable answers.)*
- Point out other feasts with which the students may be less familiar. Pay particular attention to the Easter Triduum. Explain to the students what happens during this three-day period.
- See *Background* below.
- Discuss the meaning of the term *Ordinary Time* with the students. Tell them that this season of the liturgical year has its own significance and should not be thought of as "ordinary" in the sense of uneventful and unimportant. *What do we reflect on in particular during Ordinary Time?* *(Possible answers: what it means to walk in the footsteps of Jesus, what it means to be his disciples.)*

WORKING WITH THE ACTIVITY
Media Message

- Ask a volunteer to read aloud *Media Message*.
- Allow time for the students to complete the activity. *(Answers will vary.)*
- Invite the students to share their responses, and discuss with them some of the helpful and hurtful ideas and information they get from the media that can affect their relationship with God.
- See *Reflecting on Your Faith* below.

LINK TO SOCIAL SCIENCE

Many societies throughout history have created calendars as a way of marking time and celebrating special events. We use the Julian calendar, in which the year begins with January 1. This calendar was developed by Sosigenes during the reign of Julius Caesar, adjusted somewhat by Augustus Caesar, and reformed by Pope Gregory XIII. Other calendars currently in use include the Jewish calendar, which dates from the year equal to 3761 B.C., and the Islamic calendar, which dates from A.D. 622.

REFLECTING ON YOUR FAITH

Have you ever thought about reducing the amount of time you spend watching television or browsing the Internet? What effect could this have on your relationship with God?

BACKGROUND

Liturgical colors The colors associated with the feasts and seasons of the liturgical year have different meanings. Purple and violet are used for penance. Red reminds us of the tongues as of fire on Pentecost and of how Christ and some of his followers, such as the early Christian martyrs, sacrificed their lives for love of God. Green symbolizes hope and growth in our faith life. White is a symbol of celebration and life in Christ, and it is also used on the feasts of virgins. White is also used for funerals and Masses for the dead as well as at Christmas and Easter.

Easter Triduum This term (*Triduum* is Latin for "a space of three days") refers to the 72-hour liturgical season that begins on Thursday evening, extends through Good Friday and Holy Saturday, and ends on the evening of Easter Sunday. Focused intensely on the core of the Paschal mystery—the passion, death, resurrection, and ascension of Jesus—the Easter Triduum is the center point of the entire liturgical year.

WORKING WITH THE TEXT AND PICTURES

✓ • Read the text on this page, and review the picture on pages 20 and 21.

✓ • Discuss how God is present in the sacraments. ***How can God's love affect our lives?*** *(Possible answers may include that we will become more patient, that we will get along better with others, and that we will be more generous.)*

• Review the students' examples of the effects grace can have on our lives from the discussion on page 16.

• Ask the students to look at the photograph of the labyrinth. Point out that a labyrinth is similar to a maze but that the path is easy to follow. No choices need be made. People use the labyrinth as a means of prayer and meditation. ***Why might some people find a labyrinth to be an aid to prayer?*** *(Accept all reasonable responses.)*

• See *Background* below.

WORKING WITH THE ACTIVITY

Wrap Up

• Have a volunteer read aloud the summary statements.

✓ • Allow time for the students to consider their remaining questions and write them in their books.

• Discuss any remaining questions the students may have. You may wish to have the students write their questions on separate sheets of paper so that you can collect them and respond during the next session.

Growing in Grace

The sacraments are celebrations of the Paschal mystery, enabling us to experience Christ's presence with us. They confer the grace of which they are a sign because Christ is at work in them. By celebrating the suffering, death, and resurrection of the Son of God, Jesus Christ, we enter more deeply into the life of faith to which we are called. The grace of the sacraments helps us respond to God with love and to love ourselves and others.

Think about how you get along with others. Is there a difficult person in your life who is very demanding and critical? Or maybe there is someone who is never happy and lets everyone know it. The grace of the sacraments can help you do what you know is right, such as be patient. You may not be able to make an unhappy person happy, but you may be able to put up with this person's unhappiness and not let it ruin your day or make his or her day worse. You may even find yourself able to appreciate some of this person's better characteristics!

When we meet God in the sacraments, we experience the power of his love. It is as if a close friend is always with us to support and guide us. We feel less selfish and more giving toward others. Our viewpoint gradually widens from thinking primarily about ourselves to thinking about God and other people.

Reflect on how the sacraments allow us to better understand our relationship with God. Share your thoughts with your Faith Partner.

WRAP UP

• The Paschal mystery refers to the suffering, death, and resurrection of Christ through which he saved us from the power of sin and everlasting death.

• Grace is God's life in us and the help we are given by the Holy Spirit to deepen our relationship with God.

• We celebrate the Paschal mystery through the sacraments and through the seasons of the liturgical year.

• In the sacraments we celebrate our lives as members of the Body of Christ.

What questions do you have about the content of this chapter?

_____

_____

_____

FAITH PARTNERSHIPS

Instruct the students to talk with their Faith Partners about how the sacraments help us understand our relationship with God. Remind the students that God is revealed to us and that we draw closer to him through the sacraments.

EXTENSION ACTIVITY

Skits   Arrange the students in three or four groups. Ask each group to describe how a brief, everyday event or conversation might unfold when one or more participants are not responding to God's grace. Ask the groups to describe the same situations when all the participants are responding to God's grace. Each group should present both versions of the skit to the other groups. Situations might include being pressured to shoplift and passing by someone who needs help.

ART BACKGROUND

Considered a form of "body prayer" or walking meditation, the labyrinth represents the search for meaning and guidance in life. The unicursal pattern is a metaphor for a spiritual journey.

The path leads the walker to the center and back to the starting point—the way in is the way out. Walking a labyrinth (which, unlike a maze, is neither a puzzle nor a tangle of blind alleys) is thought to promote in the seeker growth, discovery, enlightenment, and even closeness to God. Built around 1200, the labyrinth shown is on the floor of Chartres Cathedral near Paris, France.

Student Leader Connection

Consider having the Student Leader do the following:

• **Read aloud selected text.**

• **Help moderate the group discussion on ways the sacraments can affect our lives.**

• **Read aloud the *Wrap Up* summary statements.**

• **Help moderate the discussion for *Around the Group*.**

RESOURCE Center

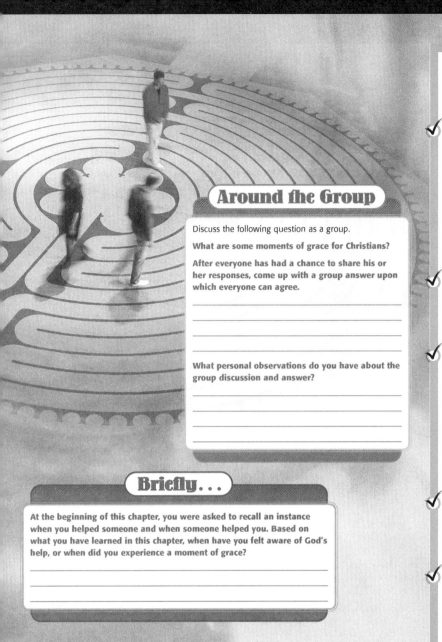

WORKING WITH THE ACTIVITIES

Around the Group

✓ • Present the question to the group, and allow time for discussion. You may need to moderate to keep the students focused on the question.

• Encourage the group members to listen to the opinions and perspectives of others.

• To help the students identify moments of grace, remind them that grace is not magic or a thing, but God sharing his life with us. Our relationship with God can change our lives.

✓ • If the group has agreed on an answer, direct the students to write it in their books. If they could not agree, direct them to list in their books the issues that were left unresolved and explain why.

✓ • Encourage the students to note in their books their personal observations about the discussion and any final thoughts they have.

• See *Reflecting on Your Faith* below.

Briefly . . .

• Encourage the students to consider how their opinions may have changed since they responded to *What Do You Think?* on page 15.

✓ • Ask the students to think about times when they wanted to help others and to do good. *In what situations might people your age discover within themselves the strength to do the right thing?*

✓ • Allow time for the students to write their responses in their books.

• See *Reflecting on Your Faith* below.

Around the Group

Discuss the following question as a group.

What are some moments of grace for Christians?

After everyone has had a chance to share his or her responses, come up with a group answer upon which everyone can agree.

What personal observations do you have about the group discussion and answer?

Briefly . . .

At the beginning of this chapter, you were asked to recall an instance when you helped someone and when someone helped you. Based on what you have learned in this chapter, when have you felt aware of God's help, or when did you experience a moment of grace?

REFLECT 21

REFLECTING ON YOUR FAITH

Around the Group: How can you help the students see that God's grace is both subtle and powerful?

Briefly: Reflect on times when you have been aware of God's grace in your life or in the lives of those with whom you are close.

EXTENSION ACTIVITY

Talking about grace Help the students talk about grace by encouraging them to put into words what a Christian's relationship with God is like. This idea may be more concrete for the students if you invite them to create one-panel cartoons expressing an insight about the relationship between God and humans. With emphasis on ideas such as faithfulness, love, and friendship, the students will be less inclined to think of grace as magical or as a "thing."

WORKING WITH THE SKILL

✓ • Remind the students that the skill for Chapters 1 and 2 is Using Religious Imagination. Discuss with the students how they have tried to use the skill since the end of Chapter 1.

✓ • Remind the students that moments of grace in their lives are steps to building the skill of Using Religious Imagination. *How do moments of grace help us develop religious imagination?* *(Possible responses: Moments of grace reveal to us the relationship we have with God and guide us to continue and improve that relationship.)*

• Discuss with the students ways that using religious imagination can help increase our faith. *How does using religious imagination help us grow in faith?* *(Possible responses: This skill helps us recognize God's presence in our lives.)*

• Ask a volunteer to read aloud *Expressions of Faith*.

✓ • Ask another volunteer to read aloud *Scripture*. Use the information presented in *Scripture Background* below to help the students use religious imagination to understand the meaning of the story—that faith inspires us to accomplish amazing things.

✓ • Ask a volunteer to read aloud *Skill Steps*. Talk with the students about how we use religious imagination. *What examples of religious imagination can you name?* *(Possible responses: works of art, hymns and songs; words that inspire us; recognizing signs of God's presence and action in our lives.)*

• See *Reflecting on Your Faith* below.

SKILLS FOR Christian Living

Using Religious Imagination

Expressions of Faith—

The skill of Using Religious Imagination can help us sense moments of grace in our lives, thereby helping us experience God's love. When we use our religious imagination, we are not limited to objects or images we can paint or sculpt. We also use our religious imagination any time we experience the presence of God in an action or event.

Scripture

But immediately Jesus spoke to them and said, "Take heart, it is I; do not be afraid." Peter answered him, "Lord, if it is you, command me to come to you on the water." He said, "Come." So Peter got out of the boat, started walking on the water, and came toward Jesus.
Matthew 14:27–29 19th Sunday of Ordinary Time

Skill Steps—

Recall what religious imagination is: the skill that can inspire us and open us to God's love in our lives. Religious imagination means using language, symbols, and gestures to express our relationship with God.

Here are some key points to remember:

● Jesus used religious imagination.

● Each of us has the ability and the obligation to use our religious imagination.

● We use language, symbols, and gestures to express our faith.

● We know God through the signs and symbols he uses to reveal himself to us.

● In Scripture the writers used religious imagination to communicate their experiences of God.

● We can use our religious imagination to motivate ourselves, renew our spirits, and grow in faith.

22 MOMENTS OF GRACE

SCRIPTURE BACKGROUND ✓

Matthew 14:27–29 illustrates the importance of religious imagination in two ways. First, the reader must use religious imagination to understand the meaning of the story. Second, Peter's own religious imagination shows in his willingness to depend upon his faith to achieve something that normally would be impossible. Although Peter loves Jesus and has faith in him, the rest of the story shows how doubt can weaken faith. (See *Matthew 14:22–33*.) You may wish to point out that this passage is part of the readings for the Nineteenth Sunday of Ordinary Time, Cycle A. Refer to page 108 of this book for more information about the liturgical year.

RESOURCE Center

REFLECTING ON YOUR FAITH
Think of three life-changing events that could occur in an adult's life. How might you treat each of these as a new beginning?

Student Leader Connection

Consider having the Student Leader do the following:

• **Read aloud *Matthew 14:22–33*.**

• **Review the skill pages from Chapter 1.**

• **Lead the group in praying the closing prayer.**

• **Organize a small group to plan a prayer service.**

Special Note: Remember to meet briefly with the Student Leader for Chapter 3. You may wish to provide him or her with the Student Leader Prep Page for Chapter 3, found on page R5.

Skill Builder–

Exercise religious imagination by thinking of the following situations as opportunities for new beginnings. What symbol might you use for each?

Share your responses and thoughts with your Faith Partner.

○ A best friend moves away.

_____

○ An older brother or sister goes to college.

_____

○ You begin attending a new school.

_____

Putting It into Practice–

Now use your religious imagination to express your experience of God's grace in your life.

○ Describe a moment in your life when you had an experience of God that moved you deeply.

_____

_____

○ Through a poem, express the feeling of being protected or empowered by God.

_____

_____

Now that you have had some practice using your religious imagination, give yourself a letter grade. _____ Explain why you graded yourself the way you did. List one area in which you need to improve.

Closing Prayer–

God of power and mercy, you are always there for us. When we are hurt and angry, you send us comfort. When we are facing a tough challenge, you give us strength. When we are not sure what to do, you grant us wisdom. Where would we be without you? Our hearts are grateful that we can depend on you. In Jesus' name, we pray. Amen.

WORKING WITH THE SKILL

✓ • Read *Skill Builder* aloud. Encourage the students to use religious imagination to think creatively about the opportunities that come with change. Have the students work with their Faith Partners to complete the activity.

✓ • Ask a volunteer to read aloud *Putting It into Practice*. To make sure the students understand the activity, discuss it with them.

✓ • Allow some time for the students to complete the activity. Encourage them to use descriptive words and phrases.

• See *Reflecting on Your Faith* below.

CLOSING PRAYER

✓ • Gather together to pray the closing prayer. You may wish to use the following music from the *Give Your Gifts* series: "Psalm 122: Let Us Go Rejoicing" *(The Songs)*, "Psalm 118: This Is the Day" *(The Basics)*, or "On That Day" *(More Songs)* (GIA Publications, Inc.; distributed by Harcourt Religion Publishers).

• You may choose to sing the hymn "Amazing Grace" with the students.

• If time permits, direct the students to create their own closing reflections or prayers. You may wish to ask a few volunteers to read aloud what they have created or to plan a prayer service. As an alternative for prayer, you may wish to use "Sacraments: Prayer Service A" from *Living Our Faith Prayer Services* by Robert Piercy and Linda Baltikas (GIA Publications, Inc.; distributed by Harcourt Religion Publishers).

REFLECTING ON YOUR FAITH

While the students are completing the *Putting It into Practice* activity, think about what your own response might be.

FAITH PARTNERSHIPS

Invite the students to share their symbols with their Faith Partners.

TEACHING TIP

Research follow-up You may wish to take time to review any research the students have been asked to complete. If the students need additional time to complete their research, set aside a few minutes at the beginning of the next session to allow them to share the information they have gathered.

LINK TO LITURGY

Have the students find a poem or a psalm that is an example of poetic inspiration about faith.

MULTIPLE LEARNING STYLES

Closing prayer You may wish to have the students create their closing prayers in the style of a formal prayer or reflection; a poem or song; or a prayer service with readings, psalm response, and music. Remind the students that the tone of their responses can be different from that of the example but should remain respectful.

ASSESSMENT

The Assessment Page for Chapter 2 can be found on page R10.

LINK TO FAMILY

The corresponding Family Resource pages for this skill are 46–50.

Baptism

KEY CONTENT SUMMARY

Baptism is the first sacrament and is a Sacrament of Christian Initiation. Through Baptism we are reborn as members of the Body of Christ. Through Baptism we share in the priesthood of Christ. Baptism calls us to be responsible members of the Church throughout our lives.

PLANNING THE CHAPTER

OPEN	PACING	CONTENT	OBJECTIVES	MATERIALS
	Suggested Time: **Parish 10 min.** **School 25 min..** Your Time: ____ min.	pp. 24–25	• Recognize that Baptism is one of the Sacraments of Christian Initiation.	• candle, matches (optional) • symbol representing chapter theme (optional) • bowl of holy water (optional)

SEARCH				
	Suggested Time: **Parish 25 min.** **School 70 min.** Your Time: ____ min.	pp. 26–29	• Identify and examine how, through Baptism, we are given new life in Christ and made members of the Body of Christ. • Explore the elements and effects of Baptism and how we celebrate the Rite for infants and for adults.	• Bibles • art supplies (optional) • symbols of Baptism (optional) • items for welcome baskets (optional)

REFLECT				
	Suggested Time: **Parish 10 min.** **School 30 min.** Your Time: ____ min.	pp. 30–31	• Reflect on what it means to be a member of the Body of Christ.	• art supplies (optional) • note paper and pens (optional)

LIVE				
	Suggested Time: **Parish 15 min.** **School 35 min.** Your Time: ____ min.	pp. 32–33	• Apply our ability to be responsible members of our family, our community, and our Church.	• Student Leader Prep Page for Chapter 4 (p. R5) (optional) • music for prayer (optional) • copies of Assessment Page for Chapter 3 (p. R11) (optional)

CATECHISM IN CONTEXT

See *Catechism of the Catholic Church*, #1213.

Baptism is a Sacrament of Christian Initiation. In Greek, *baptize* means "plunge" or "immerse," so the Sacrament of Baptism symbolizes our immersion into Christ's death and our resurrection with him into new life. Just as Christ was raised from the dead, so we are raised, through Baptism, to begin an earthly journey leading to eternal life in God.

The grace bestowed by God in Baptism brings the enlightenment of faith. Through faith we establish our relationship with God and we gather the strength to live as followers of Jesus.

Baptism sets us on our journey, marks our destination, and seals our covenant with God: "Go therefore and make disciples of all nations, baptizing them in the name of the Father and of the Son and of the Holy Spirit, and teaching them to obey everything that I have commanded you" *(Matthew 28:19–20)*.

ONE-MINUTE RETREAT

READ

"To each one of us Christ is saying: If you want your life and mission to be fruitful like mine, . . . [be] like me."
—Oscar Romero

REFLECT

What is Christ-like about my life and mission?

PRAY

Holy Spirit, through Baptism I was given new life in Christ. Help me appreciate the gift of faith and my membership in the Body of Christ. Take away my sinfulness. Guide me to be a responsible member of my family, my community, and the Church. Amen.

LIBRARY LINKS

BOOKS
FOR ADOLESCENTS

"Baptism: A Great Beginning," by James DiGiacomo SJ (*Youth Update;* St. Anthony Messenger Press).

Emphasizes the significance of Baptism and discusses reasons for apathy about this sacrament.

"Holy Spirit: Giving Your Life the Light Touch," by Christopher M. Bellito (*Youth Update;* St. Anthony Messenger Press).

Offers practical ways for young Catholics to examine their lives to find the presence of the Holy Spirit.

Words Around the Font, by Gail Ramshaw (Liturgy Training Publications, 1995).

The meaning of the words we use in Baptism and the RCIA.

FOR ADULTS

Baptism Sourcebook, ed. by J. Robert Baker, Larry J. Nyberg, and Victoria M. Tufano (Liturgy Training Publications, 1993).

A collection of key texts, prayers, and resources.

Come to the Light: An Invitation to Baptism and Confirmation, by Richard N. Fragomeni (Continuum International Publishing Group Inc., 1998).

A discussion of the contemporary context of the Sacraments of Christian Initiation.

"The RCIA: The Art of Making New Catholics," by Sandra DeGidio OSM (*Catholic Update;* St. Anthony Messenger Press).

Examines how the Catholic Church brings new members into communal life; walks readers through the four-step RCIA process.

MULTIMEDIA

Lord of Life: Baptism (video) (Harcourt Religion Publishers).

Examines our baptism as followers of Jesus; emphasizes that parents are primary caretakers of God's gift to the child in Baptism.

The Catechumenate in Brief (video) (produced by the Archdiocese of Miami; distributed by Harcourt Religion Publishers).

Explains RCIA through the steps, rituals, and terminology used in the process.

FEATURE PREPARATION

STUDENT LEADER CONNECTION

The Student Leader Prep Page for this chapter is located on page R5. You may wish to provide this information to the Student Leader as an introduction and resource for the chapter.

FAITH PARTNERSHIPS

Chapter 3 begins a new Faith Partnership. Several opportunities for Faith Partner discussions have been marked throughout the chapter. You may wish to consider other opportunities as you prepare the lesson.

SKILL NOTES

The skill for this chapter is Being Accountable. As you teach the skill lesson on pages 32 and 33, you may wish to refer to the Skill Notes marked throughout the chapter. These notes will help you identify terms and ideas related to the skill.

A check mark indicates the chapter's essential questions, statements, activities, and features. If time is limited, such as in a parish group setting, this icon will help you direct the students through the lesson.

Baptism

You may wish to review these points with the students before you begin the new chapter:

- Grace flows from our relationship with God.
- The sacraments are signs of God's grace.
- The Paschal mystery is celebrated in each sacrament and throughout the liturgical year.
- The sacraments allow us to better understand our relationship with God.
- Using Religious Imagination is a Skill for Christian Living.

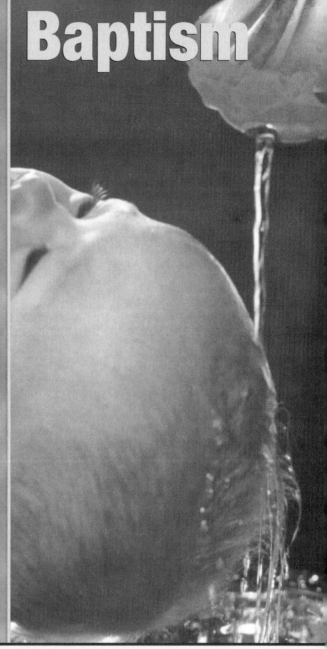

Father of us all, bless those who seek the waters of Baptism for new life in Jesus Christ your Son. And bless those of us who have already been baptized, that we may respond to your love and live as the Holy Spirit guides us.

24

✓ GATHERING

Have the students work in small groups to think of symbols for the Christian community. After each group has drawn a symbol on paper and cut the paper into puzzle pieces, have the groups exchange puzzles. Group members may then work together to reassemble the puzzles.

✓ PRAYER

Pour holy water into a bowl and invite the students to come forward and dip their fingers into the water to make the Sign of the Cross. Then pray the opening prayer as a group. If fire regulations permit, you may wish to light a candle at this time.

PRAYER ENVIRONMENT

If you have created a prayer space for the room, you may wish to display one or more sacramentals or a symbol associated with Baptism (such as water, a white garment, oil, or a candle) to represent the theme of this chapter.

FAITH PARTNER INTRODUCTION

If you haven't done so already, remind the students that it is time for them to create new Faith Partnerships. After you have assigned new Faith Partners, you may wish to give the students a few moments to complete together a Faith Partner introduction. Ask the Faith Partners to explain why they happen to have their first names. Are they named for family members? Is there a tradition attached to the name? (You may wish to begin by explaining your own given name.) Allow time for the students to answer the questions and share their responses.

RESOURCE Center

Student Leader Connection

Consider having the Student Leader do the following:

- Lead the opening prayer.
- Read aloud selected text.
- Help moderate the discussion about belonging to groups.

What Do You Think?

List the groups you have chosen to join.
What were your reasons for joining each of these groups?

Group _____

Group _____

Reasons for joining

_____

_____

Group _____

Reasons for joining

_____

_____

Group _____

Reasons for joining

_____

_____

Group _____

Reasons for joining

_____

_____

Group _____

Reasons for joining

_____

_____

Be a Part of It!

Think about why you belong to various groups. Sometimes the association is automatic, as it is with your family. But when you decide to join a group, you may have to prepare in some way before being admitted. This preparation, or initiation, helps you know more about the group, and it also helps the group know more about you. To join the school band, for instance, you must learn to play a musical instrument and practice the music the band plays.

Joining a group means becoming part of a new community. The way we look at and experience life changes. The experience of gaining membership in a group is similar to what happens in Baptism, the first Sacrament of Christian Initiation. Becoming members of the Church can bring out the best in us and help us become the people God wants us to be.

WORKING WITH THE ACTIVITY

What Do You Think?

- Allow time for the students to record their thoughts in the space provided.
- See *Reflecting on Your Faith* below.
- *What Do You Think?* is intended as a personal pre-assessment. The students should not be asked to share their responses.

WORKING WITH THE TEXT AND PICTURES

- Read the text on this page, and review the pictures on pages 24 and 25.
- Discuss some groups to which the students belong. **How did you become a member of one of these groups?** *(Accept all reasonable responses.)*
- Point out that some groups require a process of initiation before admitting new members. **Why may a period of preparation be required before a person is admitted to a group?** *(Possible answers: A period of preparation gives the new person a chance to know a group's members and goals better; this period gives the group a chance to know the prospective member better.)*
- Discuss the photographs. **What message do these pictures convey?** *(Accept all reasonable responses.)*
- Point out the details of Baptism shown in the photographs. **What significant objects and people are pictured?** *(Possible responses: a candle, a white cloth, a baptismal gown, water, parents, godparents, a priest.)*

TEACHING TIP

Dealing with personal issues   Show sensitivity when discussing questions that may touch on personal issues. Keep the conversation general, and set a tone of respect. Avoid pushing the students to talk about personal matters, and encourage all the students to be respectful of one another.

MULTIPLE LEARNING STYLES

Sculpture   Suggest that the students do the following activity at home. Invite each student to create a sculpture that tells something about one of the groups to which he or she belongs. The students might choose to create a symbol for the group, a sculpture of one of the group members, or an image of something the group does. When the students have finished creating their sculptures, invite volunteers to share them with the rest of the group.

WORKING WITH THE TEXT AND PICTURES

✓ • Read the text and review the pictures on this page.

- Invite the students to talk about wanting to have best friends. ***What are the qualities you want in someone who is a good friend?*** *(Accept all responses and be prepared to build on the gift of acceptance.)*

✓ • Direct the students' attention to the photograph from a baptismal scrapbook. Use the photograph to ask questions about the students' experiences of Baptism. They may have celebrated the Baptism of a younger sibling or an older family member, or they may have been baptized recently themselves. Ask volunteers to describe the celebration in which they participated.

- See *Background* below.

WORKING WITH THE ACTIVITY

Opening the Word

- Ask a volunteer to read aloud *Opening the Word.*

✓ • Allow the students sufficient time to read the additional Scripture passages and respond to the question. *(In the Sacrament of Baptism, the Holy Spirit comes upon us. The Scripture passage from Matthew 3:16 describes the Holy Spirit as taking the form of a dove, descending from the heavens upon Jesus.)*

✓ • See *Scripture Background* below.

Becoming a Christian

Who is your best friend? Why are the two of you so close? Is it because you share interests and participate in many activities together? Is it because you have come to know each other so well? Best friends are important. Good friends defend us and support us during difficult times.

Our relationship with Jesus is like that. We recognize all that he has done for us through his life, death, and resurrection. Believing in him, we want to be closer to him. We are fully initiated into the Church, the Body of Christ, through the Sacraments of Christian Initiation: Baptism, Confirmation, and Eucharist.

Opening the Word

Sunday After Epiphany, Cycle A

And when Jesus had been baptized, just as he came up from the water, suddenly the heavens were opened to him and he saw the Spirit of God descending like a dove and alighting on him. Matthew 3:16

Read *Matthew 3:13–17* as well as *Acts 2:38* and *Romans 6:1–4.* What do these passages tell us about Baptism?

_____
_____
_____
_____

26 **BAPTISM**

RESOURCE Center

BACKGROUND

Initiation in the Eastern Rites In the Eastern Rites of the Catholic Church, the Sacraments of Christian Initiation—Baptism, Confirmation (called Chrismation), and Eucharist—are always celebrated together at the same ceremony.

Eastern Churches in union with Rome descend historically from the patriarchates of Constantinople, Alexandria, Antioch, and Jerusalem. Members of these churches are Catholics. Eastern Churches not in union with Rome are frequently referred to as Orthodox Churches.

SCRIPTURE BACKGROUND

A different account of Jesus' baptism in the Jordan River appears in each of the four Gospels. For the writer of the Gospel of Matthew, the baptism *(Matthew 3:13–17)* is an affirmation of Jesus' righteousness and his perfect obedience to the will of his Father. The Spirit's descent upon Jesus signifies that Jesus is the Messiah, but the event is depicted as Jesus' private experience. No witnesses to the descent of the Holy

Spirit appear in this Gospel's description. You may wish to point out that this Scripture passage is part of the readings for the Baptism of the Lord, the Sunday After Epiphany, Cycle A. Refer to page 108 of this book for more information about the liturgical year.

Student Leader Connection

Consider having the Student Leader do the following:

- **Read aloud *Opening the Word.***
- **Record the results of the group discussion about Christian initiation.**
- **Read aloud one or more of the additional Scripture passages.**

The Rite of Baptism

Baptism is the first sacrament. It is the beginning of our life in Christ. Most of the baptized people you know were probably baptized as infants. But Baptism can also be celebrated when an older child or adult chooses to become a Christian. As members of the Body of Christ, we welcome new members of all ages.

Baptism is celebrated in two ways in the Latin Rite of the Catholic Church—either separately as a sacrament for infants and young children or together with Eucharist and Confirmation for older children and adults. If you were baptized as an infant, you probably celebrated your First Communion in elementary school, and if you haven't celebrated Confirmation, you may be preparing for it.

Adults and older children go through the *Rite of Christian Initiation of Adults (RCIA).* In RCIA the person seeking initiation is older than seven, the age at which, according to the Church, a person can tell right from wrong. After the pre-catechumenate, a time of inquiry, the inquirer is welcomed into the catechumenate. The catechumen, or the person preparing for Baptism, states publicly his or her intention to become a member of the Church. The person then studies for a period of time, after which the Rite of Election or Enrollment of Names is celebrated, usually on the first Sunday of Lent. During this ceremony the Church formally acknowledges the catechumen's readiness for initiation. Lent is the time of reflection and final preparation. Then, often as part of the Easter Vigil, the elect are initiated into the Church through the celebration of the Sacraments of Baptism, Confirmation, and the Eucharist.

However Baptism is celebrated, we join the community in welcoming the individual into our Church family. If you have younger family members, you probably watch out for them and guide them. The same is true of our Church family. As members of the Body of Christ, we have a duty to help younger or less experienced members learn about and live our faith.

When infants and children are baptized, godparents have a special role in the celebration. They promise to help the newly baptized person grow in faith, and they join with parents in making this promise.

Share your ideas about the role of godparents with your Faith Partner.

OUR CHRISTIAN JOURNEY

Initiation: Then and Now In the early centuries of the Church, many people became members of the Church as adults, although infants were also baptized. Adult catechumens studied, prayed, and prepared for their initiation for months or even years. Lent, the time during which the Church prepares for Easter, was the period of their final preparation. Then, during the Easter Vigil, which takes place during the hours preceding the dawn of Easter Sunday, the catechumens were baptized, confirmed, and received the Eucharist for the first time. Over the centuries this practice gradually came to an end. However, it was reinstituted after the Second Vatican Council in the form of the **Rite of Christian Initiation of Adults** (RCIA). Today our practice is similar to that of the early Church.

For more information: Speak to someone in your parish about how people can join the Church, or read your diocesan paper to learn about RCIA in your diocese.

WORKING WITH THE TEXT AND PICTURES

✓ • Read the text on this page.

✓ • Use *Vocabulary* below to help the students understand the terms *catechumen* and *godparents*.

✓ • Discuss the Rite of Christian Initiation of Adults. *How do catechumens prepare for the sacraments?* (by praying, studying, and celebrating rites such as the Rite of Election or Enrollment of Names) *What are the three Sacraments of Christian Initiation?* (Baptism, Confirmation, and Eucharist) *When are these sacraments usually celebrated in a single rite?* (at the Easter Vigil)

✓ • Discuss Christian initiation. *In what two ways is Baptism celebrated?* (as an individual sacrament for infants, with Confirmation and Eucharist for older children and adults) *Who participates in RCIA?* (older children and adults who are being initiated into the Church)

• Point out that baptized persons may also use RCIA to prepare for Confirmation and Eucharist.

• See *Reflecting on Your Faith* below.

WORKING WITH THE ACTIVITY

Our Christian Journey

• Ask a volunteer to read aloud *Our Christian Journey.*

✓ • Discuss initiation in the early Church. *How is initiation today similar to that of long ago?* (Adults prepare through study and prayer; final preparation occurs during Lent; Baptism, Confirmation, and Eucharist often take place during the Easter Vigil.)

VOCABULARY ✓

A *catechumen* is an unbaptized person who publicly declares his or her intention to become a member of the Church and prepares for Christian initiation. Catechumens pray and study during their preparation period. Although a catechumen is encouraged to attend Mass, he or she does not receive Communion.

Godparents sponsor a person at Baptism, and they help him or her grow in faith. Only a fully initiated Catholic who is at least sixteen years of age may be a godparent. Only one godparent is required; if there are two, they must be a man and a woman. A baptized non-Catholic may be a witness but not a godparent.

FAITH PARTNERSHIPS

Suggest that Faith Partners compare the role of godparents to the role of older family members in their lives.

BACKGROUND

Choosing saints' names Saints' names are often chosen for infants who will be raised in the Catholic faith. This custom began centuries ago in France and Germany and soon became the practice throughout the Catholic Church. A saint becomes the special patron of his or her namesake and may be addressed in prayer as a special source of support and guidance. The patron saint can also be an inspiration for living one's life as a Christian.

REFLECTING ON YOUR FAITH
Reflect on the symbols of Baptism. Which symbol holds particular meaning for you and can inspire you to live a deeper life of faith?

WORKING WITH THE TEXT AND PICTURES

✓ • Read the text and review the picture on this page.

✓ • Use *Vocabulary* below to help the students understand the highlighted terms.

• Discuss what happens in Baptism. **What are the essential signs of Baptism?** *(water and the words of Baptism)* **Why is water used?** *(Water is a sign of death to our old life and rebirth to new life in Christ.)* **What other symbols are part of the celebration of Baptism?** *(chrism, a white garment, and a lit candle)* **What do these symbols mean?** *(Anointing with oil marks us as God's chosen people; a white garment symbolizes new life in Christ; a lit candle signifies that the baptized person has received Christ, "The Light of the World.")* **What is the result of Baptism?** *(We are cleansed of original sin, become members of the Church, and are strengthened in divine life to live as disciples of Christ.)*

✓ • See *Skill Note* below.

WORKING WITH THE ACTIVITY

Catholics Believe

• Ask a volunteer to read aloud *Catholics Believe.*

✓ • Allow the students time to write their reflections on the meaning of the symbols of Baptism. *(Answers will vary.)*

• Distribute art supplies such as modeling clay, yarn, paper, and markers. Ask the students to create symbols of the meaning of Baptism.

✓ • Encourage the students to share with the group their thoughts about the paraphrased Catechism statement and their responses to the statement that follows.

Celebrating the Sacrament

The Sacrament of Baptism is often celebrated during Mass. The celebrant calls the family or families to the altar and welcomes all who are gathered for the celebration. The priest or deacon then blesses the baptismal water, after which the celebrant asks the person being baptized (or the parents and godparents in the case of an infant) a series of questions. These *baptismal promises* summarize key Christian beliefs. In making these promises, the person professes that he or she shares the beliefs of the community. Because we are members of Christ's Body, the Church, we renew our baptismal promises as the person being baptized first does so.

Next, the celebrant invites each family to the baptismal font for the Baptism. The one being baptized is then immersed in a pool of water or has water sprinkled or poured on him or her. Water is a sign of both life and death—death to one's old life and rebirth to a new life in Christ.

Through the waters of Baptism, we are cleansed of **original sin**—the first humans' choice to disobey God and the condition that each of us inherits. We are also strengthened to live holy lives as disciples of Christ. Water and the words of Baptism—"I baptize you in the name of the Father and of the Son and of the Holy Spirit"—are the essential signs of Baptism.

(S) After the Baptism with water, the celebrant **anoints** the child or adult with oil. In the Bible kings and prophets were anointed to mark them as God's chosen people. Similarly, we are anointed with **chrism,** a sacred oil made from olive oil scented with spices, as a sign that we are set apart for Christ.

Next, the baptized person puts on or is dressed in a white garment to symbolize his or her new life in Christ. Finally, a candle is lit from the Paschal candle as a sign that the baptized person has been enlightened by Christ and is now a light to the world.

Catholics Believe

Baptism is the basis of Christian life: we are freed from sin and reborn in Christ; we become members of the Body of Christ. *See Catechism, #1213.*

Choose one of the symbols of Baptism and describe how it holds meaning for you and how it can remind you of your Baptism.

_____

_____

_____

_____

28 **BAPTISM**

RESOURCE Center

VOCABULARY ✓

Original sin refers to the first humans' choice to disobey God, the effects of which remain with us today. Deprived of the original holiness and justice that humans had in the beginning, we have a tendency to sin. Only Jesus and Mary, his mother, were free of original sin.

In the Old Testament kings, priests, and prophets were marked with oil, or ***anointed,*** when God had a special task for them. The anointed receive the ability and strength to accomplish what God asks of them. Anointing is a symbol of the Holy Spirit and a sacramental sign.

Chrism is the sacred oil that is used for anointing at Baptism, Confirmation, and Holy Orders. It is made from olive oil and spices and is consecrated by the bishop.

(S) SKILL NOTE ✓

The text about baptismal promises can be used to discuss the skill of Being Accountable. Refer to pages 32 and 33 for more information.

BACKGROUND

Baptizing in cases of emergency In an emergency anyone with the right intention may baptize. Water and the words of Baptism are essential.

Student Leader Connection

Consider having the Student Leader do the following:

• **Read aloud *Catholics Believe.***

• **Help moderate the review of how the Sacrament of Baptism is celebrated.**

• **Collect symbols used in Baptism, and show them to the group.**

• **Help moderate a discussion on how to be faithful to baptismal promises.**

Living Our Promises

With these signs and symbols, we prepare to live our lives in the Spirit. In fact, through the Sacrament of Baptism, we are marked by the Holy Spirit with a **sacramental character.** This character permanently marks us as members of Christ's Body and calls us to live in love and holiness as Jesus did.

Keeping our baptismal promises and accepting the grace of the sacrament will show in our personal lives. For example, we will try to live honestly and generously. We will do schoolwork and chores to the best of our ability. We won't lie or cheat. We will avoid self-destructive behaviors and exploitation of the environment and work to improve the lives of others rather than harming them physically, emotionally, or spiritually. No doubt this way of life will be difficult at times. But God doesn't demand perfection from us, just our very best. Making the right choices means living honestly and morally. It means living our baptismal promises.

Through Baptism we share in Christ's ministry. For example, when we develop our prayer life and celebrate the sacraments, we share in Jesus' priesthood. As members of the Body of Christ, we join in Jesus' role of prophet by supporting and living the Church's teachings on morality and justice. And finally, we use the gifts of wisdom and forgiveness in our treatment of others, and we take responsibility for our choices and behavior. In doing so, we imitate the kingly role that Jesus demonstrated for us.

Once initiated into the Body of Christ, we are no longer the same. We are reborn in Christ. Now we live not only for ourselves but for others, as Jesus did. We celebrate God's love and give him thanks.

When we serve others, set aside our differences with one another, and live in the Spirit with love, joy, peace, kindness, goodness, and faithfulness, we participate in the life of the Body of Christ.

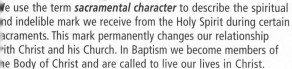

Rite Response

The Water of Baptism
Water is an essential symbol in the Sacrament of Baptism. During the ceremony the celebrant asks God to bless the baptismal water so that those who are baptized in it "may be washed clean of sin and be born again" to live as children of God.

SEARCH 29

WORKING WITH THE TEXT AND PICTURES
- Read the text and review the pictures on this page.
- Discuss the photographs showing two methods of Baptism. *At what age may a person be baptized?* *(at any age)*
- Use *Vocabulary* below to help the students understand the term *sacramental character.*
- Discuss our new life in Christ. *What is the sacramental character of Baptism?* *(We become members of the Body of Christ and are called to live in love and holiness as Jesus did.)*
- Discuss how we remain true to our baptismal promises, and ask the students for concrete examples. *What are the qualities of people who live in the Spirit as Christ calls us to do?* *(Possible answers include living in love, peace, kindness, and faithfulness.)*
- Discuss sharing in Christ's ministry through Baptism. *How do we share in Christ's role as priest, prophet, and king?* *(as priest, by developing a prayer life and celebrating the sacraments; as prophet, by supporting and living the Church's teachings on morality and justice; as king, by being wise and good leaders and forgiving in our treatment of others)*

WORKING WITH THE ACTIVITY
Rite Response
- Ask a volunteer to read aloud *Rite Response.*
- The water used at Baptism is blessed. *As he blesses the water, what does the celebrant ask of God?* *(that those being baptized may be cleansed of sin and born again as children of God)*

VOCABULARY
We use the term *sacramental character* to describe the spiritual and indelible mark we receive from the Holy Spirit during certain sacraments. This mark permanently changes our relationship with Christ and his Church. In Baptism we become members of the Body of Christ and are called to live our lives in Christ.

EXTENSION ACTIVITY
Walking through the rite   Take the students to the baptismal area of the church. Ask a staff member to walk through the rite of Baptism with them. Be sure all the items used in Baptism are available and explained.

MULTIPLE LEARNING STYLES
Symbolic garments   Have the students work in small groups to provide a list of clothing related to particular groups or activities. Show them an infant baptismal gown or the white garment used by adults who are being initiated. Discuss with the students how the garment symbolizes putting on Christ by beginning a new life in Christ. The garment reminds us that we are reborn and called to live lives of holiness and care for others as Jesus did. Because people in this age group readily recognize the importance of clothing as a symbol of personhood, the symbolism of the garment can be a powerful reminder to the students of a new life in Christ.

WORKING WITH THE TEXT AND PICTURES

✓ • Read the text on this page, and review the picture on pages 30 and 31.

✓ • Talk with the students about how they can live their faith every day. ***When do you experience situations that challenge you to do what is right even when the right choice is difficult?*** (Answers will vary.)

✓ • See *Skill Note* below.

WORKING WITH THE ACTIVITY

Wrap Up

• Have a volunteer read aloud the summary statements.

✓ • Allow time for the students to consider their remaining questions and write them in their books.

• Discuss any remaining questions the students may have. You may wish to have the students write their questions on separate sheets of paper so that you can collect them and respond during the next session.

In the Body of Christ

When we are baptized, we become members of the Body of Christ. Called to follow Jesus, we rely on the Holy Spirit to help us do what is right even when the right choice is difficult. The choices we make can bring us closer to God and keep as our most important focus our relationship with him.

We live our faith in the ordinary events of our lives. The Holy Spirit is with us to guide us whenever we need help and support. For example, perhaps you have a friend who is abusing alcohol or drugs. You realize that your friend is heading for serious trouble. You can rely on the Holy Spirit for the courage to face your friend and tell him or her that the drinking or drug abuse has to stop. You can support your friend while he or she gets help. Courage to confront your friend in this way shows real concern for him or her as well as respect for your friendship. This gift of the Spirit builds honesty and compassion in our relationships with others.

(S) Being a member of the Body of Christ means that we are part of a community. This community, the Church, celebrates the sacraments and worships together. Baptism brings us into this community, and we live our relationship with God in the Church. We depend on and help the other members of the Body of Christ so that all of us together live in the light of God's love and extend that love to those who have not yet experienced it. We have been reborn to a new life to honor Christ and serve others.

Make a poster showing what it means to be a member of the Body of Christ. Share your thoughts with your Faith Partner.

WRAP UP

• Through the Sacraments of Christian Initiation, Christ transforms us with new life in him.

• In Baptism our sins are forgiven, we are made members of the Body of Christ, and we are saved from the power of sin and everlasting death.

• The waters of Baptism cleanse us of original sin.

• Water and the words of Baptism are the signs of our rebirth to a new life in Christ.

What questions do you have about this chapter?

_____

_____

_____

30 BAPTISM

RESOURCE Center

FAITH PARTNERSHIPS

Have the partners work together to discuss what being a member of the Body of Christ means to each of them. Encourage the students to recall examples from the group discussion and to make the connection to their own lives. Distribute art supplies, and have the Faith Partners create posters that illustrate their ideas about being members of the Body of Christ.

LINK TO LITURGY

Point out to the students that we make our baptismal promises more than once. At our First Holy Communion, at Confirmation, and during the Easter Vigil and on Easter Sunday, all the members of the Body of Christ renew their baptismal promises. This renewal reminds us that we are called to live our lives as Jesus did. It also helps us support and guide one another. Encourage the students to participate fully in the renewal of their baptismal promises as a way of affirming their initial celebration of the sacrament.

(S) SKILL NOTE ✓

Being a member of the Body of Christ means, in part, that we are accountable to the rest of the membership. It also means that we have the responsibility to reflect on what the Body of Christ represents. Refer to pages 32 and 33 for more information.

Student Leader Connection

Consider having the Student Leader do the following:

• Read aloud the *Wrap Up* summary statements.

• Help moderate the discussion about how to live faith every day.

• Help moderate the discussion for *Around the Group*.

• Record the results of the group discussion.

Do you believe in
Jesus Christ, his only Son?

This is our faith.

Do you believe in
the Holy Spirit?

Around the Group

Discuss the following question as a group.

What are some ways you can share in Christ's mission as priest, prophet, and king?

After everyone has had a chance to share his or her responses, come up with a group answer upon which everyone can agree.

_____
_____
_____
_____

What personal observations do you have about the group discussion and answer?

_____
_____
_____

Briefly . . .

At the beginning of this chapter, you were asked about the reasons you had for joining some of the groups to which you belong. If you were choosing to be baptized now, what reasons would you give for your choice?

_____
_____

WORKING WITH THE ACTIVITIES

Around the Group

- Present the question to the group, and allow time for discussion. You may need to moderate to keep the students focused on the question.

- Encourage the group members to listen to the opinions and perspectives of others.

- Help the students make the connection between Christ's mission as priest, prophet, and king and their own baptism by reminding them to think about what it means to be anointed and by referring them to the text on page 29.

- If the group has agreed on an answer, direct the students to write it in their books. If they could not agree, direct them to list in their books the issues that were left unresolved and explain why.

- Encourage the students to note in their books their personal observations about the discussion and any final thoughts they have.

- See *Reflecting on Your Faith* below.

Briefly . . .

- Encourage the students to consider how their opinions may have changed since they responded to *What Do You Think?* on page 25.

- Ask the students to consider reasons they would now give for choosing to be baptized. Direct the students to note in their books some of these reasons.

- Allow time for the students to write their responses in their books.

- See *Reflecting on Your Faith* below.

REFLECTING ON YOUR FAITH

Around the Group: What did the students' discussion about their participation in Christ's mission tell you about the challenges to faith that they face? How might you help them?

Briefly: Consider the reasons you might have for choosing to be baptized at this point in your life.

EXTENSION ACTIVITY

Notes of encouragement Help the students discover the strength of their own faith and nurture the faith of others by having them write notes of encouragement to the catechumens and candidates in your parish RCIA program. Invite the students to share their reasons for thinking that joining the Church is a good idea. They might choose to close their letters with a promise to pray for the catechumens to whom they have written. (**Alternative during Lent:** Learn the number of people being initiated, and have the students make a card for each person or work in small groups so that each person initiated receives a card signed by everyone in the group.)

WORKING WITH THE SKILL

✓
- Review with the students the fact that Baptism is a Sacrament of Christian Initiation. **How might our initiation through Baptism make us accountable to one another?** *(Baptism makes us members of the Church. As such, we are obligated to help one another as we try to follow the example of Jesus and live as he wishes us to.)*

- Ask a volunteer to read aloud *Expressions of Faith.*

✓
- Help the students understand that being members of the Body of Christ means that we help one another live holy lives. **How do people your age help one another and family members live holy lives?** *(Accept all reasonable answers.)*

- Have a volunteer read *Scripture* aloud. **According to this passage, what is the most important thing Christians can do?** *(Love one another.)*

✓
- See *Scripture Background* below.

✓
- Ask a volunteer to read aloud the text and directions for *Think About It.* Give the students sufficient time to complete the activity.

- See *Reflecting on Your Faith* below.

✓
- Talk with the students about their experiences of being able to count on other people for support and advice. **How does it feel to depend on other people and know they will be there for you?** *(Possible responses should express the relief, strength, and comfort we get from depending on others.)*

- Draw the students' attention to the photograph. **What does this picture represent?** *(Possible answers should express the idea that we all help each other.)*

SKILLS for Christian Living

Being Accountable

Expressions of Faith—

Because we have been baptized, we are members of the Body of Christ. This means we help one another live holy lives. We are accountable to one another for our thoughts, words, and actions. We are expected to base our decisions on our Christian values.

Scripture

Owe no one anything, except to love one another; for the one who loves another has fulfilled the law. The commandments . . . are summed up in this word, "Love your neighbor as yourself."
Romans 13:8–9   23rd Sunday of Ordinary Time, Cycle

Think About It—

Every day people make demands of us. We have chores to do. We have homework. We are expected to show up at a certain time and place. Sometimes we can meet these demands. Other times it seems impossible. Being accountable requires us to do our best to make sure that we act responsibly and that our behavior is based on Jesus' teachings.

Being part of a community of faith, the Body of Christ, we have people we can turn to when we need help in choosing to live as baptized Christians.

Identify persons of virtue who fit the following characteristics— a truthful person, an unselfish person, a prayerful person, a wise person, a loving person. Place their names around the table.

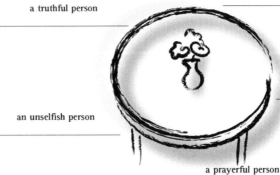

a truthful person

a loving person

a wise person

an unselfish person

a prayerful person

32 BAPTISM

REFLECTING ON YOUR FAITH

While the students are completing *Think About It,* take a few moments to consider how you would complete the activity.

TEACHING TIP

Helping adolescents be responsible   Adolescents are trying to balance their responsibilities with their need for independence. When they are focused on meeting their need for independence, they may not understand why others sometimes consider their behavior irresponsible. Use examples of friendship from their lives to help the students understand accountability as a matter of mutual support.

SCRIPTURE BACKGROUND ✓

Romans 13:8–9 repeats Jesus' command that we love one another. This obligation is essential in the life of every

Christian. Loving one's neighbor is part of being accountable as a member of the Body of Christ. You may wish to point out that this passage is part of the readings for the Twenty-Third Sunday of Ordinary Time, Cycle A. Refer to page 108 of this book for more information about the liturgical year.

Student Leader Connection

Consider having the Student Leader do the following:

- **Read aloud *Expressions of Faith.***

- **Help moderate a discussion on the meaning of the Scripture quote.**

- **Organize a small group to plan a prayer service.**

Special Note: Remember to meet briefly with the Student Leader for Chapter 4. You may wish to provide him or her with the Student Leader Prep Page for Chapter 4 found on page R5.

Skill Steps

Think of two or three people you know and admire. Consider them your personal advisors. If you are faced with a tough decision, try imagining what their advice would be. Then act on it.

The key to using your personal advisors is to be honest about what you know each person would say. If you admire them for the right reasons, you will find God's grace and wisdom in their answers.

Now imagine that you are faced with one of the following situations. Circle one situation and describe the advice you think each of your personal advisors would give.

- You're at a friend's house after school, and he or she offers you a beer.
- Your younger sister needs help with her homework, but you promised a friend that you'd go to his soccer game.
- A friend confided in you that she is thinking about running away from home. She has asked you not to tell anyone.

Person 1: _____

Person 2: _____

Person 3: _____

Check It Out

Place a check mark next to the sentences that apply to you.

- ○ I look out for others and try to act responsibly.
- ○ I try to base my behavior on Jesus' teachings.
- ○ I see many examples every day of ways to stay accountable.
- ○ I turn to my faith community for support and guidance.
- ○ I try to focus on what it means to live as a baptized member of the Body of Christ.

On a scale of 1 to 10 (1 being the easiest), how hard is it for you to practice this skill? _____

Closing Prayer

Lord God, send the power of the Holy Spirit to us when we need encouragement and guidance. Through water and the Holy Spirit, you brought us to new life. As members of the Body of Christ, help us share your love with everyone we meet.

LIVE 33

WORKING WITH THE SKILL

- Ask a volunteer to read *Skill Steps* aloud. Then talk about the concept of accountability. **What does it mean to be accountable?** *(It means that you are responsible for your actions, including asking for advice when you need it.)*
- Describe to the students the process of imagining what advice they would receive from two or three people they admire. **What is the key to using imaginary advisors?** *(Be honest about what you know each person would say.)*
- Give the students sufficient time to complete the *Skill Steps* activity. Encourage the students to keep in mind what it means to be accountable by considering what they think their imaginary advisors would tell them.
- Allow time for the students to complete *Check It Out*. Answer any questions the students may have about the skill, and give them time to express their opinions. Elicit from the students examples of ways that teens are accountable every day.
- See *Reflecting on Your Faith* below.

CLOSING PRAYER

- Gather together to pray the closing prayer. You may wish to use the following music from the *Give Your Gifts* series: "Blessed Be the Lord" *(The Songs),* "All Things New" *(The Basics),* or "Give Your Gifts" *(More Songs)* (GIA Publications, Inc.; distributed by Harcourt Religion Publishers).
- If time permits, direct the students to create their own closing reflections or prayers. You may wish to ask a few volunteers to read aloud what they have created or to plan a prayer service.

REFLECTING ON YOUR FAITH

Consider your responses to the *Check It Out* activity. How do you assess your own mastery of this skill?

TEACHING TIP

Research follow-up You may wish to take time to review any research the students have been asked to complete. If the students need additional time to complete their research, set aside a few minutes at the beginning of the next session to allow them to share the information they have gathered.

MULTIPLE LEARNING STYLES

Closing prayer You may wish to have the students create their closing prayers in the style of a formal prayer or reflection; a poem or song; or a prayer service with readings, psalm response, and music. Remind the students that the tone of their responses can be different from that of the example but should remain respectful.

ASSESSMENT

The Assessment Page for Chapter 3 can be found on page R11.

LINK TO FAMILY

The corresponding Family Resource pages for this skill are 64–67.

Confirmation

4

KEY CONTENT SUMMARY

Confirmation is a Sacrament of Christian Initiation. Through Confirmation our baptismal grace is perfected, and through the power of the Holy Spirit, our faith is strengthened. Confirmation strengthens our bond with the Church and helps us bear witness to our faith in our words and actions.

PLANNING THE CHAPTER

OPEN	PACING	CONTENT	OBJECTIVES	MATERIALS
	Suggested Time: **Parish 10 min.** **School 25 min.** Your Time: ___ min.	pp. 34–35	• Recognize that Confirmation is a Sacrament of Christian Initiation.	• candle, matches (optional) • symbol representing chapter theme (optional)

SEARCH				
	Suggested Time: **Parish 25 min.** **School 70 min.** Your Time: ___ min.	pp. 36–39	• Identify and examine how we celebrate the Rite of Confirmation. • Explore the elements and effects of Confirmation.	• Bibles • hymnals (optional) • art supplies (optional)

REFLECT				
	Suggested Time: **Parish 10 min.** **School 30 min.** Your Time: ___ min.	pp. 40–41	• Reflect on what it means to be sealed with the Spirit in Confirmation.	• old magazines, art supplies (optional)

LIVE				
	Suggested Time: **Parish 15 min.** **School 35 min.** Your Time: ___ min.	pp. 42–43	• Apply ideas about responsible and mature behavior to our lives.	• Student Leader Prep Page for Chapter 5 (p. R6) (optional) • music for prayer (optional) • *Living Our Faith Prayer Services* (optional) • copies of Assessment Page for Chapter 4 (p. R12) (optional)

CATECHISM IN CONTEXT

See Catechism of the Catholic Church, #1285.

Like Baptism, Confirmation is a Sacrament of Christian Initiation. The anointing of the forehead with chrism, a perfumed oil, "marks" the confirmand forever with the spiritual seal of the Holy Spirit; that is, the anointed is recognized as belonging to Christ and his Church. This spiritual and indelible mark, like that of Baptism, means that the sacrament can be conferred only once.

Anointing is richly symbolic for a number of reasons. Traditionally, it sets an individual apart for a leadership role or for a particular task. Chrism enhances and beautifies, cleanses and heals, and represents abundance and joy—all gifts of the Spirit. Through Confirmation the Holy Spirit strengthens our bond with the Church, increases our understanding of the Church's mission, and makes us more effective witnesses and servants for Christ. The confirmed rise to the challenges and responsibilities of being full members of the Church.

ONE-MINUTE RETREAT

READ

"The soul is a breath of [L]iving [S]pirit, that with excellent sensitivity, permeates the entire body to give it life." —Hildegarde of Bingen

REFLECT

What gifts of the Spirit can I use to build up the Body of Christ?

PRAY

Holy Spirit, breathe the grace of the Father within me. Stir the fire of your love in my soul so that my relationship with the Son may continue to grow. Grant that my gifts may be used for building up the Body of Christ.

LIBRARY LINKS

BOOKS
FOR ADOLESCENTS

"Confirmation: Seven Symbols in One Sacrament," by Thomas Richstatter OFM (*Youth Update;* St. Anthony Messenger Press).

Explains the symbols of Confirmation and explores the role of Confirmation in the Christian community.

"Gifts of the Holy Spirit: Yours to Open and Use," by Sara Kirtlink (*Youth Update;* St. Anthony Messenger Press).

Broadens understanding of the applications of the Spirit's gifts to daily life.

"What Difference Does Confirmation Make?" by Joseph Martos (*Youth Update;* St. Anthony Messenger Press).

Ways to inspire or rekindle appreciation for Confirmation.

FOR ADULTS

Anointing with the Spirit: The Rite of Confirmation, by Gerard Austin OP (The Liturgical Press, 1992).

Reflections on anointing in Confirmation and the symbolism of sacred oils.

The Awe-Inspiring Rites of Initiation: The Origins of the RCIA, by Edward Yarnold SJ (The Liturgical Press, 1994).

A revised edition of the classic explanation of how Baptism, Confirmation, and Eucharist are linked.

When a Teenager Chooses You—as Friend, Confidante, Confirmation Sponsor: Practical Advice for Any Adult, 2nd edition, by Joseph Moore (St. Anthony Messenger Press, 2000).

Helps adults act as spiritual companions on teens' journey of faith.

MULTIMEDIA

Confirmation: Sealed with the Spirit (video) (Harcourt Religion Publishers).

Twelve 5-minute episodes appropriate for studying about or preparing for Confirmation.

Lord of Light: Confirmation (video) (Harcourt Religion Publishers).

Focuses on Confirmation as the "mirror of Baptism," underscoring the challenges and responsibilities of Christian life.

FEATURE PREPARATION

STUDENT LEADER CONNECTION

The Student Leader Prep Page for this chapter is located on page R5. You may wish to provide this information to the Student Leader as an introduction and resource for the chapter.

FAITH PARTNERSHIPS

Chapter 4 has the same Faith Partners as Chapter 3. Several opportunities for Faith Partner discussions have been marked throughout the chapter. You may wish to consider other opportunities as you prepare the lesson.

SKILL NOTES

The skill for this chapter is Being Accountable. You may wish to build on what the students have learned in the previous chapter as you teach this chapter. A few Skill Notes have been called out to help you. The skill lesson for this chapter can be found on pages 42 and 43.

A check mark indicates the chapter's essential questions, statements, activities, and features. If time is limited, such as in a parish group setting, this icon will help you direct the students through the lesson.

Confirmation

KEY POINTS FROM CHAPTER 3

You may wish to review these points with the students before you begin the new chapter:

- Baptism is the first sacrament and is a Sacrament of Christian Initiation.
- Through Baptism we are reborn as members of the Body of Christ.
- Through Baptism we share in the priesthood of Christ.
- Baptism calls us to be responsible members of the Church throughout our lives.
- Being Accountable is a Skill for Christian Living.

✓ GATHERING

Have the students take turns giving compliments to one another. Remind the students to resolve to give at least one compliment a day to other friends or family members.

✓ PRAYER

Have the students gather in a circle. Invite them to pray by raising their hands with palms up. Pray the opening prayer together. If fire regulations permit, you may wish to light a candle at this time.

Come,

Holy Spirit,

awaken our

hearts to

God's love.

Come,

Holy Spirit,

make us wise

and gentle.

Come,

Holy Spirit,

strengthen us

to live as

we should.

Amen.

34

RESOURCE Center

PRAYER ENVIRONMENT

If you have created a prayer space for the room, you may wish to display one or more sacramentals or a symbol associated with Confirmation such as oil, a flame, or a dove to represent the theme of this chapter.

MULTIPLE LEARNING STYLES

Signing prayer Before praying with the students, have them read the prayer and decide what movements and gestures they could use to accompany it. For example, they might place their hands over their hearts for the first sentence. Invite them to think of simple gestures for the words "wise," "gentle," and "strengthen," and the phrase "Come, Holy Spirit." If anyone in the group is familiar with American Sign Language, perhaps he or she could teach the rest of the group the signs for these words. Or you might use the Internet or a book on American Sign Language from your local library. Then pray the prayer together.

Student Leader Connection

Consider having the Student Leader do the following:

- Lead the group in prayer.
- Read aloud selected text.
- Help moderate the discussion about the meaning of responsibility.
- Research the American Sign Language words for the prayer.

What Do You Think?

Place the name of a historical figure or a person you know and respect on the line next to the quality you think that figure or person represents.

trustworthy _____   supportive _____

courageous _____   honest _____

humble _____   respectful _____

generous _____   polite _____

cheerful _____   responsible _____

What characteristics do you admire about yourself?

_____

_____

_____

Taking a
Stand

If someone you know is described as being responsible, what does this mean? It probably means that he or she speaks truthfully and can always be counted on. A responsible person doesn't try to mislead anyone and always does his or her best.

As Catholics we are called to live responsibly according to the values that Jesus taught us. Sometimes, though, it can be difficult to live as Jesus would want us to. Knowing we are part of a larger community of believers helps support and strengthen us to stand up for our beliefs even when we are on our own. The Sacrament of Confirmation, a Sacrament of Christian Initiation, seals us with the Spirit, which strengthens us in our faith. Confirmation enables each of us to live a virtuous and loving Christian life.

WORKING WITH THE ACTIVITY

What Do You Think?

✓ • Allow time for the students to record their thoughts in the space provided.

• See *Reflecting on Your Faith* below.

✓ • *What Do You Think?* is intended as a personal pre-assessment. The students should not be asked to share their responses.

WORKING WITH THE TEXT AND PICTURES

✓ • Read the text on this page, and review the pictures on pages 34 and 35.

• Brainstorm words the students associate with responsibility. **What does the word responsible *mean to you?** (Possible responses: thoroughness, honesty, dependability.)*

✓ • Encourage the students to think about people they admire. **What qualities do you admire in others?** *(Possible answers: particular talents or skills or such qualities as the ability to help others feel positive about themselves.)*

• Discuss the pictures. **What do the symbols on these pages mean?** *(Possible responses: The students may associate the dove with the Spirit because this symbol was noted in Chapter 2. They may pair the cruet with anointing, which was also discussed in Chapter 2. You may wish to point out that one symbol of the Spirit, a flame, signifies strength and the removal of impurities.)*

REFLECTING ON YOUR FAITH

Reflect on the people you know and respect and the particular characteristics you admire in them. What characteristics do you admire in yourself?

EXTENSION ACTIVITY

Exploring responsibility   Arrange the students in three or four groups. Have each group compile a list of characteristics of responsible people and explain why these characteristics are important. Then have the large group discuss each list, rating all the suggested characteristics and listing the top three. Ask the students how these three characteristics reflect a Christian lifestyle.

TEACHING TIP

Modeling prayerful behavior   Help the students make prayer more meaningful by encouraging a quiet, reflective atmosphere. Pause for several moments of quiet before praying. You might have the students bow their heads or close their eyes. When praying aloud, speak slowly and clearly. Never rush through prayer, but speak the words with meaning and reverence. This modeling of prayerful behavior will help the students learn appropriate attitudes and actions for prayer.

WORKING WITH THE TEXT AND PICTURES

✓ • Read the text on this page, and review the pictures on pages 36 and 37.

✓ • Use *Vocabulary* below to help the students understand the terms *Pentecost* and *gifts of the Holy Spirit.*

• Discuss privileges the students wish to have. **What responsibilities come with privileges?** *(Possible answers: taking care of oneself, avoiding choices that hurt oneself or others.)*

✓ • Discuss Confirmation. **What happened at Pentecost?** *(The Spirit descended on the apostles, inspiring them to bear witness in Jesus' name and giving them the courage to preach and baptize.)*

✓ • Discuss the picture. **How does the picture illustrate what you are learning?** *(The picture shows a young person helping a child and so living as Jesus asks.)*

✓ • Ask the students to connect being responsible people with being responsible Christians. **How do we bear witness to Jesus?** *(Possible answers: by living our faith and finding ways to spread the faith.)*

WORKING WITH THE ACTIVITY

Opening the Word

• Ask a volunteer to read aloud *Opening the Word.*

✓ • Allow time for the students to read the additional Scripture passages and respond to the question. *(Possible answers: The Spirit is God, who brings understanding, joy, and truth; one of the Spirit's roles is to inspire.)*

✓ • See *Scripture Background* below.

Strengthened in the Spirit

Young adults seem to have so much freedom. They stay out as late as they want. They make their own decisions about what to wear, what friends to spend time with, and what music to listen to. In wishing for that kind of freedom for ourselves, we often fail to realize the responsibility that comes with these choices. When we are older, we can't blame anyone else when we show up late for work. And although we can buy nonessential things, we first have to pay for such basics as housing, insurance, and medical care.

Opening the Word

Pentecost

When the day of Pentecost had come, they were all together in one place. . . . Divided tongues, as of fire, appeared among them, and a tongue rested on each of them. All of them were filled with the Holy Spirit. Acts 2:1, 3–4

Read *Acts 2:1–8* as well as *Luke 1:39–42, John 16:12–14,* and *1 Corinthians 2:9–13.* According to your reading, who is the Holy Spirit and what does the Spirit do?

_____
_____
_____
_____
_____

As confirmed Catholics we are given more privileges, but we also have to be more responsible in sharing our talents and our faith. Through the Sacrament of Confirmation, another Sacrament of Christian Initiation, we are strengthened by the Holy Spirit to live with an awareness of our faith and the traditions of our Church.

In the Acts of the Apostles, we read that after Jesus ascended into heaven, the apostles met together on the Jewish Feast of Pentecost. This holiday was, and remains, the day when the Jewish people celebrate their covenant with God and the giving of the Torah, the books of the Law. (See *Exodus 34:10–11, 22.*) For Christians **Pentecost** is the day to celebrate the Holy Spirit descending upon the apostles, empowering them to bear witness in Jesus' name. The apostles gathered together because Jesus had just been crucified and they were afraid for their lives. Many of them were even afraid to admit they were followers of Jesus. But, strengthened by the Holy Spirit, the apostles received the courage to go out and live, preach, and baptize in Jesus' name. Through their words and actions, the fullness of the Holy Spirit overflowed in the new followers of Jesus as well. (See *Acts 2:1–4, 37–42.*)

Like the apostles we will often have questions about our faith. But also like them, we are called to celebrate and spread the gospel message to others. In Confirmation the **gifts of the Holy Spirit** are increased in us.

36 CONFIRMATION

RESOURCE Center

VOCABULARY

Pentecost, from a Greek word meaning "the fiftieth day," is celebrated fifty days after Easter. It commemorates the descent of the Holy Spirit on the apostles. Called the birthday of the Church, this feast marks the occasion when the apostles began to spread the Christian faith throughout the world.

Received in Baptism and strengthened in Confirmation, the seven **gifts of the Holy Spirit** are powerful qualities that help us grow in our relationship with God and others. These gifts—wisdom, understanding, counsel (right judgment), courage (fortitude), knowledge, reverence (piety), and wonder and awe (fear of the Lord)—show the influence of the Holy Spirit in our lives.

SCRIPTURE BACKGROUND

Acts 2:1–8 describes the coming of the Holy Spirit upon the apostles at Pentecost. The story indicates that courage and miraculous occurrences marked early Christian efforts to spread the faith. The emphasis on "tongues" shows the universality of the Christian mission and demonstrates the power of the apostles, activated by the Holy Spirit, to prophesy and preach the word. The importance of Pentecost lies in its depiction of a universal Christian faith destined to reach everyone, regardless of language or culture. You may wish to point out that this account is part of the readings for Pentecost, Cycles A, B, and C. Refer to page 108 of this book for more information about the liturgical year.

Student Leader Connection

Consider having the Student Leader do the following:

• Using the format of a game show, help moderate the discussion about being responsible.

• Read aloud *Opening the Word.*

• Read aloud *Focus On.*

• Introduce skits about the gifts of the Holy Spirit.

The Gifts of the
ⓢHoly Spirit

To bear witness to Christ we must be strong, informed, and confident. So the Spirit helps us develop the gifts of *wisdom, understanding, counsel, courage (fortitude), knowledge, reverence (piety),* and *wonder and awe (fear of the Lord).*

Wisdom is a gift frequently associated with the Holy Spirit. In *2 Chronicles 1:10* King Solomon prays to God for the wisdom to be a good leader. For us, having wisdom means that we use common sense and that we see things with the eyes of faith.

The gift of *understanding* is closely related to wisdom. When we use the gift of understanding, we are aware of what is going on around us. We also recognize that certain actions will result in certain consequences. Understanding focuses on seeing the relationship between things.

Counsel is also called right judgment. In the same way that school counselors advise students, so we are often called on to advise others and to be open to advice ourselves. Good counsel involves taking the time to make a good decision after we consider the options and the consequences and praying for guidance.

Courage, or fortitude, is one of the gifts of the Holy Spirit that we associate most closely with the Sacrament of Confirmation. Courage is the strength of character that enables us to know what is right and to do what is right even when it would be easier to give in.

Knowledge helps us distinguish between truth and falsehood. Knowing the facts helps us avoid confusion and poor judgment. We gain knowledge by studying, but we also gain knowledge by trying to live as members of the Body of Christ.

Symbols of the Spirit
There are several symbols for the Holy Spirit found in Scripture. At Jesus' baptism the Spirit came upon him in the form of a dove, and at Pentecost the Spirit came down upon the apostles like tongues of fire, or flames, and a great wind. (See *Matthew 3:16* and *Acts 2:2–3.*)

SEARCH 37

WORKING WITH THE ACTIVITY
Focus On
• Ask a volunteer to read aloud the text on the symbols of the Spirit.
• Discuss the meanings of the symbols of the Holy Spirit. Have volunteers explain the symbols of the dove, tongues as of fire, and wind. ***What do these symbols mean?*** *(Accept all reasonable answers that describe the action of the Spirit in our lives.)*
• Discuss people whose lives have been affected by the Spirit. ***Can you name someone who has experienced the power of the Holy Spirit in his or her life?*** *(Possible answers: the apostles and the saints. Have the students explain the reasons for their choices. Point out that we can admire people whose lives reflect the joy, generosity, honesty, and peace that show the Spirit's presence.)*

WORKING WITH THE TEXT AND PICTURES
• Read *The Gifts of the Holy Spirit* on pages 37 and 38.
• Discuss the gifts of the Holy Spirit with the students. Answer any questions they have about each gift.
• Invite the students to examine the gifts of the Holy Spirit. Ask for examples of how each gift can be lived every day. *(Accept all reasonable answers.)*
• Arrange the students in groups and assign one of the gifts of the Holy Spirit to each group. Have the group members prepare a brief skit illustrating how to live the gift assigned to them. Allow sufficient time for each group to prepare and present a skit.
• See *Skill Note* below.

ⓢ SKILL NOTE ✓
Use the text on this page to discuss what it means to be accountable as a Christian. Refer to pages 42 and 43 for more information.

LINK TO MUSIC
It may interest the students to learn that music and hymns used in prayer and worship are sacramentals. Early liturgical music featured the Christian Scriptures in such hymns as the "Magnificat" and "Glory to God." Some of the most well-known and traditional music of the Catholic Church is Gregorian chant, or plain song, popularized by Pope Saint Gregory the Great (540–604). You may wish to distribute hymnals and arrange for the students to learn an old or a modern hymn of their choice, emphasizing that music can be a form of prayer.

EXTENSION ACTIVITY
Creating symbols of the Spirit Distribute art supplies, and have the students create their own symbols to represent the ways in which the Holy Spirit works in our lives. Give the students sufficient time to create their symbols, and then ask volunteers to share their symbols with the group. You may choose to display the students' work in a centrally located place where the students can be reminded of the Spirit's power in their lives.

WORKING WITH THE TEXT AND PICTURES

✓ • Review the text and the picture on this page.

• Point out the photographs on pages 38 and 39. *What gifts do you think the pictures depict?* (Accept all reasonable responses.)

✓ • Ask the students for specific ways that we can show reverence for God.

WORKING WITH THE ACTIVITY

Our Christian Journey

• Ask a volunteer to read aloud *Our Christian Journey.*

• Discuss the life and work of Thomas Merton. *Describe how Trappist monks live.* (The Trappist lifestyle is characterized by community prayer, prayerful silence, and manual labor.) *For what did Thomas Merton become well known?* (He became known for his writings on freedom, social justice, and spirituality.)

✓ • Ask the students to name some of Thomas Merton's ideas. *What did Thomas Merton think about the power of the Holy Spirit in our lives?* (Thomas Merton rejected the idea that to be holy means to avoid the world. He wrote that the Holy Spirit challenges us to be deeply involved in the world and in every dimension of our lives.)

• Draw the students' attention to the time line. Have a volunteer read it aloud. Talk about the significance of the events described. *Why did Merton emphasize the importance of being involved in the world?* (Many significant events of the twentieth century occurred during his lifetime.)

• See *Background* below.

Witness to the Spirit

Thomas Merton was a Trappist monk who spent most of his life in a religious community near Bardstown, Kentucky. Though the Trappists emphasize silence, manual labor, and little or no traveling, Merton became known throughout the world for his writings on freedom, social justice, and spirituality. Philosophically, he insisted that we are not what we may superficially think ourselves to be. Merton also thought that we should neither avoid the world nor hide from it. Rather, through the power of the Spirit, we should be passionately involved in the world. Toward the end of his life, Merton became interested in what other religions, especially Buddhism, taught about holiness. While traveling in Asia to meet religious leaders, he died in Bangkok, Thailand.

For further information: Visit the official Web site of the Abbey of Gethsemani, where Merton was a monk, at **www.monks.org.** You may also wish to look in your library for books and movies about Merton's life.

1900   **1975**

1915-1968
THOMAS MERTON'S LIFE

1939-1945
WORLD WAR II

1954-1968
CRUCIAL PERIOD IN THE
U.S. CIVIL RIGHTS MOVEMENT

1962
UGANDA BECOMES AN
INDEPENDENT STATE

Reverence, or piety, is the deep sense of love that helps us live as children of God and members of the Body of Christ. This gift means being faithful and devout. We celebrate the Eucharist often, pray and help others every day, and respect ourselves, our neighbors, the Church, and God. We are reverent toward all creation because it reflects God, whom we honor.

Wonder and awe, or the gift of fear of the Lord, is sometimes misunderstood to mean that we must be afraid of God. But our heavenly Father is a merciful God. Wonder and awe is our response to God who is holy, powerful, wise, beautiful, and almighty. We feel overwhelmed by the realization of all that God is, and we are flooded with thanks and praise for him.

When we celebrate the Sacrament of Confirmation, the Holy Spirit acts within us to nourish these gifts. Those preparing to celebrate the sacrament must be open to the Spirit's gifts, which will help them bear witness to their faith in Christ.

38 CONFIRMATION

EXTENSION ACTIVITY

"Spirit" poem   Invite the students to write poems or songs on the Holy Spirit, the gifts of the Holy Spirit, or the work of the Holy Spirit. Ask volunteers to share their work with the group.

BACKGROUND

Time line   Thomas Merton became a Catholic when he was twenty-three years old. He recorded his troubled early life and experiences, as well as his conversion and his decision to become a Trappist, in his autobiography, *The Seven Storey Mountain.*

World War II resulted from Germany's attempt to conquer Europe and a simultaneous bid by Japan for expansion and domination in the East.

The Civil Rights movement began as an effort to secure the racial equality promised by the Thirteenth, Fourteenth, and Fifteenth Amendments to the U.S. Constitution.

After declaring independence from Great Britain, the African country of Uganda endured thirty years of instability before replacing its leaders and rewriting its constitution in 1995.

RESOURCE Center

Student Leader Connection

Consider having the Student Leader do the following:

• **Help moderate the discussion on how Confirmation is celebrated.**

• **Read aloud *Catholics Believe.***

• **Research and present information on one of the items on the time line from *Our Christian Journey.***

Becoming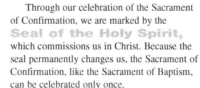

Confirmation continues our baptismal celebration. In fact, as part of the sacramental celebration, the candidates are asked to renew their baptismal promises. Like godparents in the Sacrament of Baptism, the **sponsor** of each candidate promises to help the candidate live his or her faith. Unlike Baptism, however, Confirmation is presided over in most cases by a bishop. As with all sacraments, God's word is proclaimed.

The two symbolic and essential actions during the ceremony are the **laying on of hands** and the anointing of the candidates' foreheads with chrism. During the anointing the one presiding says the words "Be sealed with the Gift of the Holy Spirit." The laying on of hands is an ancient practice found in the Bible. (See *Numbers 27:22–23* and *Acts 6:6, 8:17.*) With the laying on of hands, the outpouring of the Holy Spirit is invoked. The anointing with chrism on the forehead is the sign that the Holy Spirit brings us closer to Christ to be his witnesses and the sign that gives us the grace we need to live in Christ.

Through our celebration of the Sacrament of Confirmation, we are marked by the **Seal of the Holy Spirit,** which commissions us in Christ. Because the seal permanently changes us, the Sacrament of Confirmation, like the Sacrament of Baptism, can be celebrated only once.

Through the Sacrament of Confirmation, our relationship with God is deepened. We experience more completely that God is our loving Father and that we are his children. We also become more aware of the importance of Christ in our lives and are drawn more closely to him.

Further initiated into the Church community, we have a responsibility to be active members according to our age and abilities. As confirmed Christians we are given the strength and the courage to be witnesses for Christ and to reach out in word and action to bring others to him.

Discuss the responsibilities of a Confirmation sponsor with your Faith Partner.

Catholics  *Believe*

(S) *The baptized are strengthened by the Holy Spirit through the Sacrament of Confirmation.* See *Catechism, #1285.*

What gift of the Spirit do you need to strengthen your life? In what ways can this gift help you?

_____
_____
_____

WORKING WITH THE TEXT AND PICTURES

✓ • Read the text and review the picture on this page.

✓ • Use *Vocabulary* below to help the students understand the highlighted terms.

• Confirmation continues our baptismal celebration. ***How are Baptism and Confirmation related?*** *(Both are Sacraments of Christian Initiation. At Confirmation baptismal promises are renewed, and each candidate has a sponsor whose role is similar to a godparent's.)*

✓ • Discuss how we celebrate Confirmation. ***What are the essential actions and words of Confirmation?*** *(Laying on of hands and anointing with chrism while saying the words, "Be sealed with the Gift of the Holy Spirit.")* ***What does anointing signify?*** *(The Spirit gives us grace to live in Christ and strength to be witnesses for Christ.)*

✓ • Confirmation strengthens us to bear witness for Christ. ***What does bearing witness for Christ mean?*** *(We confidently affirm our beliefs and spread the good news of faith.)*

• See *Reflecting on Your Faith* below.

✓ • See *Skill Note* below.

WORKING WITH THE ACTIVITY

Catholics Believe

• Ask a volunteer to read aloud *Catholics Believe.*

✓ • Allow time for the students to write their reflections on the question. *(Answer will vary.)*

• Encourage the students to share with the group their thoughts about the paraphrased Catechism statement and their responses to the questions that follow.

VOCABULARY ✓

A *sponsor* is a person who presents a candidate for the anointing of Confirmation and helps him or her fulfill baptismal promises.

In the celebration of some sacraments, a *laying on of hands* occurs. This gesture invokes the Holy Spirit upon the person celebrating the sacrament and signifies blessing, healing, or the conferral of an office or a special task.

The *Seal of the Holy Spirit* is the spiritual and indelible character conferred in Confirmation through the anointing and the presider's words. In celebrating Confirmation we accept the rewards and responsibilities of Christians growing in faith.

FAITH PARTNERSHIPS

Ask the students to discuss why they would or would not wish to be Confirmation sponsors.

(S) SKILL NOTE ✓

We practice accountability by recognizing the areas of our lives that need strength and support. Refer to pages 42 and 43 for more information.

BACKGROUND

Laying on of hands When the laying on of hands appears in Scripture, it usually expresses a healer's prayer that one who is sick may become well. (See *Mark 5:23.*) The gesture may also imply protection and blessing, as when Jesus laid his hands on the children brought to him. (See *Mark 10:16.*) The laying on of hands is used in celebrating Confirmation, Holy Orders, and other sacraments. Accompanied by prayer, the gesture invokes the Holy Spirit to bless and sanctify those celebrating these sacraments.

WORKING WITH THE TEXT AND PICTURES

✓ • Read the text on this page, and review the picture on pages 40 and 41.

✓ • Have a volunteer read aloud the text entitled *Living Through the Spirit*. Discuss with the students how we bear witness to our faith in our treatment of others. ***What are some examples of how we live a deeper level of commitment to our faith as a result of the Sacrament of Confirmation?*** *(Possible answers: When we meet someone who is having a bad day, we will comfort that person; when we are corrected, we will try to understand and improve our behavior; when family members argue with us or embarrass us, we will try to understand and place higher priority on getting along with them; when we're tempted in the areas of sex, alcohol, drugs, tobacco products, vandalism, and gangs, we'll choose to do the right thing.)* Invite the students to suggest their own examples.

• See *Background* below.

WORKING WITH THE ACTIVITY

Wrap Up

• Ask a volunteer to read aloud the summary statements.

✓ • Allow time for the students to consider their remaining questions and write them in their books.

• Discuss any remaining questions the students may have. You may wish to have the students write their questions on separate sheets of paper so that you can collect them and respond during the next session.

Living Through the Spirit

Sealed with the Holy Spirit through Confirmation, we are called to live our faith with a deeper level of commitment than we had before we celebrated this sacrament. If we are open to the power of the Holy Spirit, our faith will not be something abstract and unfamiliar. We will live our lives as witnesses of Jesus' love and strength.

Faith will affect every decision and every action. If you meet someone who is having a bad day because he or she failed a test, don't hesitate to comfort that person. His or her feelings matter more than your "image."

If a teacher corrects your behavior in class, you might feel embarrassed at first, but try to understand that you were acting inappropriately. Instead of talking back, work on improving your future behavior. Respect your teacher's authority.

Our increased faith will also allow us to reconsider the importance of our family members. Instead of arguing with or feeling embarrassed by your family, try to understand them. Although you probably see them every day, how well do you really know them? What is your sister's favorite color? What is your mom's favorite song? The answers to these questions may seem insignificant, but they help you get to know more about the most important people in your life.

When we are responsible, respectful, and kind to others, we show them the love that Christ has for all of us. We bear witness to our faith.

Reflect on what it means to be sealed with the Spirit in Confirmation. Share your thoughts and responses with your Faith Partner.

> **WRAP UP**
>
> • **Confirmation is a Sacrament of Christian Initiation.**
> • **In Confirmation the Holy Spirit brings us closer to Christ.**
> • **In Confirmation the Holy Spirit strengthens us, as the apostles were strengthened at Pentecost, to bear witness for Christ.**
> • **Confirmation makes us more responsible for our faith.**
> • **The gifts of the Holy Spirit are wisdom, understanding, counsel, courage, knowledge, reverence, and wonder and awe.**
>
> **What questions do you have about this chapter?**
> _____
> _____
> _____

40 CONFIRMATION

RESOURCE Center

FAITH PARTNERSHIPS

Suggest that the Faith Partners consider what it means to be sealed with the Spirit in Confirmation.

BACKGROUND

Confirmation Over time, Catholics have emphasized different aspects of the Sacrament of Confirmation. In the 1950s the image "Soldiers of Christ," explained the strength we need to bear witness and was the primary focus of Confirmation. During the 1970s it was emphasized that the celebration of Confirmation was a mark of maturity in faith. Throughout the 1990s emphasis was on strengthening our faith and the Sacrament of Christian Initiation. Today we recognize that many images and ideas describe how the Spirit acts in us through Confirmation.

EXTENSION ACTIVITY

Examples of bearing witness Have the students compile a "Top Ten" list of situations in which people their age can bear witness to their faith. Then have the students identify ten situations when it is hard to be followers of Jesus. Ask the students to suggest ways to live faithfully in these instances.

Student Leader Connection

Consider having the Student Leader do the following:

• **Read aloud the *Wrap Up* summary statements.**

• **Help moderate the discussion of ways to live faithfully.**

• **Arrange for the display of the completed montage.**

Around the Group

Discuss the following questions as a group.

In the United States, Confirmation is celebrated at different ages depending on the diocese: before First Communion, while in middle school, and while in high school. At what age does your diocese celebrate Confirmation? What are some good reasons to be confirmed at this age?

After everyone has had a chance to share his or her responses, come up with a group answer upon which everyone can agree.

_____
_____
_____
_____

What personal observations do you have about the group discussion and answer?

_____
_____
_____
_____
_____

Briefly . . .

At the beginning of this chapter, you were asked about the characteristics you admire in yourself. Which of these characteristics do you think are made stronger by celebrating the Sacrament of Confirmation?

WORKING WITH THE ACTIVITIES

Around the Group

- Present the questions to the group, and allow time for discussion. You may need to moderate to keep the students focused on the question.
- Encourage the group members to listen to the opinions and perspectives of others.
- If the students have not yet been confirmed, tell them the age at which they will be celebrating Confirmation. Then have them discuss reasons for celebrating the sacrament at that age.
- If the group has agreed on an answer, direct the students to write it in their books. If they could not agree, direct them to list in their books the issues that were left unresolved and explain why.
- Encourage the students to note in their books their personal observations about the discussion and any final thoughts they have.
- See *Reflecting on Your Faith* below.

Briefly . . .

- Encourage the students to consider how their opinions may have changed since they responded to *What Do You Think?* on page 35.
- Allow time for the students to write their responses in their books.
- See *Reflecting on Your Faith* below.

REFLECT 41

REFLECTING ON YOUR FAITH

Around the Group: What did the students' reasons for celebrating Confirmation tell you about their understanding of what commitment to Christ means? How can you help them continue to grow in their understanding?

Briefly: How has your commitment to your faith in Christ been challenged or deepened by working through this lesson with the students?

TEACHING TIP

Understanding commitment Help the students broaden their understanding of what it means to bear witness by discussing with them how most people live their faith in ordinary ways. Emphasize that living a life of commitment to their faith does not mean that they must live dramatically or achieve greatness. Offer examples of simple ways to live faithfully every day, and ask the students to suggest their own examples.

MULTIPLE LEARNING STYLES

Images of faithfulness Distribute magazines, construction paper, scissors, and glue, and invite the students to find words and images that express the life of a faithful Christian. Have the students paste these to the construction paper to create a montage representing what being a faithful Christian means.

WORKING WITH THE SKILL

✓ • Remind the students that the skill for Chapters 3 and 4 is Being Accountable. Discuss with the students how they have tried to use the skill since the end of Chapter 3.

✓ • Remind the students that Confirmation, like Baptism, is a Sacrament of Christian Initiation. *How does Confirmation help us develop the skill of Being Accountable?* *(Confirmation affirms us as mature members of the Body of Christ, underscoring our responsibility to one another and to Christ. The grace conferred on us in Confirmation, as well as the gifts of the Holy Spirit, enables us to accept accountability for Christian conduct throughout our daily lives.)*

• Ask a volunteer to read aloud *Expressions of Faith.*

• Read *Scripture* aloud. *What does the writer of this passage say is the difference between a servant and a friend?* *(The relationship between master and servant is a business arrangement; the relationships of friends are close, personal, and enduring.)*

✓ • See *Scripture Background* below.

✓ • Ask a volunteer to read aloud *Skill Steps.* Review the material in Chapter 3 about being accountable. Remind the students of the technique of using imaginary personal advisors to help them make good decisions.

✓ • Allow time for the students to complete and discuss *Skill Builder.* Then discuss this example: Two students are planning to embarrass Maria in front of the whole class. Maria is new to this country and is learning to speak English.

• See *Reflecting on Your Faith* below.

SKILLS FOR Christian Living

Being Accountable

Expressions of Faith-

Along with the Eucharist, both Baptism and Confirmation are Sacraments of Christian Initiation—the sacraments by which we become ready to live Christ's call to us as members of his Body. When someone decides to celebrate the Sacrament of Confirmation, one thing he or she is doing is accepting the responsibility of being accountable to Christ in response to his call.

Scripture

I do not call you servants any longer, because the servant does not know what the master is doing; but I have called you friends, because I have made known to you everything that I have heard from my Father. You did not choose me but I chose you. And I appointed you to go and bear fruit....
John 15:15–16 6th Sunday of Easter, Cycle B

Skill Steps-

There are two steps to being accountable. First, remember the values that Jesus taught us. Let his life be a model for your life. Second, remember to ask your imaginary advisors. Think of the people around you who represent the people of God and who act with love, respect, and concern for others. How might they react?
Here are some key points to remember:

● You are accountable because of your Baptism.
● When you are accountable, you remain spiritually strong.
● Your behavior should be based on Jesus' teachings.
● The commandment to love your neighbor can help you make good decisions.

Skill Builder-

Imagine you are advising friends who are faced with the following situations.

○ Instead of collecting information on the Internet for his class project, Michael is surfing white-supremacist sites.
_____
_____

○ Tanya is planning to have a party when her parents are not home. Her friends want to bring alcohol to the party.
_____
_____

SCRIPTURE BACKGROUND ✓

John 15:15–16 uses the images of servant and friend to emphasize that our relationship with Jesus is not the impersonal one between employee and employer—Jesus calls us to grow close to him in friendship. The original language in this Gospel suggests that the word *friend* means the special closeness shared by a teacher and student or a master and apprentice. Although this friendship can be a close and personal one, the writer deliberately avoids the connotation of equality. We are to grow close to Jesus, but we are not his equals. You may wish to point out that this passage is part of the readings for the Sixth Sunday of Easter, Cycle B. Refer to page 108 of this book for more information about the liturgical year.

REFLECTING ON YOUR FAITH
How can you be more accountable in your life? How might you practice the techniques for improving this skill?

TEACHING TIP

Becoming closer to Christ Remind the students that being accountable helps them grow closer to Christ: the way they treat others is the way they treat Christ. When they show love, respect, and concern, they demonstrate their accountability to Christ.

Student Leader Connection

Consider having the Student Leader do the following:

• **Read aloud *Expressions of Faith.***

• **Read aloud *Scripture.***

• **Organize a small group to plan a prayer service.**

Special Note: Remember to meet briefly with the Student Leader for Chapter 5. You may wish to provide him or her with the Student Leader Prep Page for Chapter 5 found on page R6.

utting It into Practice-

Now complete the following activity to practice being accountable.

- List five people whom you respect to be your imaginary advisors. Include Jesus as one member of the group.

1. _____   4. _____

2. _____   5. _____

3. _____

- What is an important decision that you recently made or that you will soon have to make?

_____

- What kind of advice do you think each person would provide?

1. _____

2. _____

3. _____

4. _____

5. _____

Using what you have learned about the skill of Being Accountable, take time each day to put it into practice. Before you make a decision, do the following:

- Remember to think of at least two possible actions you could take.
- Imagine the consequences of what might happen in each case.
- Remember to use Jesus and your other imaginary advisors to think about possible solutions.

Based on your experience with the skill so far, which of these steps of being accountable is easiest for you? Which of them requires more work?

_____

_____

losing Prayer-

Father, send us your Spirit to help us follow your Son. May the Holy Spirit dwell in us to guide us and help us. May the Spirit turn our fears to courage, our weakness to strength, and our selfishness to generosity. May the Holy Spirit inspire us as the apostles were inspired at Pentecost. Amen.

LIVE 43

WORKING WITH THE SKILL

✓ • Ask a volunteer to read aloud *Putting It into Practice.* Give the students time to complete the activity.

✓ • Talk about how the students chose their imaginary advisors. **What do you look for in an advisor? Why would you trust his or her advice?** *(Answers will vary but should express confidence in the wisdom, maturity, experience, and responsibility of the selected advisors.)*

- Discuss what the students have learned about being committed and faithful Christians. **How does Confirmation help us become responsible Christians?** *(Confirmation strengthens us to bear witness to Christ and to accept the responsibility of being accountable to Christ.)*

- See *Reflecting on Your Faith* below.

- Ask volunteers to share what they have learned about being accountable.

CLOSING PRAYER

✓ • Gather together to pray the closing prayer. You may wish to use the following music from the *Give Your Gifts* series: "Come and Follow Me" *(The Songs)*, "Send Down the Fire" *(The Basics)*, or "With You by My Side" *(More Songs)* (GIA Publications, Inc.; distributed by Harcourt Religion Publishers).

- If time permits, direct the students to create their own closing reflections or prayers. You may wish to ask a few volunteers to read aloud what they have created or to plan a prayer service. As an alternative for prayer, you may wish to use "Sacraments: Prayer Service B" from *Living Our Faith Prayer Services* by Robert Piercy and Linda Baltikas (GIA Publications, Inc.; distributed by Harcourt Religion Publishers).

REFLECTING ON YOUR FAITH

Think about an important decision you recently made or will make soon. How can you best find the support and advice you need? Who are your advisors?

TEACHING TIP

Research follow-up You may wish to take time to review any research the students have been asked to complete. If the students need additional time to complete their research, set aside a few minutes at the beginning of the next session to allow them to share the information they have gathered.

MULTIPLE LEARNING STYLES

Closing prayer You may wish to have the students create their closing prayers in the style of a formal prayer or reflection; a poem or song; or a prayer service with readings, psalm response, and music. Remind the students that the tone of their responses can be different from that of the example but should remain respectful.

ASSESSMENT

The Assessment Page for Chapter 4 can be found on page R12.

LINK TO FAMILY

The corresponding Family Resource pages for this skill are 64–67.

Eucharist

KEY CONTENT SUMMARY

The Sacrament of the Eucharist completes the Sacraments of Christian Initiation. The Eucharist is the "source and summit" of our Christian life. The Eucharist is a sacrifice and a sacred meal. The Body and Blood of Christ provide us with spiritual nourishment.

PLANNING THE CHAPTER

	PACING	CONTENT	OBJECTIVES	MATERIALS
OPEN	Suggested Time: Parish **10 min.** School **25 min.** Your Time: ____ min.	pp. 44–45	• Recognize that the Sacrament of the Eucharist is a Sacrament of Christian Initiation.	• candle, matches (optional) • symbol representing chapter theme (optional) • art supplies (optional)
SEARCH	Suggested Time: Parish **25 min.** School **70 min.** Your Time: ____ min.	pp. 46–49	• Identify and examine the two major parts of the celebration of the Eucharist. • Explore the elements of the Eucharist and the fruits of Communion.	• Bibles • lectionary (optional) • hymnals (optional)
REFLECT	Suggested Time: Parish **10 min.** School **30 min.**. Your Time: ____ min.	pp. 50–51	• Reflect on the central role of the Eucharist in our lives.	• art supplies (optional)
LIVE	Suggested Time: Parish **15 min.** School **35 min.** Your Time: ____ min.	pp. 52–53	• Apply the Eucharist's hope and spiritual nourishment to our everyday lives.	• picture of a yoke (optional) • Student Leader Prep Page for Chapter 6 (p. R6) (optional) • music for prayer (optional) • copies of Assessment Page for Chapter 5 (p. R13) (optional)

CATECHISM IN CONTEXT

See Catechism of the Catholic Church, #1382.

As Catholics we believe that the Eucharist, a Sacrament of Christian Initiation, nourishes us not with bread and wine but with the Body and Blood of Christ. Through the Real Presence in Communion, we are intimately united with Christ, who offered himself for us. Real Presence refers to the unique, true presence of Christ in the Eucharist under the appearances of bread and wine.

Participation in the Eucharist is an act that preserves, increases, and renews the grace of Baptism and anticipates our place at the heavenly banquet that is eternal life. When we celebrate the Eucharist each time we are at Mass, we commemorate Christ's Last Supper and resolve to grow in Christian life as we accept and are strengthened by the spiritual gifts of the Trinity.

"Those who eat my flesh and drink my blood abide in me, and I in them" (John 6:56).

ONE-MINUTE RETREAT

READ

". . . He made himself the Bread of Life to be our life of love and joy. No one else can give what he gives and he is there all the time. We have only to realize that." —Mother Teresa

REFLECT

How does the realization of Jesus as the Bread of Life bring nourishment to my life?

PRAY

Bread of Life, you are the hope and nourishment of my life. In gratitude I praise you for the gift of your sacrifice in the sharing of your Body and Blood. May my hunger for you in the Eucharist be the source and summit of my life.

LIBRARY LINKS

BOOKS
FOR ADOLESCENTS

"Eucharist: Say Yes!" by Mary Cummins Wlodarski (*Youth Update;* St. Anthony Messenger Press).

Challenges teens to make a deeper commitment to the Body of Christ.

"Top 10 Reasons for Going to Mass," by Jim Auer (*Youth Update;* St. Anthony Messenger Press).

Leads teens to explore the value of Mass and its place in their spiritual journey.

We Gather in Christ: Our Identity as Assembly, from the Worship Office of the Archdiocese of Cincinnati (Liturgy Training Publications, 1997).

How to be a fully participating member of the Eucharistic community.

FOR ADULTS

The Future of Eucharist: How a New Self-Awareness Among Catholics Is Changing the Way They Believe and Worship, by Bernard Cooke (Paulist Press, 1997).

A noted sacramental theologian takes a look at the changes and challenges facing Catholic worship in the new century.

The Mystery and Meaning of the Mass, by Joseph M. Champlin (Crossroad Publishing Co., 1999).

A thorough and engaging presentation of the meaning behind liturgical practices and prayers.

Responses to 101 Questions on the Mass, by Kevin W. Irwin (Paulist Press, 1999).

A sourcebook for educators, youth ministers, and liturgists.

MULTIMEDIA

Give Your Gifts (CD, tape, book) (GIA; Harcourt Religion Publishers).

This program of music and printed resources helps young people develop their own Eucharistic liturgies and prayer services.

The History and Meaning of the Eucharist (video) (Harcourt Religion Publishers).

Part I explains how the Eucharist has developed from the Last Supper to the present. Part II helps young people relate more personally to the parts of the Mass.

The Last Supper (video) (Ark Enterprises; Harcourt Religion Publishers).

Depicts Passover and the events from Palm Sunday through Holy Thursday.

FEATURE PREPARATION

STUDENT LEADER CONNECTION

The Student Leader Prep Page for this chapter is located on page R6. You may wish to provide this information to the Student Leader as an introduction and resource for the chapter.

FAITH PARTNERSHIPS

Chapter 5 begins a new Faith Partnership. Several opportunities for Faith Partner discussions have been marked throughout the chapter. You may wish to consider other opportunities as you prepare the lesson.

SKILL NOTES

The skill for this chapter is Staying Hopeful. As you teach the skill lesson on pages 52 and 53, you may wish to refer to the Skill Notes marked throughout the chapter. These notes will help you identify terms and ideas related to the skill.

A check mark indicates the chapter's essential questions, statements, activities, and features. If time is limited, such as in a parish group setting, this icon will help you direct the students through the lesson.

KEY POINTS FROM CHAPTER 4

You may wish to review these points with the students before you begin the new chapter:

- Confirmation is a Sacrament of Christian Initiation.
- Through Confirmation our baptismal grace is perfected, and through the power of the Holy Spirit, our faith is strengthened.
- Confirmation strengthens our bond with the Church and helps us bear witness to our faith in our words and actions.
- Being Accountable is a Skill for Christian Living.

GATHERING

Invite the students to discuss their favorite food.

PRAYER

Have the students offer each other a sign of peace before praying together the opening prayer. If fire regulations permit, you may wish to light a candle at this time.

Eucharist

Almighty God, you always remember us, taking care of our every need. Whether we are strong or weak, troubled or happy, fearful or brave, you look out for us and watch over us. We turn to you with thanks and love. Through Christ our Lord. Amen.

44

PRAYER ENVIRONMENT

If you have created a prayer space for the room, you may wish to display one or more sacramentals or a symbol associated with Mass or the Eucharist, such as a basket with bread or grapes, to represent the theme of this chapter.

FAITH PARTNER INTRODUCTION

If you haven't done so already, remind the students that it is time for them to create new Faith Partnerships. After you have assigned new Faith Partners, you may wish to give the students a few moments to complete together a Faith Partner introduction. Ask each Faith Partner to describe for the other his or her favorite holiday and the foods associated with it. Suggest that the students compare notes on ingredients and how the foods are prepared. Allow time for the students to answer the questions and share their responses.

RESOURCE Center

Student Leader Connection

Consider having the Student Leader do the following:

- Begin the opening prayer by extending a sign of peace to everyone. Lead the prayer.
- Help moderate the discussion about experiences of thankfulness.
- Help moderate the discussion about things that make people thankful to God.

What Do You Think?

List three things that are valuable to you and explain why you consider them valuable.

1. _____   _____
2. _____   _____
3. _____   _____

Name three people for whom you are thankful and explain why.

1. _____   _____
2. _____   _____
3. _____   _____

Describe a situation in which someone went out of his or her way to be generous to you. How did you thank him or her?

_____
_____
_____
_____

Giving Thanks

Think of a time when you felt thankful. Maybe your team won an important game, or a friend helped you through a tough time.

(S) When we are thankful to someone, we are aware that our happiness is influenced by that person's action. We appreciate the fact that this person thought of us. When we have such an experience, we feel wonderful. We want to express our thanks and let him or her know how we feel.

Our relationship with God is like this. God constantly takes care of us and gives us gifts to bring us closer to him. To express our thanks, we celebrate the Eucharist, also called the Mass. We gather together as members of the Body of Christ, and we give thanks and praise to God for all that he does for us.

OPEN 45

WORKING WITH THE ACTIVITY

What Do You Think?

✓ • Allow time for the students to record their thoughts in the space provided.

• See *Reflecting on Your Faith* below.

✓ • *What Do You Think?* is intended as a personal pre-assessment. The students should not be asked to share their responses.

WORKING WITH THE TEXT AND PICTURES

✓ • Read the text on this page, and review the pictures on pages 44 and 45.

• Talk with the students about their experiences of thankfulness. *When are you thankful?* (Accept all reasonable responses.)

✓ • Encourage the students to explain how they express thankfulness. *What are some of the things you do and say to express thanks?* (Answers will vary.)

• Discuss some of the things that make people especially thankful to God. *Why do people give thanks to God?* (Answers will vary.)

• Talk with the students about how we give thanks to God by celebrating the Eucharist. Draw the students' attention to the photographs. Point out that when we give thanks to God we draw closer to him and those around us.

✓ • See *Skill Note* below.

REFLECTING ON YOUR FAITH

Think about what makes you thankful to God. How does your experience of thankfulness renew your spirit?

(S) SKILL NOTE ✓

...e text on this page can be used to introduce the skill of Stay-...g Hopeful. Refer to pages 52 and 53 for more information.

...XTENSION ACTIVITY

...reminder of thankfulness Distribute art supplies to ...e group, and invite each student to create a bumper sticker or ...allet card that completes the sentence "Thankfulness means . . ." ...ave the students decorate their work, and encourage them to ...splay their bumper stickers or carry their cards in their wallets ... remind them of the power of thankfulness in their lives.

BACKGROUND

Our word *Mass* comes from the Latin expression *Ite, missa est,* or "Go, the Mass is [ended]." Evidence indicates that as early as the second century, the basic structure of the Mass as a celebration of the Eucharist consisted of Scripture readings, prayer, preaching, the offering of bread and wine, and a Communion rite. The individual parts of the Mass have been expanded and elaborated over time into the celebration with which we are familiar today. Since the Second Vatican Council of the early 1960s, the Mass has departed from centuries-old tradition in significant ways. Among the most important changes are the use of the vernacular rather than Latin, the priest's facing the congregation rather than turning his back to them, and the expanded role of lay people in the liturgy.

WORKING WITH THE TEXT AND PICTURES

✓ • Read the text and review the picture on this page.

✓ • Use *Vocabulary* below to help the students understand the terms *Passover* and *Eucharist*.

• Ask the students to tell the story of Moses and the Exodus. **What is Passover?** *(the day that the Jewish people commemorate their deliverance from slavery in Egypt)*

• In biblical times animals, grain, and fruit were sacrificed to God. Relate this practice to the Passover lamb and to Christ by explaining that we refer to Jesus as the Lamb of God because of his sacrifice for us on the cross.

✓ • Discuss *Eucharist*. **What does Eucharist mean?** *(thanksgiving)* **For what are we thankful?** *(We give thanks for Jesus' sacrifice—Paschal mystery—through a community meal.)*

✓ • See *Skill Note* below.

WORKING WITH THE ACTIVITY

Opening the Word

• Ask a volunteer to read aloud *Opening the Word.*

✓ • Allow time for the students to read the additional Scripture passages and answer the question. *(Possible answers: the connection between Passover and Eucharist and between the manna fed to the Israelites in the desert and the Eucharist; also, the description of Eucharist as a community meal.)*

• Compare the Last Supper to the Mass. **How are the Mass and the Last Supper similar?** *(Possible answers: the bread and wine, the repetition of Christ's words, and the breaking and distribution of bread.)*

✓ • See *Scripture Background* below.

Symbolic Action

Several retellings of the Last Supper appear in the New Testament, each with its own focus. In fact, no two are exactly the same.

In the Gospels, the Last Supper takes place around the time of **Passover,** the Jewish feast celebrating the delivery of the Israelites from slavery in Egypt. But the author of the Gospel according to John structures the story to make an important point. Because the Last Supper occurs in John's Gospel on the day before Passover, Jesus' crucifixion—which occurred the day after the Last Supper—would have taken place on Passover. The readers of John's Gospel, therefore, would have compared Jesus' sacrifice with the sacrificial lamb the Jews slaughtered on Passover. Jesus' saving action would become the new and perfect Passover lamb.

Opening the Word

Corpus Christi, Cycle B

While they were eating, he took a loaf of bread, and after blessing it he broke it, gave it to them, and said, "Take; this is my body." Mark 14:22

Read *Mark 14:22–26* as well as *Matthew 26:17–30, John 6:30–38,* and *1 Corinthians 11:17–34.* What do these passages tell us about Eucharist?

_____
_____
_____
_____

Our Celebration of Thanks

(S) In biblical times meals were symbolic: they celebrated God's ability to provide for his children and thanked him for his saving presence. The breaking of bread signified unity and reconciliation. When people came together to "break bread," they celebrated a bond of family unity or friendship.

When we gather for the Sacrament of the Eucharist, we celebrate in the same spirit. We acknowledge our thankfulness to God the Father and his Son through a community meal. In fact, the word **Eucharist** comes from a Greek word meaning "thanksgiving."

As with all the sacraments, the Eucharist celebrates the Paschal mystery. We recall and celebrate Jesus' suffering, death, and resurrection. We give thanks that Jesus brings us to his Father, and we celebrate the Holy Spirit, who acts in our lives to make us a holy people. Throughout the liturgical year we celebrate the Eucharist by worshiping together as members of the Body of Christ, dedicating ourselves to a Christian life.

At the Last Supper Jesus took bread, blessed it, broke it, and gave it to his disciples to eat. This happens again whenever we gather to celebrate the Eucharist. The priest, in the name of Jesus, takes the bread, blesses it, and gives it to us.

46 **EUCHARIST**

VOCABULARY ✓

The Jewish holiday of thanksgiving is *Passover.* This day commemorates the Jewish Exodus from Egypt when the Lord "passed over," or spared, the firstborn of the children of Israel. This event is celebrated every year with a special meal called the *Seder,* at which the Exodus story is retold.

The word *Eucharist* means "gratitude" or "thanksgiving" in Greek. The Sacrament of the Paschal mystery and Jesus' presence is the Eucharist. We celebrate it by receiving Christ's Body and Blood in the form of bread and wine. The Eucharist is the "source and summit" of our Christian lives.

SCRIPTURE BACKGROUND ✓

In *Mark 14:22* the story of the Last Supper is connected to Jesus' death on the cross, a death understood in the Old Testament tradition of sacrifice. The realism of the language underscores the power of the words, "Take, this is my body." Jesus blesses, breaks, and shares the bread, inviting his followers to participate in his death as a sacrifice that will result in their

presence at the banquet in the kingdom of God. The Last Supper is not an isolated event but is connected to the heavenly banquet. You may wish to point out that this passage is part of the readings for the Feast of Corpus Christi, Cycle B. Refer to page 108 of this book for more information about the liturgical year.

(S) SKILL NOTE ✓

Point out that remembering the love of God and the sacrifice Jesus made for us in the Eucharist can help us stay hopeful. For more information about this skill, see pages 52 and 53.

Student Leader Connection

Consider having the Student Leader do the following:

• **Read aloud** *Exodus 12:29—14:30* **about Passover.**

• **Research and report on the Jewish celebration of Passover.**

• **Help moderate the discussion about the Creed.**

The Liturgy of the Word

Our celebration of the Eucharist begins with the *Introductory Rites*. We gather together singing a hymn, and the celebrant greets us. During the *Penitential Rite* that follows, we acknowledge our sins and praise God for his mercy. The priest then prays a prayer of forgiveness. Sometimes we pray or sing the *Glory to God*. The *Opening Prayer* relates to the theme of the mass.

The first great part of the Mass is called the **Liturgy of the Word.** During this liturgy we listen to the word of God in readings from the Old and New Testaments. Through Scripture God reveals himself to us and guides us to him. We respond to the first reading with a joyful psalm, or song from Scripture. After

the second reading and Alleluia verse, the celebrant proclaims the good news of Jesus' life and teachings as recounted in one of the four Gospels.

Next, the priest or deacon speaks to us about the readings we have heard. This is the *homily*, which helps us understand how we can apply the message of the readings to our lives. Then, we recite together the *Profession of Faith*, or declaration of our Christian beliefs. Finally, during the *General Intercessions*, we offer prayers for the needs of the community, the Church, and the world.

With your Faith Partner make a list of your community's needs.

Rite Response

Objects Used at Mass

During the Mass we use special objects to help us celebrate. The *paten* is the plate that holds the *hosts*, or bread, that becomes the Body of Christ. The *chalice* is the cup that holds the wine that becomes the Blood of Christ. The *flagon* also holds wine. The *sacramentary* is the book that contains the prayers for the Mass. The *cruets* are the small containers, usually made of glass, that hold the wine and water used at Mass. The *ciborium*, or Eucharistic dish, is the covered container used to keep consecrated hosts. The ciborium is kept in the *tabernacle*, a special box-like receptacle. The *ambo* is the reading stand from which the Scripture is read and the homily is given.

WORKING WITH THE TEXT AND PICTURES

• Read the text and review the pictures on this page.

• Use *Vocabulary* below to help the students understand the term *Liturgy of the Word*.

• Review the first part of the Mass. **What happens during the Liturgy of the Word?** *(We listen to the word of God in Old and New Testament readings; we learn to apply the message to our lives; we declare our beliefs by reciting the creed; and we pray for the community, the Church, and the world.)*

• Refer to the lectern shown in the photograph and explain that it is also called an *ambo*.

• Review the sequence of events for the Liturgy of the Word. **In what order do the events of the Liturgy of the Word occur?** *(Encourage use of accurate terms: homily, Profession of Faith, and General Intercessions.)*

• Review the Profession of Faith. **What beliefs do we affirm in the Nicene Creed?** *(Answers should include belief in God, Jesus Christ, and the Spirit; the incarnation; Jesus' death, resurrection, and ascension; and the final judgment.)*

WORKING WITH THE ACTIVITY

Rite Response

• Ask a volunteer to read aloud *Rite Response*.

• Using their correct names, discuss the pictured sacred vessels. **How are these vessels used in celebrating the Eucharist?** *(Each item's purpose should be described.)*

• Discuss other sacred objects used in celebrating the sacraments. **How does using sacred objects make a celebration special?** *(Using objects only at a special time gives an occasion more meaning.)*

VOCABULARY ✓

The first great part of the Mass is called the **Liturgy of the Word.** On Sundays and important feasts, it includes an Old Testament reading, a New Testament reading, a Gospel reading, the homily, the Creed, and General Intercessions. During this part of the Mass, we celebrate God's word.

EXTENSION ACTIVITY

Reading about the Last Supper Encourage the students to learn more about the Last Supper by arranging the students in four groups and assigning one of the Gospels to each group. Have group members read their Gospel's account of the Last Supper or, in the case of the Gospel according to John, browse through the account. Ask the students to note anything that they didn't know before, are wondering about, or find interesting. When the groups have finished reading and taking notes, have them report their findings.

FAITH PARTNERSHIPS

Suggest that each pair of Faith Partners review the completed list and decide which item is the most important.

LINK TO LITURGY

If possible, pass around a lectionary for the students to examine. A lectionary is a book that contains Scripture readings, labeled by the day for which they are intended. Remind the students that the Scripture readings for Sundays and Solemnities are determined by a three-year cycle, A, B, and C, each of which begins with the first Sunday in Advent. The three-year lectionary allows us to hear a wide selection of texts. The weekday cycle is a two-year cycle, and there are also readings for saints' feast days and a variety of other Masses. Weekday Masses usually have only two readings—one from the Old or New Testament and one from one of the Gospels. See page 108 of this book for more information.

WORKING WITH THE ACTIVITY

Our Christian Journey

- Ask a volunteer to read aloud *Our Christian Journey.*

✓ • Discuss belief in the Eucharist. **What do we receive in the Eucharist?** *(the Body and Blood of Christ)* Point out that some Christians believe that the bread and wine are only signs or noneffective symbols.

- See *Background* below.

WORKING WITH THE TEXT AND PICTURES

✓ • Read *The Liturgy of the Eucharist* on pages 48 and 49, and review the photo on this page.

✓ • Use *Vocabulary* below to help the students understand the term *Liturgy of the Eucharist.*

✓ • Discuss the Liturgy of the Eucharist. **Why is the Liturgy of the Eucharist a "great" part of the Mass?** *(Possible answer: The Liturgy of the Eucharist is so designated because in it we offer to God in and through Christ all that we are as members of the Body of Christ, and we thank God for sharing with us the sacrificial meal of the Body and Blood of Jesus. The Eucharist is the great celebration of our faith and God's grace.)*

- Discuss the Concluding Rite. **What does it mean to be sent forth?** *(We are renewed in the Spirit and continue our celebration by the way we live and how we treat others.)*

✓ • Consider the Mass as it is celebrated in your parish. **For you, what are the highlights of the Mass in your parish?** *(Answers will vary.)*

Our Christian Journey

Something to Celebrate The celebration of the Eucharist is the central event of the Church. Over the centuries many Church councils, or official meetings of bishops and Church advisors, have dealt with the topic of the Eucharist. The Council of Trent, one of the most important councils in the history of the Church, issued an important statement about the Eucharist. In this decree the Council fathers wished to affirm the official Church position that the bread and wine become the Body and Blood of Christ during the celebration of the sacrament. They used the word **transubstantiation** to explain that the bread and wine offered at Mass are actually changed in their substance to Christ's Body and Blood, even though they keep the appearance of bread and wine. Catholics, then, believe that Christ is truly present in the consecrated Bread and Wine. This is called the **Real Presence.**
For more information: Research Pius X and the changes he made regarding the reception of Communion. Ask a librarian for good sources, use a Catholic encyclopedia, or consult the Internet.

1450   1575

1451-1506
CHRISTOPHER
COLUMBUS'S LIFE

1506-1552
SAINT FRANCIS
XAVIER'S LIFE

1545-1563
COUNCIL OF TRENT

1549
JESUIT MISSION
TO JAPAN

The Liturgy of the Eucharist

The second great part of the Mass is called the **Liturgy of the Eucharist.** We begin this part of the celebration by bringing our offerings, including the bread and wine, to the altar. This is the *Preparation of the Gifts.* In the name of the community, the priest receives the gifts and prays over them.

During the *Eucharistic Prayer,* a prayer of thanksgiving, the priest gathers our prayers with the prayers of all the Church and asks God the Father to send the Spirit upon our gifts. He asks that by the power of the Holy Spirit, our gifts of bread and wine may become the Body and Blood of Christ. The priest, through the power of God, consecrates the bread and wine.

We call the Eucharist a *sacrifice,* something special done or given out of love, because Jesus lived and died to save us. Our celebration of the Eucharist is also a sacred meal because our heavenly Father gives us his only Son, who is the Bread of Life.

48 **EUCHARIST**

VOCABULARY ✓

The second part of the Mass is the *Liturgy of the Eucharist,* which includes the Preparation of the Gifts, the Eucharistic Prayer, and Communion. The entire Mass is sometimes called the Liturgy of the Eucharist.

BACKGROUND

Time line Hoping to take part in the profitable spice trade, Italian explorer Christopher Columbus, financed by Spain, sought a new route to the East.

Saint Francis Xavier is the patron saint of Catholic missions. His work in India and east Asia helped spread the gospel message to new lands.

The Council of Trent affirmed the seven sacraments and the necessity of good works. It declared the Latin Vulgate to be the authentic version of the Bible.

The Jesuits brought Christianity to Japan; their mission continued until the Japanese eventually expelled all foreigners.

MULTIPLE LEARNING STYLES

Touring the sanctuary If possible, have a staff member take the students on a tour of the sanctuary and sacristy of the church. Invite the students to look at and reverently examine the vessels and vestments used at Mass. This activity can deepen the students' appreciation of the celebration of the Eucharist.

Student Leader Connection

Consider having the Student Leader do the following:

- **Review what happens during the Liturgy of the Eucharist.**
- **Read aloud *Our Christian Journey.***
- **Research and present information on one of the items on the time line from *Our Christian Journey.***

The next part of the Liturgy of the Eucharist is the *Communion Rite*. We pray together the Lord's Prayer and the Doxology, a prayer glorifying and praising the Trinity. Then, during Communion, we receive the Body and Blood of Christ. To recognize and experience hunger for this holy meal, the Church asks us not to eat or drink anything except water for one hour before Communion.

When we have received Communion, we once again thank God for his generosity. Finally, in the *Concluding Rite*, renewed in the Spirit, we pray the *Prayer After Communion*, and we are sent forth to live in Christ. We are called to spread his peace and justice throughout the world to become the Body of Christ for others.

The Fruits of Communion

The Eucharist is the source and summit of our Christian life. It is a celebration of the totality of our faith and the renewal of grace that comes to us through all the sacraments. The effects of the Eucharist are present in everything we do. Through the Eucharist we are nourished with the abundance of gratitude, love, joy, and hope that comes from full membership in the Body of Christ. We anticipate the heavenly banquet and the eternal happiness that will be ours.

When we participate in the Mass, we experience the saving love of Christ and the grace of God. We become more sensitive to those who are hurting and those who are in need. Because of Christ's example, we will work to change the structures of society that bring pain and suffering to people.

As part of our celebration of thanksgiving, we recognize that through the Eucharist our venial sins have been forgiven. And because of our renewed relationship with Christ, we are better able to avoid sin in the future. We are strengthened to make good moral decisions and to do works of justice and charity.

The Eucharist is a sign of the unity that ought to be present in the Church. It should lead us to pray and work for the union of Christian Churches. This may mean being tolerant of others' beliefs rather than criticizing them for being different.

Ⓢ Each time we gather for Eucharist, we celebrate our membership in the Body of Christ. The Eucharist is a time, place, and way in which we bring our lives to God as offering and thanksgiving. Through the grace of the Father, the example of his Son, and the power

of his Spirit, we receive the nourishment to continue to grow as the Body of Christ in the Eucharist. This sacrament is a celebration of what "has been" and what "can be" through faith and grace.

Catholics Believe

When we receive Communion, we receive Christ himself.
See Catechism, #1382.

What can you do to prepare yourself to receive Christ in Communion?

_____
_____
_____

WORKING WITH THE TEXT AND PICTURES

✓ • Read *The Fruits of Communion,* and review the picture on this page.

✓ • Discuss the effects of the Eucharist. *(forgiveness of venial sin, nourishment by the Spirit, a hint of eternal happiness to come, and strength to make good moral decisions)*

✓ • See *Skill Note* below.

• Name and briefly discuss various liturgical ministries open to young people. *(lectors, commentators, servers, greeters, ushers, musicians)*

WORKING WITH THE ACTIVITY
Catholics Believe

• Ask a volunteer to read aloud *Catholics Believe.*

• Explain why we must prepare to receive the Eucharist. **Why do we prepare for Communion?** *(Receiving Christ is central to our faith: we should be ready to greet him with thanks and joy.)*

✓ • Allow time for the students to answer the question. *(Possible answer: we reconcile with others and fast for one hour.)*

• See *Reflecting on Your Faith* below.

• Encourage the students to share with the group their thoughts about the paraphrased Catechism statement and their responses to the question that follows.

REFLECTING ON YOUR FAITH
Reflect on ways you might improve your preparation for receiving Christ in Communion.

Ⓢ SKILL NOTE ✓
In celebrating the Eucharist we find our faith and hope renewed. For more information on the skill of Staying Hopeful, see pages 52 and 53.

LINK TO MUSIC
Have the students select two or three songs frequently sung by your parish community during Communion. Distribute hymnals and have the students examine the lyrics. Discuss the meaning of the hymns with the students. How is the importance of the Eucharist expressed in these hymns? What words and images are used? If possible, arrange to have the students sing the songs together or use them in future liturgies planned by the students.

BACKGROUND
Fasting before Communion When we receive Communion, we receive Christ himself. The Church asks us to prepare for this special moment by fasting for one hour before we receive Holy Communion: We may not eat, but we may drink water. Fasting is rooted in the earliest days of the Church. This practice of limiting the amount of food we eat and when we eat it helps us grow spiritually by placing less emphasis on the needs of our bodies. Fasting before Communion is just one of the ways we can prepare to celebrate the Sacrament of the Eucharist.

EXTENSION ACTIVITY
Keeping a journal Have the students begin a daily or weekly "gratitude" journal as a way of preparing for the Eucharist. You may wish to set aside time each week for the students to write in their journals. Remind the students that journals are private. If you ask the students to hand the journals in to you, tell them that in most cases nothing they write will be shared with anyone. Only if their writing indicates possible harm or danger to themselves or others would a confidence not be kept.

A Eucharistic People

WORKING WITH THE TEXT AND PICTURES

✓ • Read the text on this page, and review the picture on pages 50 and 51.

• Discuss with the students what it means to be good. *Who or what inspires you to be good?* (Accept all reasonable responses.)

✓ • Invite the students to think about what they have learned about the Eucharist. *What do you think it means to say that the sacraments, especially the Eucharist, are the center and source of our life in Christ?* (Possible answer: our relationship with Jesus is rooted in the sacraments, especially the Eucharist.)

• Encourage the students to understand the importance of the sacraments, especially the Eucharist, in their lives as Catholics. *What does it mean to be a Eucharistic person?* (Possible answers: As Catholics we can depend on our relationship with Jesus in the sacraments, especially the Eucharist, to help us know what is right and to have the strength to see it through; we are nourished to live in Christ and to share his peace and love with everyone.)

WORKING WITH THE ACTIVITY

Wrap Up

• Have a volunteer read aloud the summary statements.

✓ • Allow time for the students to consider their remaining questions and write them in their books.

• Discuss any remaining questions the students may have. You may wish to have the students write their questions on separate sheets of paper so that you can collect them and respond during the next session.

For us as Catholics the sacraments are the center and source of our life in Christ. Our relationship with Jesus is rooted in the sacraments, especially the Eucharist. Some of the sacraments, like Baptism and Confirmation, are celebrated only once in our lives. But the Sacrament of the Eucharist should be celebrated often. We participate in the life of the community and celebrate this sacred meal with the rest of the Church. The Eucharist plays a central role in our lives as Christians. This is why we are often called a Eucharistic people.

Think about your life. Do you consider yourself a Eucharistic person? Who or what inspires you to do good? Where do your beliefs and ideals come from? If Jesus is important to you, draw closer to him through the Eucharist. If someone encourages you to go against your principles, such as pressuring you to have sex or use drugs, how do you decide what to do? As a Catholic you can depend on your relationship with Jesus in the Eucharist to help you know what is right for you and to have the strength to see it through.

In the Eucharist Jesus offers himself to his Father out of love for us. Whenever we celebrate this sacrificial meal, our venial sins are forgiven and God's grace is strengthened within us. We experience the Real Presence of Jesus with us. We are renewed and nourished to live in Christ and to share his peace and love with everyone.

Reflect on the central role of the Eucharist in our lives. Share your thoughts with your Faith Partner.

WRAP UP

- The Eucharist is a Sacrament of Christian Initiation and the source and summit of our Christian life.
- The Eucharist is the sacrament of Jesus' presence with us.
- In the Eucharist we receive the Body and Blood of Christ.
- At Mass we gather together as the Church to give thanks and to praise God.
- Through the Eucharist we anticipate the heavenly banquet, eternal life in the fullness of the kingdom.

What questions do you have about this chapter?

_____
_____
_____

50 **EUCHARIST**

FAITH PARTNERSHIPS

Have the students work with their Faith Partners to discuss the central role of the Eucharist in their lives. Encourage the students to think about what their faith means to them and to consider the effects that receiving Christ in Communion can have on their lives.

EXTENSION ACTIVITY

Celebrating together To stress the importance of the Sacrament of the Eucharist to our lives as Catholics, arrange for the celebration of the Eucharist or a Communion service for the group. If neither of these is possible, work with the students to create a prayer celebration that is especially meaningful to them, and arrange to share a light snack with them afterward. (Be sure to ask the students whether any of them have food allergies before deciding on the snack.) The experience of celebrating our faith in Christ and giving thanks to God as a community of faith is central to our Catholic identity.

LINK TO LITURGY

Have the group host the hospitality time after the liturgy on a particular Sunday.

Student Leader Connection

Consider having the Student Leader do the following:

• **Help the group create a graffiti wall about what it means to be Eucharistic people.**

• **Read aloud the *Wrap Up* summary statements.**

• **Help moderate the discussion for *Around the Group*, or record the results of the discussion.**

• **Collect or record any questions the students have, and help find answers to these.**

RESOURCE Center

Around the Group

Discuss the following question as a group.

How can we live as Eucharistic people?

After everyone has had a chance to share his or her responses, come up with a group answer upon which everyone can agree.

_____
_____
_____
_____

What personal observations do you have about the group discussion and answer?

_____
_____
_____
_____

Briefly . . .

At the beginning of this chapter, you were asked to list things which you find valuable and people for whom you are thankful. How was your faith reflected in your response? Based on what you have learned in this chapter, do you want to add anything to your original response?

_____
_____
_____

WORKING WITH THE ACTIVITIES

Around the Group

✓ • Present the question to the group, and allow time for discussion. You may need to moderate to keep the students focused on the question.

• Encourage the group members to listen to the opinions and perspectives of others.

• Encourage the students to examine how celebrating the Eucharist strengthens their relationship with Jesus.

✓ • If the group has agreed on an answer, direct the students to write it in their books. If they could not agree, direct them to list in their books the issues that were left unresolved and explain why.

✓ • Encourage the students to note in their books their personal observations about the discussion and any final thoughts they have.

• See *Reflecting on Your Faith* below.

Briefly . . .

• Encourage the students to consider how their opinions may have changed since they responded to *What Do You Think?* on page 45.

• Invite the students to consider how faith influences an attitude of thankfulness.

✓ • Allow time for the students to write their responses in their books.

• See *Reflecting on Your Faith* below.

REFLECTING ON YOUR FAITH

Around the Group: Think about how your understanding of what it means to be part of a Eucharistic people is different from or similar to what the students understand. How have their insights deepened your own?

Briefly: Consider how your faith can more completely influence the people and things for which you are thankful.

EXTENSION ACTIVITY

Building a graffiti wall Have the students create short phrases or slogans that reflect what it means to be Eucharistic people. Provide a few examples, such as "Baptized in Jesus" or "Guided by the Light." Supply the students with sheets of poster board and markers, and have them post their completed work on one wall of the room. If there is no suitable wall or backdrop, ask the students to write their slogans in a random pattern on the board. Supply colored chalk for this purpose.

TEACHING TIP

Participating at Mass Help the students understand that their celebration of the Eucharist will be more meaningful to them if they participate actively. Remind the students that celebrating the Eucharist is an act of worship. It requires more than passive observation. Encourage the students to appreciate the Mass as a celebration of *their* faith. Arrange an opportunity for the students to sign up for any liturgical ministries open to them.

WORKING WITH THE SKILL

✓ • *How does the Eucharist help us remain hopeful?* (The Eucharist reinforces the virtues of faith, hope, and love in us as we accept Jesus in this sacrament.) **What are the characteristics of a hopeful person?** (A hopeful person is optimistic and resourceful and enjoys meeting people and trying new activities.)

• Ask a volunteer to read aloud *Expressions of Faith.*

• Ask a volunteer to read aloud *Scripture.* Discuss the image used in the verse. *What is a yoke?* (a wooden bar laid across the shoulders to enable a person to carry a heavy load) If possible, show the students a picture of a yoke so that they understand what it means to be burdened in this way. Invite them to express their opinions about this Scripture verse. **What does this Scripture passage mean?** (Answers will vary.)

✓ • See *Scripture Background* below.

✓ • Ask a volunteer to read aloud *Think About It.* Give the students enough time to complete the activity. Invite the students to decide how much work each has to do to become a hopeful person.

• See *Reflecting on Your Faith* below.

✓ • Explain that hopefulness is an attitude everyone can develop. *What can make you feel more hopeful when you are having a bad day?* (Possible answers: praying, talking with a friend, listening to music, spending some quiet time, enjoying a snack.) **What can you do when you are facing really serious problems or pressures?** (You can pray, seek advice from an adult, talk to a counselor, and if possible, avoid dangerous situations.)

SKILLS FOR Christian Living

Staying Hopeful

Expressions of Faith—

In the Sacrament of the Eucharist, we are reminded that we have every reason to be hopeful people. Yet it can be hard to stay hopeful every day.

We face troubles and anxieties that overshadow the promises God has made us. As Catholics we may know why we should be hopeful, but sometimes we don't know how to go about it. Often we need to use our faith to gain the courage to stay hopeful. Staying hopeful will help you live as one of Christ's followers.

Scripture

"Come to me, all you that are weary and are carrying heavy burdens, and I will give you rest. Take my yoke upon you, and learn from me; for I am gentle and humble in heart, and you will find rest for your souls. For my yoke is easy, and my burden is light."
Matthew 11:28–30

14th Sunday of Ordinary Time, Cycle A

Think About It—

No one is happy and enthusiastic every day. Sometimes we have good reasons for being unhappy or sad. Sometimes we just need a little practice being more optimistic and hopeful. Hopefulness is a feeling of looking forward to the future and believing that even though bad things happen, good things happen, too. In the following examples, place an abbreviation before each of the statements (Really True—RT, Somewhat True—ST, and Not True—NT).

_____ 1. Bad things tend to happen to me and those I care about.

_____ 2. I tend to give up easily.

_____ 3. I don't like taking on new tasks.

_____ 4. I usually don't make a good impression on new people I meet.

_____ 5. In general I'm a hopeful person.

_____ 6. God helps me when I need it.

_____ 7. If someone doesn't answer me when I say hello, I tend to think the person didn't hear me.

_____ 8. I can usually succeed at a new project.

Are you a hopeful person?
If you answered RT to 1–4, or NT to 5–8, you might have trouble staying hopeful. If you answered NT to 1–4, or RT to 5–8, you are probably a person who finds it easy to stay hopeful. Whatever your answers, you can decide that you will be a hopeful person.

52 EUCHARIST

REFLECTING ON YOUR FAITH

Reflect on how hopeful you are by completing the *Think About It* activity. Name one thing you can do to grow in hope.

BACKGROUND

General intercessions The general intercessions include prayers for our community, the Church, and the world. In placing these prayers before the Lord, we show our faith and hope in him.

SCRIPTURE BACKGROUND ✓

Matthew 11:28–30 describes Jesus as the giver of wisdom, the revealer of truth, and the source of comfort and rest. In this passage we realize that depending on Jesus relieves us of the burdens of everyday life. You may wish to point out that this passage is part of the readings for the Fourteenth Sunday of

Ordinary Time, Cycle A. Refer to page 108 of this book for more information about the liturgical year.

Student Leader Connection

Consider having the Student Leader do the following:

• **Help moderate the discussion about the traits of a hopeful person.**

• **Show a picture of a yoke, and explain what the Scripture passage means to him or her.**

• **Help the group practice the three-step process of staying hopeful by using an example from real life.**

• **Organize a small group to plan a prayer service.**

Special Note: Remember to meet briefly with the Student Leader for Chapter 6. You may wish to provide him or her with the Student Leader Prep Page found on page R6.

RESOURCE Center

Skill Steps

Sometimes we may feel so overwhelmed by our emotions and concerns that we are not sure what we are feeling. There is a simple way to handle any emotion that is so strong that it seems to be taking control. Remember three easy steps: name it, tame it, and claim it.

Name it means identifying exactly what you are thinking and feeling. *Tame it* means that you try to gain control over the emotion by admitting that you are experiencing it. Is this a permanent situation? Do I have the power to change it? Is this the way things frequently happen to me?

After you have *named it* and *tamed it*, then you can *claim it*. None of us are completely in control of everything that happens to us. We can, however, choose how we respond to things. The key is not to let our emotions control who we are and how we act.

How do you name, tame, and claim feelings of hopelessness?

Let's say you are feeling hopeless because you are having trouble in your English class.

- First, name it. Identify how you are feeling. "I feel stupid and way behind."
- Then, tame it. Ask yourself the three questions: Is this a permanent situation? "Not necessarily." Do I have the power to change it? "Yes, if I admit that I'm having trouble and ask for help." Is this the way things usually happen to me? "No, I usually do well in school."
- Finally, claim it. What can you do to learn from this? How can you put this experience or emotion to productive use? Maybe you can tell yourself not to give up so easily or not to wait so long before asking for help. Claiming a situation means finding a productive way to improve your situation while also looking to God and others for support and guidance.

Check It Out

Place a check mark next to one of the following responses.

When it comes to managing my emotions, which is the most difficult for me?

○ Naming It
○ Taming It
○ Claiming It

What does this tell you about yourself?

_____

_____

Closing Prayer

God our Father, you call us to the Eucharistic banquet table to feed us and renew our hearts. We give thanks to you for your Son, Jesus Christ, who gave himself for us so that we could be close to you. May your Holy Spirit help us live every day with thanks and praise for your mercy and kindness. Amen.

WORKING WITH THE SKILL

- Introduce the process of staying hopeful to the students as it is presented in the text. ***Have you ever been emotionally over-whelmed by a situation? How did you handle it?*** *(Answers will vary.)*

- Have a volunteer read aloud *Skill Steps*.

✓ - Discuss the three steps of the process with the students. What does it mean to "Name It"? To "Tame It"? To "Claim It"? *(Responses should accurately reflect the description of each part in* Skill Steps*.)*

- Once the students have worked through the example in the text, invite volunteers to suggest another common problem that teens face. With the rest of the group, work through the three parts of the staying hopeful process so that the students gain experience in working with the technique. Answer any questions the students have.

- See *Reflecting on Your Faith* below.

✓ - Direct the students' attention to *Check It Out*, and give them sufficient time to complete the activity.

CLOSING PRAYER

✓ - Gather together to pray the closing prayer. You may wish to use the following music from the *Give Your Gifts* series: "For Living, for Dying" *(The Songs)*, "Psalm 34: Taste and See" *(The Basics)*, or "Raise Me Up" *(More Songs)* (GIA Publications, Inc.; distributed by Harcourt Religion Publishers).

- If time permits, direct the students to create their own closing reflections or prayers. You may wish to ask a few volunteers to read aloud what they have created or to plan a prayer service.

REFLECTING ON YOUR FAITH

Use a situation or emotional experience in your own life to work through the three-part process described in *Skill Steps*. How does the process help you gain control and perspective?

TEACHING TIP

Research follow-up You may wish to take time to review any research the students have been asked to complete. If the students need additional time to complete their research, set aside a few minutes at the beginning of the next session to allow them to share the information they have gathered.

MULTIPLE LEARNING STYLES

Closing prayer You may wish to have the students create their closing prayers in the style of a formal prayer or reflection; a poem or song; or a prayer service with readings, psalm response, and music. Remind the students that the tone of their responses can be different from that of the example but should remain respectful.

ASSESSMENT

The Assessment Page for Chapter 5 can be found on page R13.

LINK TO FAMILY

The corresponding Family Resource pages for this skill are 82–85.

Reconciliation

KEY CONTENT SUMMARY

Reconciliation is a Sacrament of Healing. Contrition, confession, and penance are integral parts of the sacrament. God's mercy and forgiveness strengthen us to live virtuous lives.

PLANNING THE CHAPTER

OPEN	PACING	CONTENT	OBJECTIVES	MATERIALS
	Suggested Time: Parish **10 min.** School **25 min.** Your Time: ____ min.	pp. 54–55	• Recognize that the Sacrament of Reconciliation is a Sacrament of Healing.	• candle, matches (optional) • symbol representing chapter theme (optional) • instrumental music for prayer • Bibles (optional)
SEARCH				
	Suggested Time: Parish **25 min.** School **70 min.** Your Time: ____ min.	pp. 56–59	• Identify the fact that because of sin, we require God's forgiveness. • Explore the elements and effects of the Rite of Penance and how we are called to reconciliation with ourselves, with those we hurt, and with God.	• Bibles • list of sins of commission and sins of omission (optional)
REFLECT				
	Suggested Time: Parish **10 min.** School **30 min.** Your Time: ____ min.	pp. 60–61	• Reflect on how we can live reconciling and virtuous lives.	
LIVE				
	Suggested Time: Parish **15 min.** School **35 min.** Your Time: ____ min.	pp. 62–63	• Apply God's mercy and forgiveness to our own lives and to our personal relationships.	• Student Leader Prep Page for Chapter 7 (p. R7) (optional) • music for prayer (optional) • *Living Our Faith Prayer Services* (optional) • copies of Assessment Page for Chapter 6 (p. R14) (optional)

CATECHISM IN CONTEXT

See Catechism of the Catholic Church, #1431.

In the Sacrament of Reconciliation, we confess our sins. Sincere contrition for our sins means that we reorder our lives and convert, or turn away from, wrong choices we have made and turn toward God. When we regret our sinful thoughts and actions and seek absolution, we are open to Jesus' gifts of mercy, forgiveness, and healing. With renewed hope we pray and perform good works in Christ to make up for the harm we have done. In doing so, we express our sorrow and learn to change the behavior that leads us to sins of omission and commission.

Through the grace of Reconciliation, we gain the ability to recognize evil, the strength to resist temptation, and a peacefulness of mind and heart. When we determine once more to live as Jesus did, we can lead virtuous lives and fulfill our roles in the mission and ministry of his Church.

ONE-MINUTE RETREAT

READ

"Forgiveness does not mean ignoring what has been done. . . . It means, rather, that the evil act no longer remains as a barrier to the relationship." —Martin Luther King Jr.

REFLECT

How are my relationships strengthened through forgiveness?

PRAY

Jesus, Reconciler, I ask your mercy. Forgive my sins. Lift away the barriers I have placed between myself and those I have hurt. Turn me away from sin and toward you.

LIBRARY LINKS

BOOKS
FOR ADOLESCENTS

"'Bless Me, Father, I'm Not Sure I Want to Be Here!'" by Kathleen M. Paiva (*Youth Update;* St. Anthony Messenger Press).

Reviews the theology of the Sacrament of Reconciliation, helps heal negative experiences, and celebrates forgiveness.

"Preparing for Confession: Taking Your Spiritual Temperature," by Rev. Thomas M. Casey OSA (*Youth Update;* St. Anthony Messenger Press).

Provides a thorough and practical examination of conscience (based on the Ten Commandments) for young people to use in preparing for the sacrament.

"Right or Wrong: How Can I Know?" by Jim Heft SM (*Youth Update;* St. Anthony Messenger Press).

Presents the concept of conscience formation and counteracts the attitude that "being good is no fun."

FOR ADULTS

A Reconciliation Sourcebook, ed. by Joseph Favazzaa and Kathleen Hughes (Liturgy Training Publications, 1997).

A collection of key texts, prayers, and resources.

A Time for Embracing: Reclaiming Reconciliation, by Julia Upton (The Liturgical Press, 1999).

Encourages participation in the sacrament as a source of healing.

Why Go to Confession? Questions and Answers About Sacramental Reconciliation, by Rev. Joseph M. Champlin (St. Anthony Messenger Press, 1996).

A classic reference work on sacramental reconciliation.

MULTIMEDIA

A Father and Two Sons (video) (American Bible Society; distributed by Harcourt Religion Publishers).

Contemporary biblical story features black-and-white images and a blues vocal track. Includes study guide and activities.

Reconciliation: Closing the Gap (video) (Harcourt Religion Publishers).

Presents a history of Reconciliation and encourages young people to resolve conflicts by following Jesus' example.

FEATURE PREPARATION

STUDENT LEADER CONNECTION

The Student Leader Prep Page for this chapter is located on page R6. You may wish to provide this information to the Student Leader as an introduction and resource for the chapter.

FAITH PARTNERSHIPS

Chapter 6 has the same Faith Partners as Chapter 5. Several opportunities for Faith Partner discussions have been marked throughout the chapter. You may wish to consider other opportunities as you prepare the lesson.

SKILL NOTES

The skill for this chapter is Staying Hopeful. You may wish to build on what the students have learned in the previous chapter as you teach this chapter. A few Skill Notes have been called out to help you. The skill lesson for this chapter can be found on pages 62 and 63.

A check mark indicates the chapter's essential questions, statements, activities, and features. If time is limited, such as in a parish group setting, this icon will help you direct the students through the lesson.

Reconciliation

KEY POINTS FROM CHAPTER 5

You may wish to review these points with the students before you begin the new chapter:

- The Sacrament of the Eucharist completes the Sacraments of Christian Initiation.
- The Eucharist is the "source and summit" of our Christian life.
- The Eucharist is a sacrifice and a sacred meal.
- The Body and Blood of Christ provide us with spiritual nourishment.
- Staying Hopeful is a Skill for Christian Living.

✓ **GATHERING**

Invite volunteers to share how the day has been going on a scale of 1 to 10 (1 being the lowest, 10 the highest). Have them include in their evaluation the things they have enjoyed or struggled with, things they wish they had done differently, and things they are proud of.

✓ **PRAYER**

Have the students stand in a circle for prayer. Play a few moments of soothing instrumental music, and, if practical, turn off the lights to create a prayerful, meditative environment. Pray the opening prayer together, and make a sign of peace to one another. If fire regulations permit, you may wish to light a candle at this time.

Jesus, sometimes we hurt others by making wrong choices and acting selfishly. Forgive us, and help us choose what is right. Bring us to forgiveness and healing, and help us change our hearts.

54

RESOURCE Center

PRAYER ENVIRONMENT

If you have created a prayer space for the room, you may wish to add an image (perhaps a drawing or picture of people shaking hands or praying together) that suggests reconciliation, the theme of this chapter.

EXTENSION ACTIVITY

Learning about forgiveness Distribute Bibles and arrange the students in three groups. Assign to each group one of the Gospels according to Matthew, Mark, or Luke. Ask each group to find situations in which Jesus forgives someone or talks about forgiveness. Have the groups share their findings.

Student Leader Connection

Consider having the Student Leader do the following:

- Find or create a symbol for the prayer space.
- Gather the students by inviting them to share their reactions to the day.
- Play music, turn off the lights, and lead the opening prayer
- Read aloud or review selected text.
- Help moderate a discussion about the harmful effects of sin.
- Help moderate the discussion about experiences of reconciliation.

What Do You Think?

Complete the following sentences to describe the experience of sin and our desire to make things right again.

When a friend lies to me, I feel _____

_____

If someone insults me out of anger, I _____

_____

If I want to apologize for something I did, I _____

_____

Describe a time when you did not want to reconcile with someone but are glad that you did it anyway.

_____

_____

The Loneliness of Sin

When you and your friends or family have a disagreement, how do you get over your anger and hurt? Do you apologize? Do you try to make up for the misunderstanding in some way?

Sin causes separation. It harms and sometimes destroys relationships and drives people apart. Because of sin, we distrust one another, and often we feel lonely and isolated. When we experience the separation and hurt caused by sin, God wants to act in our lives to heal us. He invites us to *reconcile*, or be brought back together, with him, with those we have hurt or who have hurt us, with the Church, and with ourselves. In turning toward God, we find ways to make amends for the wrongs we have done and to be forgiving of others.

(S) The Sacrament of Reconciliation, one of the Sacraments of Healing, is also one of the sacraments through which God forgives sins. In this sacrament we celebrate God's mercy and forgiveness. With God's grace we are no longer separated. Instead, we are united in celebrating God's forgiveness and the peace it brings.

OPEN 55

WORKING WITH THE ACTIVITY

What Do You Think?

✓ • Allow time for the students to record their thoughts in the spaces provided.

• See *Reflecting on Your Faith* below.

✓ • *What Do You Think?* is intended as a personal pre-assessment. The students should not be asked to share their responses.

WORKING WITH THE TEXT AND PICTURES

✓ • Read the text on this page, and review the pictures on pages 54 and 55.

✓ • Discuss the effects of sin. **How does sin affect our relationships with people?** *(Possible answers: Sin harms and sometimes destroys relationships; distrust and deceit drive people apart; hurt can lead to anger and revenge.)*

• Discuss reconciliation. **What are some characteristics of reconciliation?** *(forgiveness, willingness to forget, a mutual desire to heal the relationship)* **When might we need to reconcile with God and the Church?** *(When we reject what is good and do what is wrong.)*

• Discuss the icons. **What do the icons suggest about the Sacrament of Reconciliation?** *(Possible answers: The position of the hand may suggest prayer or an extension of healing and forgiveness. The book may suggest Scripture, from which we learn about God's love and his willingness to forgive our sins.)*

• Ask the students when full reconciliation with someone might be impossible. *(Someone may refuse to reconcile or may have died.)*

✓ • See *Skill Note* below.

TEACHING TIP

Talking about sensitive issues When talking about examples of sin, avoid judging the students or their behavior. Encourage a general discussion of the experiences of sin that some young people might encounter rather than have the students give specific examples of their own sinfulness. Students this age are able to apply privately ideas that they have discussed in general.

EXTENSION ACTIVITY

Eliciting advice Have the students create a two-column chart on the board or on large sheets of chart paper. Label one column *Words and Actions That Hurt* and the other column *Words and Actions That Heal*. Ask the students to brainstorm words and actions that can make a situation or a relationship better or worse. For example, the students may suggest using "I" words during a disagreement rather than making accusatory statements addressed to "you," or they may suggest ways to walk away from a conflict without losing dignity.

(S) SKILL NOTE ✓

When we celebrate God's mercy and forgiveness, our hope is restored. For more information on the skill of Staying Hopeful, see pages 62 and 63.

WORKING WITH THE TEXT AND PICTURES

- ✓ Read the text and review the picture on this page.
- ✓ Use *Vocabulary* below to help the students understand the term *conscience*.
- Discuss the picture of the woman washing Jesus' feet. **Why did the woman approach Jesus? Could you have approached Jesus as she did? Why?** (Answers will vary.)
- ✓ Discuss forgiveness. **How can we ask for forgiveness?** (We can speak to the one who has been hurt, write a note of apology, or do something kind for the person.)
- Explain the difference between mistakes and deliberate choices.
- See *Background* below.
- ✓ Discuss sins of commission and omission. **What is an example of a sin of commission? A sin of omission?** (Answers will vary.)

WORKING WITH THE ACTIVITY

Catholics Believe

- Ask a volunteer to read aloud *Catholics Believe*.
- ✓ Allow time for the students to write their reflections on the question. (Answers will vary.)
- ✓ Explain that intention lies behind every deliberate choice. **How do our attitudes affect the choices we make?** (Answers will vary.)
- See *Reflecting on Your Faith* below.
- Encourage the students to share with the group their thoughts about the paraphrased Catechism statement and their responses to the question that follows.

Recognizing **Our Sinfulness**

Sin hurts our relationship with God, self, and others. But through the Sacrament of Reconciliation, we celebrate God's forgiveness and learn to heal our relationships. If we recognize the pain we have caused and are sorry for our sinful thoughts or actions, we can be forgiven. We can learn from our poor choices and work to live more virtuous lives.

During a meal that Jesus attended in the house of a Pharisee, a woman whom people judged to be a sinner entered and approached Jesus. She washed his feet with her tears and dried them with her hair. She then kissed his feet and anointed them with oil. The Pharisee was surprised that Jesus allowed the woman to do this because she was known as a sinful person. But Jesus said that because the woman had shown great love, her sins were forgiven. (See *Luke 7:36–50*.)

Like the woman in the story, we are called to seek forgiveness and ask for God's mercy and grace in our lives. How do you know when you need to seek God's forgiveness? You know because sin is a deliberate choice you make. Perhaps you drink a beer at a friend's house, something you know is wrong (a sin of *commission*). Or perhaps you hear some hurtful gossip about someone and you know that the gossip is untrue, but you do nothing to stop it (a sin of *omission*).

God gives us the gift of **conscience,** the ability to tell right from wrong and to choose what is right. Because of our conscience, we know the difference between a sin and something that goes wrong by accident. As we develop a habit of choosing what is right, it becomes easier to do so.

Share with your Faith Partner your thoughts about how we develop our conscience.

Catholics Believe

Jesus' call to conversion and penance means changing our hearts. This will lead to changing the way we act. See Catechism, #1430.

What do you think it means to "change our hearts"?

_____
_____
_____

56 **RECONCILIATION**

VOCABULARY ✓

Although we face difficult decisions and strong temptations throughout our lives, **conscience,** a gift from God, helps us recognize the difference between right and wrong. The more a person informs his or her conscience and relies on it, the more strength he or she has to choose what is right. Conscience, free will, grace, and reason work together to help us make good decisions.

FAITH PARTNERSHIPS

Suggest that the Faith Partners discuss specific situations that helped them develop a sense of right and wrong.

BACKGROUND

Making choices Emphasize that we all make mistakes for various reasons, among them fatigue, lack of information, or feeling unwell. While we need to correct and often to apologize for our mistakes, we also must recognize that we did not intend harm by our words or actions. On the other hand, choosing to do wrong means that we deliberately say or do something to cause harm to ourselves or others. In these situations we must not only apologize and make amends, we must also recognize that we have chosen to turn away from God and the values of Christian living—and we must turn back to God for forgiveness through the Sacrament of Reconciliation.

REFLECTING ON YOUR FAITH

In what areas of your life do you need to change your heart and become more open and sensitive to others?

Student Leader Connection

Consider having the Student Leader do the following:

- Read aloud *Luke 7:36–50*.
- Help the group create an examination of conscience.
- Research and present information on one of the items on the time line from *Our Christian Journey*.

RESOURCE Center

Looking at Your Life

When we prepare for the Sacrament of Reconciliation, we look at how well we are living the Christian life. This is called an **examination of conscience,** a prayerful way of recognizing our strengths and weaknesses and admitting to the presence of sin in our life.

Venial sin, or less serious sin, weakens our relationship with Jesus and with other members of the Body of Christ. The Sacrament of Reconciliation helps us overcome the petty habits and selfishness that characterize venial sin and strengthens our union with Jesus. Even when sin is very serious, or *mortal* (such as murder), the Sacrament of Reconciliation is always available. A mortal sin breaks the bond with Christ and his Church completely. But anyone who is truly sorry and who seeks God's forgiveness can turn to this Sacrament of Healing.

Although you can examine your conscience at any time, anywhere, a quiet place and time are helpful. Before you start, pray to the Holy Spirit for guidance. Then ask yourself questions about your attitudes and actions as they affect your relationships with God, others, and self. You might use the Ten Commandments to review your decisions. For example, do I put God first in all things? Do I lie? Do I steal? The Beatitudes may also help you decide whether your attitudes and actions are truly Christian. Do you forgive easily? Do you try to find peaceful solutions to disagreements?

After you become used to reviewing your attitudes and actions, you will develop your own questions. You may refer to Scripture for help, or you may personalize your questions based on areas of your life that you know need work.

OUR CHRISTIAN JOURNEY

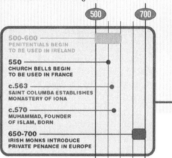

Medieval Penitential Books While today we emphasize the forgiveness and healing of the Sacrament of Reconciliation, people of earlier times focused on how to make up for their wrongdoing. Priests during the Middle Ages used special books, known as penitentials, when listening to confessions. These manuals listed specific penances for sins. The penances were based on the sin committed and the social rank of the sinner. Usually, a penance was the length of time a sinner had to fast, but a penance could also include reciting the psalms and other practices. The penitentials, written by priests and monks experienced in hearing confessions, were never official Church documents.

For further information: Research or talk to someone of a different faith about the role of reconciliation in other religions.

500   700

500-600
PENITENTIALS BEGIN
TO BE USED IN IRELAND

550
CHURCH BELLS BEGIN
TO BE USED IN FRANCE

c.563
SAINT COLUMBA ESTABLISHES
MONASTERY OF IONA

c.570
MUHAMMAD, FOUNDER
OF ISLAM, BORN

650-700
IRISH MONKS INTRODUCE
PRIVATE PENANCE IN EUROPE

WORKING WITH THE TEXT AND PICTURES

- Read the text and review the picture on this page.

- Use *Vocabulary* below to help the students understand the term *examination of conscience.*

- Discuss examination of conscience. **What can help us examine our consciences regularly?** *(daily prayer, retreats, taking time to relax in peaceful places, reading, journaling)*

- Define the word *sin*. **What is the difference between mortal and venial sin?** *(Mortal sin severs the relationship between the sinner and Christ and between the sinner and the Church. Though venial sin is less serious, it can lead to mortal sin if a habit of sinning is established.)*

- Have the students identify sources of guidance for evaluating their lives. **What are guides for examining your conscience?** *(the Ten Commandments, the Beatitudes, Jesus' life and teachings, the Church's teachings, reason)*

WORKING WITH THE ACTIVITY

Our Christian Journey

- Ask a volunteer to read aloud *Our Christian Journey.*

- Discuss fasting. **Why do we fast?** *(Possible answer: Limiting the amount of food we eat places our spiritual needs above our physical needs.)*

- Discuss penitentials. **If penitentials were in use today, what might you find in them?** *(Answers will vary.)*

- See *Background* below.

VOCABULARY ✓

An *examination of conscience* is a prayerful way of looking at our lives in light of the Ten Commandments, the Beatitudes, the life of Jesus, the teachings of the Church, and reason to determine how we may have sinned against God. Examining our consciences helps us avoid major problems in life and is a source of inspiration and strength.

MULTIPLE LEARNING STYLES

Exploring the hurtfulness of sin You may wish to arrange the students in groups and invite each group to create a skit. Illustrating potentially harmful relationships and situations common among adolescents, the skits should help the students analyze the causes and effects of sin. Topics may include mocking and teasing, drinking, spreading rumors, and expressing anger inappropriately. After each skit, have the students change roles so that they can interpret both the feelings of one who chooses to sin and the reactions of one who is sinned against.

BACKGROUND

Time line Appearing first in Irish and Welsh monasteries, penitentials soon spread throughout Europe. They were used extensively until the eleventh century.

Before clocks were common, church bells were used to call the faithful to worship.

After founding monasteries in his native Ireland, Saint Columba (521–597) brought Christianity to Scotland by establishing a monastery on Iona, an island off the Scottish coast.

Followers of Islam, or Muslims, call God *Allah* (AH•luh) and believe that the Qur'an (kuh•RAN), the book of Muhammad's teachings, is divinely inspired.

Because of the Irish monks' influence, private confession to a priest became the norm, and the custom of public penance disappeared.

WORKING WITH THE TEXT AND PICTURES

✓ • Read the text and review the picture on this page.

✓ • Use *Vocabulary* below to help the students understand the highlighted terms.

• Explain how conversion affects behavior. **How does behavior change when someone your age experiences conversion?** *(Possible answers: We treat family members better; we are more sensitive to other students; we are more respectful toward teachers, coaches, and other authority figures.)*

✓ • Discuss contrition. **When do we experience contrition?** *(when we see the harm our sins have caused; when we recognize destructive behavior)*

WORKING WITH THE ACTIVITIES

Media Message

• Ask a volunteer to read aloud the text about video game violence.

✓ • Allow time for the students to write answers to the questions. *(Answers will vary.)*

✓ • Discuss why some people enjoy watching violence. *(They may enjoy the excitement or the demonstration of superiority, power, and control.)* **Does watching violence conflict with Christian values? Explain.** *(Christians do not accept violence as a solution to any problem. Watching violence can conflict with Christian values when such exaggerated behavior desensitizes people to the suffering of others and emphasizes a "might makes right" philosophy.)*

Conversion

When we recognize and regret our sins, we begin the process of **conversion,** or turning back to God. In conversion we seek God's grace and rely on him with trust and hope. We know that he will help us become less self-centered and more attentive to the needs of others.

If we lie about going to a place our parents or guardians don't approve of, we can lose our family's trust and respect. As part of our conversion, we admit that our decision to go was wrong and that we lied to cover it up. Even though we admit our wrongdoing, we still must work to rebuild the trust that was broken.

When we are truly sorry for the wrongs we have done, we become more aware of the choices that led us to sin, and we can decide to change our behavior. Our sorrow, also called **contrition,** helps us grow in our relationships and in our faith. Contrition reminds us to love others as Jesus loves us all.

Media Message

VIDEO GAME VIOLENCE How do the media affect the good and bad choices we make? Do you think the media affect you at all? For example, some people say that violent video games encourage violence. Others say that violent video games can be a safe and healthy way to channel aggression or frustration. Still others say that violent video games become a problem only when the person playing them becomes obsessed with such games.

What do you think? Do violent video games make a person more likely to act violently in everyday life? Explain.

_____
_____
_____
_____
_____

58 **RECONCILIATION**

VOCABULARY ✓

Conversion is the process of turning away from sin and evil and turning toward God, who calls us to conversion.

Contrition is the deep sorrow that we feel when we have sinned. Contrition moves us to resolve to do better and to turn our lives toward God.

EXTENSION ACTIVITY

Role-playing reconciliation Many young people aren't regular in the practice of the Sacrament of Reconciliation and may have forgotten how it is celebrated. On the board or on chart paper, list the essential elements of the Sacrament of Reconciliation: contrition, confession, absolution, and penance. Walk through these elements with the students, alternately role-playing the part of the priest and the penitent. Ask volunteers to assist you as the students become more familiar with the process.

BACKGROUND

Seeking forgiveness The prayer of absolution in the Sacrament of Reconciliation declares the forgiveness we have in Christ. The reference to "Father of mercies" reminds us of God's generosity and willingness to forgive sin. In seeking forgiveness, we receive pardon and peace both through and by the Church.

Student Leader Connection

Consider having the Student Leader do the following:

• **Direct the activity in *Media Message* about video game violence.**

• **Help the group identify examples of conversion.**

• **Help moderate a discussion about how people show contrition.**

RESOURCE Center

Celebrating the Sacrament

We can celebrate the Sacrament of Reconciliation individually or we may be part of a communal, or group, celebration. (In cases of grave necessity, a bishop may allow general confession and general absolution.) During the communal celebration, we may listen to Scripture readings and together reflect on an examination of conscience. In both forms of the sacrament, we confess our sins to a priest. Talking with a priest helps us see more clearly and take responsibility for our attitudes and actions. The priest then advises us about how we might avoid a particular pattern of sin. After we confess our sins, we pray an Act of Contrition, a prayer of sorrow. In the name of Christ and the Church, the priest offers us **absolution.** This prayer is an effective sign of God's forgiveness and of the grace he offers to help us live as Christians.

Although our sins are forgiven, forgiveness alone does not eliminate the pain and problems our sins can cause. So before the priest absolves us, he asks us to complete a **penance** to show we are serious about changing our lives. Usually a penance includes prayers or actions that help make up for the harm our sins have done. If we have stolen, we must return what we took or pay the owner back. If we lied, we must apologize and tell the truth. If we harmed another's reputation, we must take back our hurtful statements, admit our wrong, and work to rebuild trust with that person.

Focus On

Seal of the Sacrament
A priest is never allowed to tell anyone what he is told in confession. This is called the Seal of the Sacrament, and it guarantees that you can be open and honest in your confession, even if you did something illegal.

Opening the Word

7th Sunday of Ordinary Time, Cycle B

When Jesus saw their faith, he said to the paralytic, "Son, your sins are forgiven." Mark 2:5

Read *Mark 2:1–12* as well as *Matthew 18:21–22, Luke 15:11–32,* and *Luke 19:1–12.* What do these passages say about forgiveness?

_____

_____

_____

_____

A Chance to Grow

Reconciliation is our chance to make things right—to return to a life in union with God. Of course, facing up to our sins can be uncomfortable, but we should see beyond the initial discomfort. When we apologize to a friend for something we did, a true friend forgives us. Together we can continue a friendship that brings us happiness and love.

The same is true of our relationship with God. He has promised that if we are truly sorry for our sins, we will be forgiven. In turn, we are rewarded with stronger relationships with our friends and with God.

WORKING WITH THE TEXT AND PICTURES

- Read the text on this page.
- Use *Vocabulary* below to help the students understand the highlighted terms.
- Discuss how we reconcile with others. *(by apologizing, by atoning for sin, by seeking forgiveness)*
- Discuss the meaning of penance. *(Penance is a prayer or an action that shows that we intend to change our lives; penance begins that change.)*
- Discuss how God and the Church are part of our relationships. *(Our relationship with God must come first in our lives; as a result, this relationship to him and to his Church affects how well we maintain all other relationships.)*
- See *Skill Note* below.

WORKING WITH THE ACTIVITY

Opening the Word

- Ask a volunteer to read aloud *Opening the Word.*
- Allow time for the students to read the additional Scripture passages and respond to the question. *(If we are truly sorry, the forgiveness by the "Father of mercies" is effective no matter what we have done.)*
- See *Scripture Background* below.

Focus On

- Ask a volunteer to read aloud *Focus On.*
- Discuss the Seal of the Sacrament. **What does the Seal of the Sacrament accomplish?** *(The Seal allows people to seek forgiveness with absolute trust that confidentiality and privacy will not be violated. The Seal also promotes frankness on the part of the penitent.)*

VOCABULARY

In the Sacrament of Reconciliation, we receive *absolution*—God's forgiveness of sin through the Church. The priest, through the power of Christ given to the Church, and as the representative of the Church, pardons the sins of the penitent. This is an essential element of the sacrament.

In the Sacrament of Reconciliation, we are assigned a *penance,* prayers or actions that help us in Christ make up for the harm our sins have caused. Completing a penance shows our sorrow and helps us resolve to avoid sin. Penance completes our conversion.

SKILL NOTE

We can always make things right by seeking God's forgiveness. His mercy allows us to stay hopeful. For more information about the skill, see pages 62 and 63.

EXTENSION ACTIVITY

The prodigal son   Refer the students again to the story of the prodigal son. (See *Luke 15:11–32.*) Discuss the story, emphasizing the son's need for forgiveness and the father's willingness to forgive. Point out the contrite son's surprise at

the love and joy with which his father greets his return. How are we sometimes like the father, the older son, and the younger son? Consider asking volunteers to create a rap about the story or a contemporary version of the story.

SCRIPTURE BACKGROUND

Mark 2:1–12 explains the role of the Body of Christ in helping us turn to God for forgiveness and healing. In this Scripture passage a paralyzed man's friends help him reach Jesus. When the door to Jesus' home is blocked by crowds, the determined friends open a section of the roof and lower the paralyzed man into Jesus' presence. Moved by the profound demonstration of belief among the friends, Jesus forgives the man's sins and heals him. Similarly, as members of the Body of Christ, we place our relationship with God first in our lives. Our faith strengthens all of our other relationships, and we seek to influence one another only in ways that bring us all closer to God. You may wish to point out that this passage is from the readings for the Seventh Sunday of Ordinary Time, Cycle B. Refer to page 108 of this book for more information about the liturgical year.

WORKING WITH THE TEXT AND PICTURES

✓ • Read the text on this page, and review the pictures on pages 60 and 61.

✓ • Brainstorm with the students about the qualities of a virtuous person. *(Possible answers: honesty, generosity, patience, loyalty, sensitivity, compassion.)* Be sure the students understand that one need not be perfect to be virtuous.

• See *Reflecting on Your Faith* below.

WORKING WITH THE ACTIVITY

Wrap Up

• Have a volunteer read aloud the summary statements.

✓ • Allow time for the students to consider their remaining questions and write them in their books.

• Discuss any remaining questions the students may have. You may wish to have the students write their questions on separate sheets of paper so that you can collect them and respond during the next session.

Growing in
Goodness

Jesus knew that we would need support and guidance to follow him. That is why he sent us the Holy Spirit and why we are made members of Christ's Body, the Church. Through the sacraments we celebrate together as the Church, especially Eucharist and Reconciliation, we are strengthened in our relationship with God. And his grace helps us resist temptations to sin and strengthens us in holiness.

Think of examples of virtuous people you know. What qualities do you admire in them? How do they show these qualities in their everyday lives? How might you imitate some of these qualities?

When you are shopping, the clerk gives you too much change. Instead of keeping the money, you return it. Or perhaps you have done something your parents or guardians asked you not to do. You know you can tell a convincing lie and avoid trouble, but instead of lying you tell the truth and accept the consequences. When you make these right choices, you are living honestly. Each day you have the opportunity to sin or to live virtuously.

Reflect on how you can live a virtuous life. Share your thoughts with your Faith Partner.

FaiTH ParTNerSHiP

WRAP UP

•The Sacrament of Reconciliation is one of the Sacraments of Healing.

•When we sin, we hurt our relationship with God, self, and others.

•God has given us the gift of conscience—the ability to tell right from wrong and to choose what is right.

•We seek forgiveness for our sins in the Sacrament of Reconciliation.

•Through the Sacrament of Reconciliation, we are healed of the pain and separation that sin can cause, our sins are forgiven, and we are brought back into relationship with God and with others.

What questions do you have about this chapter?

_____
_____
_____

60 **RECONCILIATION**

FAITH PARTNERSHIPS

Have the students discuss with their Faith Partners how they can live virtuous lives.

EXTENSION ACTIVITY

Living virtuously Divide the group into two teams. Have one team speak in defense of Dolores, Mike, and Rachel in the following scenarios, and have the other team challenge the characters for lack of virtue. (1) Dolores tries on a dress at the store and when approaching the counter to pay for it discovers a lipstick stain on the collar. She isn't sure whether it's her own lipstick, but she decides to ask for a reduction in price on the dress. (2) Mike really enjoys a CD he borrowed from his brother. He decides to make a copy of it so that one of his friends who doesn't have the money for the CD can enjoy the music, too. (3) Rachel sees a pile of change on the kitchen counter. She remembers that at school today there will be a collection for the missions. Knowing how generous her mother is, Rachel takes the money to school.

REFLECTING ON YOUR FAITH

Consider the qualities you admire in a virtuous person. How can you become more like this person?

Student Leader Connection

Consider having the Student Leader do the following:

• Help moderate the brainstorming activity about the qualities of a virtuous person.

• Read aloud the *Wrap Up* summary statements.

• Help moderate the *Around the Group* discussion.

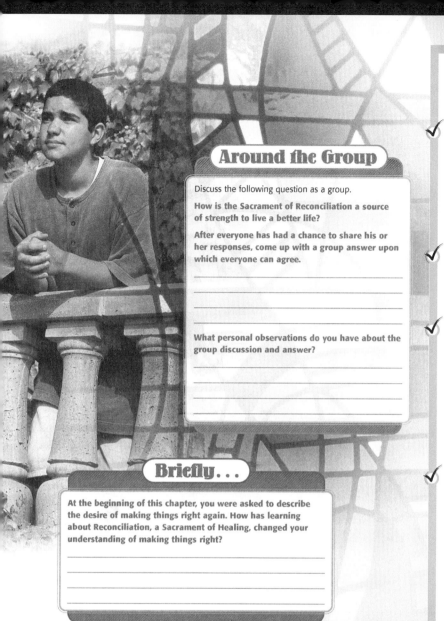

Around the Group

Discuss the following question as a group.

How is the Sacrament of Reconciliation a source of strength to live a better life?

After everyone has had a chance to share his or her responses, come up with a group answer upon which everyone can agree.

_____

_____

_____

_____

What personal observations do you have about the group discussion and answer?

_____

_____

_____

Briefly . . .

At the beginning of this chapter, you were asked to describe the desire of making things right again. How has learning about Reconciliation, a Sacrament of Healing, changed your understanding of making things right?

_____

_____

_____

_____

REFLECT 61

WORKING WITH THE ACTIVITIES

Around the Group

- Present the question to the group, and allow time for discussion. You may need to moderate to keep the students focused on the question.

- Encourage the group members to listen to the opinions and perspectives of others.

- Have the students discuss the effects of sin on their relationships, especially the relationship with God and the Church.

- If the group has agreed on an answer, direct the students to write it in their books. If they could not agree, direct them to list in their books the issues that were left unresolved and explain why.

- Encourage the students to note in their books their personal observations about the discussion and any final thoughts they have.

- See *Reflecting on Your Faith* below.

Briefly . . .

- Encourage the students to consider how their opinions may have changed since they responded to *What Do You Think?* on page 55.

- Allow time for the students to write their responses in their books.

- See *Reflecting on Your Faith* below.

REFLECTING ON YOUR FAITH

Around the Group: How can you best explain to the students the ways in which the Sacrament of Reconciliation is a source of strength for them? How is the Sacrament of Reconciliation a source of strength for you? You may wish to share this with the students.

Briefly: How has this lesson and working with the students deepened your understanding of the importance the Sacrament of Reconciliation has in making things right in your life?

EXTENSION ACTIVITY

Facing peer pressure Discuss peer pressure and the pain that can result from it. Invite the students to consider the words and actions people their age might use to identify with a group and shut out nonmembers. Encourage the students to decide whether some of the words and actions might hurt someone accidentally or become sinful. Ask the students for examples of how they can be loyal to their friends while practicing reconciliation in their lives. You may also wish to have the students provide examples of instances when peer pressure has been a positive influence in their lives. To start the discussion, ask the students to reflect on good behavior they have learned from peers.

WORKING WITH THE SKILL

- ✓ • Remind the students that the skill for Chapters 5 and 6 is Staying Hopeful. Discuss with the students how they have tried to use the skill since the end of Chapter 5.

- ✓ • Discuss how the Sacrament of Reconciliation helps us practice the skill of Staying Hopeful. *(Reconciliation allows us, in Christ, to make things right with God and with others so that we can begin anew to live as disciples of Jesus.)*

- • Ask a volunteer to read aloud *Expressions of Faith.*

- • Invite a volunteer to read *Scripture* aloud. **Why did Jesus tell the woman that her faith had saved her?** *(The woman's faith gave her the courage and hope to trust that her sins would be forgiven.)*

- ✓ • See *Scripture Background* below.

- ✓ • Review each bulleted point in *Skill Steps.* **Which of these points might be especially meaningful to someone? Why?** *(Answers will vary but should show a grasp of the connection between hope and faith.)*

- • Point out the photograph and discuss hope. **How does this image express hope?** *(The picture shows happiness, encouragement, and being part of a group.)*

- • Ask a volunteer to read *Skill Builder* aloud.

- ✓ • Allow the students time to complete the activity. Let volunteers share their responses with the group. **How might this three-step process work in a person's life?** *(Some people may find themselves more in control of a problem than they thought; identifying a problem makes it seem less overwhelming; solutions and support may be easier to obtain.)*

Staying Hopeful

Expressions of Faith—

The Sacrament of Reconciliation celebrates forgiveness—God forgives our sins and heals us, reconciling us with himself, the Church, ourselves, and others. Knowing that God is willing to forgive us when we recognize what we have done wrong and are contrite restores our hope and strengthens us to live virtuously.

Scripture

Then he said to her, "Your sins are forgiven." But those who were at the table with him began to say among themselves, "Who is this who even forgives sins?" And he said to the woman, "Your faith has saved you; go in peace."
Luke 7:48–50   11th Sunday of Ordinary Time, Cycle

Skill Steps—

Remember the steps for staying hopeful when you're feeling down. *Name It* by identifying what you are thinking and feeling. *Tame It* by finding a way to keep the emotion under control. *Claim It* by using the emotion in the most productive way.

Here are some key points to remember:

- ● We are a hopeful people because Christ has promised us eternal life.
- ● We can stay hopeful by recognizing that our emotions need not overwhelm us.
- ● Through the sacraments God acts in our everyday lives, giving us the strength and insight we need to work out our problems.

Skill Builder—

Practice staying hopeful by using the *Name It, Tame It, Claim It* strategy. For each of the following situations, imagine what you might feel and then use the strategy for staying hopeful.

Remember to consider questions such as the following to *Tame It. Is the situation permanent? Do you have the power to change it? Is this the way things usually happen in your life?* Then suggest ways you might be able to handle the situation to *Claim It:*

Name It: I am failing math because I don't understand it.
Tame It: _____
Claim It: _____
Name It: My family is always criticizing me.
Tame It: _____
Claim It: _____

Share your responses and thoughts with your Faith P

FAITH PARTNERSHIP

SCRIPTURE BACKGROUND ✓

In *Luke 7:36–50* a woman comes to Jesus seeking forgiveness. To show her remorse for her sins and her love for Jesus, she humbly washes, dries, and anoints his feet. Jesus rewards the woman's faith and contrition by generously and lovingly forgiving her sins. When some Pharisees criticize Jesus for this response, he reminds them that love and forgiveness are linked. Those who approach God in love, humility, and faith are never refused his love, mercy, and forgiveness. You may wish to point out that this passage is from the readings for the Eleventh Sunday of Ordinary Time, Cycle C. Refer to page 108 of this book for more information about the liturgical year.

FAITH PARTNERSHIPS

Have the Faith Partners discuss their responses to the *Skill Builder* activity. Caution them to be sure their examples and suggestions for problem solving are realistic.

RESOURCE Center

Student Leader Connection

Consider having the Student Leader do the following:

- **Review with the group what they have learned about staying hopeful.**
- **Read *Scripture* aloud.**
- **Explain the *Skill Builder* activity.**
- **Organize a small group to plan a prayer service.**

Special Note: Remember to meet briefly with the Student Leader for Chapter 7. You may wish to provide him or her with the Student Leader Prep Page found on page R7.

Putting It into Practice-

Use the *Name It, Tame It, Claim It* strategy in your own life by thinking of a personal problem you are dealing with and working through the process by answering the questions below. Choose a situation that does not involve temptation or sin and is fairly typical of people your age.

○ Name It

The problem is _____

When I think about the problem, I hear myself thinking _____

_____

When I think about the problem, I feel _____

_____

○ Tame It

Is this problem permanent? _____

Do I have the power to change this problem? _____

Has this ever happened to me before? Does it happen to me frequently?

_____

○ Claim It

How can I use this experience in a productive way? _____

_____

What have I learned from this? _____

_____

As soon as you can identify the kinds of feelings that affect how you feel, you can work to change your behavior.

What aspects of staying hopeful are you good at?

_____

What things do you still need to work on?

_____

Closing Prayer-

Lord, we are sorry for the wrong things we choose to do and the good things we choose not to do. When we sin, we turn away from you, the one who loves us most. Forgive us and help us open our hearts to your grace. Guide us in leading good lives and fill our hearts with your mercy. Heal us of all pain and sadness and give us hope. Amen.

WORKING WITH THE SKILL

- Have a volunteer read aloud *Putting It into Practice,* and invite the students to complete the activity.
- See *Reflecting on Your Faith* below.
- Ask a few volunteers to share what they have learned about how to stay hopeful.

CLOSING PRAYER

- Gather together to pray the closing prayer. You may wish to use the following music from the *Give Your Gifts* series: "You Are Mine" *(The Songs),* "Psalm 141: Let My Prayer Rise Up" *(The Basics),* or "You Are My Shepherd" *(More Songs)* (GIA Publications, Inc.; distributed by Harcourt Religion Publishers).
- If time permits, direct the students to create their own closing reflections or prayers. You may wish to ask a few volunteers to read aloud what they have created or to plan a prayer service. As an alternative for prayer, you may wish to use "Sacraments: Prayer Service C" from *Living Our Faith Prayer Services* by Robert Piercy and Linda Baltikas (GIA Publications, Inc.; distributed by Harcourt Religion Publishers).

REFLECTING ON YOUR FAITH

Consider your own responses to the *Putting It into Practice* activity. In what area might you need to improve: naming a problem, taming it, or claiming it?

TEACHING TIP

Research follow-up You may wish to take time to review any research the students have been asked to complete. If the students need additional time to complete their research, set aside a few minutes at the beginning of the next session to allow them to share the information they have gathered.

MULTIPLE LEARNING STYLES

Closing prayer You may wish to have the students create their closing prayers in the style of a formal prayer or reflection; a poem or song; or a prayer service with readings, psalm response, and music. Remind the students that the tone of their responses can be different from that of the example but should remain respectful.

ASSESSMENT

The Assessment Page for Chapter 6 can be found on page R14.

LINK TO FAMILY

The corresponding Family Resource pages for this skill are 82–85.

Anointing
of the Sick

KEY CONTENT SUMMARY

Anointing of the Sick is a Sacrament of Healing. Jesus' life and teachings illustrate the important role that healing plays in our faith. The Sacrament of the Anointing of the Sick strengthens our bodies and our spirits.

PLANNING THE CHAPTER

OPEN	PACING	CONTENT	OBJECTIVES	MATERIALS
	Suggested Time: **Parish 10 min.** **School 25 min.** Your Time: _____ min.	pp. 64–65	• Recognize that Anointing of the Sick is a Sacrament of Healing.	• candle, matches (optional) • art supplies (optional) • symbol representing chapter theme (optional)

SEARCH				
	Suggested Time: **Parish 25 min.** **School 70 min.** Your Time: _____ min.	pp. 66–69	• Identify and examine the importance of healing in Christ's life and teaching. • Explore the elements and effects of the Sacrament of the Anointing of the Sick.	• Bibles

REFLECT				
	Suggested Time: **Parish 10 min.** **School 30 min.** Your Time: _____ min.	pp. 70–71	• Reflect on how anointing can heal us both physically and spiritually.	• art supplies (optional)

LIVE				
	Suggested Time: **Parish 15 min.** **School 35 min.** Your Time: _____ min.	pp. 72–73	• Apply the knowledge of how we honor the body.	• magazines (optional) • Student Leader Prep Page for Chapter 8 (p. R7) (optional) • music for prayer (optional) • copies of Assessment Page for Chapter 7 (p. R15) (optional)

CATECHISM IN CONTEXT

See Catechism of the Catholic Church, #1513.

Through the Sacrament of the Anointing of the Sick, Jesus shows his compassion and mercy for those who are gravely ill, facing major surgery, or passing from this world to the next. In this sacrament Jesus reveals himself as the spiritual physician. Even in the absence of physical healing, those who celebrate this sacrament can receive the strength and courage to face and cope with infirmity, pain, and the prospect of death.

In the ritual of the Sacrament of the Anointing of the Sick, sins are forgiven and faith and hope are renewed. Through anointing and prayer the person is made ready for the final transition from earthly life to life everlasting.

ONE-MINUTE RETREAT

READ

"In every child who is born and in every person who lives and dies, we see the image of God's glory."
—Pope John Paul II

REFLECT

How can I become more conscious of God's image in others?

PRAY

Divine Healer, I trust in the power of your love. Strengthen me in body and spirit so that my life may honor you. Help me see the glory of your image in everyone I meet on my journey to you.

LIBRARY LINKS

BOOKS
FOR ADOLESCENTS

"Facing the Death of Friends," by Karen Callinan (*Youth Update;* St. Anthony Messenger Press).

Helps young people cope with death through an understanding of grief and loss. Includes ways to express sympathy and suggestions of how to be helpful in difficult times.

"For Our Healing: The Sacrament of the Anointing of the Sick," by Woodeene Koenig-Bricker (*Youth Update;* St. Anthony Messenger Press).

Explores the theology and spirituality of the sacrament and its renewal after Vatican II and traces the sacrament back to Jesus' healing ministry.

"Helping a Friend Face Serious Illness," by Lynn Marie-Ittner Klammer (*Youth Update;* St. Anthony Messenger Press).

Helps engender empathy for peers and encourages Christian compassion for all those who are ill.

FOR ADULTS

"Jesus the Physician: What the Gospels Say About Healing," by Donald Senior CP (*Catholic Update;* St. Anthony Messenger Press).

Discusses Jesus' healing power in his own time and the healing power of faith today as signs of compassion and solidarity with suffering people.

Praying with the Sick: Prayers, Services, Rituals, by Sandra DeGidio OSM (Twenty-Third Publications, 1998).

A resource handbook for pastoral ministers and others who visit and pray with those who are ill.

Who Cares? Simple Ways You Can Reach Out, by Marcy Heidish (Ave Maria Press, 1997).

Practical ways to implement the art of caring.

MULTIMEDIA

Making Sense of Suffering (audio) (St. Anthony Messenger Press).

Pastoral minister Carol Riley CDP talks about spiritual growth for those who suffer and for their caregivers.

No One Cries the Wrong Way: Helping Children Cope with Grief, Suffering, and Death (video, booklet) (produced by Salt River Production Group; Harcourt Religion Publishers).

Helps children understand and share in the goodness of God and the mystery of human suffering.

FEATURE PREPARATION

STUDENT LEADER CONNECTION

The Student Leader Prep Page for this chapter is located on page R7. You may wish to provide this information to the Student Leader as an introduction and resource for the chapter.

FAITH PARTNERSHIPS

Chapter 7 begins a new Faith Partnership. Several opportunities for Faith Partner discussions have been marked throughout the chapter. You may wish to consider other opportunities as you prepare the lesson.

SKILL NOTES

The skill for this chapter is Honoring the Body. As you teach the skill lesson on pages 72 and 73, you may wish to refer to the Skill Notes marked throughout the chapter. These notes will help you identify terms and ideas related to the skill.

A check mark indicates the chapter's essential questions, statements, activities, and features. If time is limited, such as in a parish group setting, this icon will help you direct the students through the lesson.

KEY POINTS FROM CHAPTER 6

You may wish to review these points with the students before you begin the new chapter:

- Reconciliation is a Sacrament of Healing.
- Contrition, confession, and penance are integral parts of the sacrament.
- God's mercy and forgiveness strengthen us to live virtuous lives.
- Staying Hopeful is a Skill for Christian Living.

 GATHERING

Begin by asking the students to give only the first name of someone who is ill, elderly, or dying.

✓ **PRAYER**

Invite the students to sit quietly for a moment and recall the ill, elderly, or dying people mentioned in *Gathering*. Then pray the opening prayer aloud together. If fire regulations permit, light a candle to signify this time of prayer.

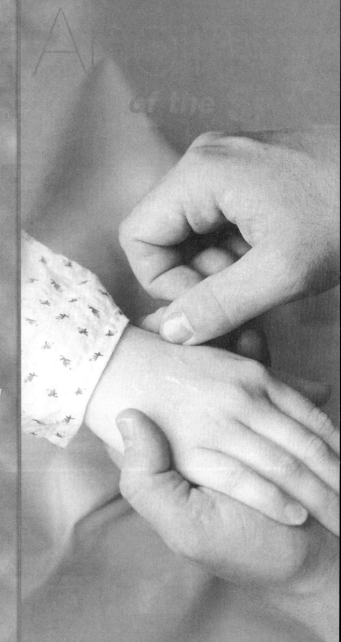

Holy Spirit, remember our friends and family members who are ill. Bring them strength and patience. Ease their pain and help them know that they are not alone.

64

PRAYER ENVIRONMENT

If you have created a prayer space for the room, you may wish to display a picture of Mother Teresa at work, some literature from a local hospice, or photographs of someone helping a person who is elderly or ill.

FAITH PARTNER INTRODUCTION

If you haven't done so already, remind the students that it is time for them to create new Faith Partnerships. After you have assigned new Faith Partners, you may wish to give the students a few moments to complete together a Faith Partner introduction. Ask each Faith Partner to describe for the other a time when he or she was ill with a typical childhood ailment such as an ear infection, a bad cold, or the flu. What people or items did each of the partners find most comforting during the illness? Why?

RESOURCE Center

Student Leader Connection

Consider having the Student Leader do the following:

- Invite the students to say aloud the names of those who are ill before the group prays the opening prayer.
- Read aloud selected text.
- Bring in an item for the prayer space.

What Do You Think?

Explore some of your attitudes and experiences of illness and death by checking *Yes* or *No* in response to the following statements.

Yes	No	
○	○	I have had to go to the hospital when I was hurt or ill.
○	○	Eventually medical science will cure all illnesses.
○	○	I have experienced the death of someone close to me.
○	○	Getting well is a matter of fixing the body.
○	○	I don't like being around people who are ill.
○	○	I have attended a wake or a funeral.
○	○	People need to be healed spiritually as well as physically.
○	○	I have visited someone in a hospital or other care center.
○	○	I think I would enjoy caring for those who are ill or frail.

Describe your experience of facing either your own illness or that of someone else.

_____

_____

_____

Health and Healing

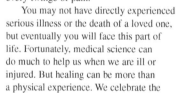

(S) When we are healthy, we may not think about our bodies much at all. But when we become ill, we may suddenly become aware of every movement and every twinge of pain.

You may not have directly experienced serious illness or the death of a loved one, but eventually you will face this part of life. Fortunately, medical science can do much to help us when we are ill or injured. But healing can be more than a physical experience. We celebrate the Sacrament of the Anointing of the Sick, a Sacrament of Healing, to help heal those with serious illnesses or those who are facing death because of illness, injury, or old age.

WORKING WITH THE ACTIVITY

What Do You Think?

✓ • Allow time for the students to record their thoughts in the space provided.

• See *Reflecting on Your Faith* below.

✓ • *What Do You Think?* is intended as a personal pre-assessment. The students should not be asked to share their responses.

WORKING WITH THE TEXT AND PICTURES

✓ • Read the text on this page, and review the pictures on pages 64 and 65.

• Invite the students to share their ideas about how to stay healthy. ***Will medical science be able to cure all illnesses someday?*** *(Answers will vary.)*

• Discuss funerals and the students' experiences with the deaths of people they have known. ***Describe what it is like to attend a funeral or a wake.*** *(Answers will vary.)*

✓ • Point out the photograph of the get-well card, and discuss the concept of healing. Suggest that how we think about illness can affect our experience of it. ***What might help us feel better when we are ill?*** *(Possible answer: having someone visit, listen to us talk about how we feel, send a card, or bring a small gift.)*

• Draw attention to the photograph on page 64. ***Why might anointing play a role in healing?*** *(When we are anointed with oil, the Spirit strengthens us.)*

✓ • See *Skill Note* below.

EXTENSION ACTIVITY

Exploring health and healing Ask a volunteer to lie down on a plain cloth sheet or several attached sheets of chart paper. Outline his or her body with a felt marker. Then invite the students to use markers on the drawing to write about or draw symbols of their attitudes, beliefs, and expectations about health and healing. The students may choose to write a slogan or a piece of advice, such as "Turn down the sound," or they may design a symbol that sends a message, such as drawing an *X* on top of a package of cigarettes.

(S) SKILL NOTE ✓

Note that because we live our lives as physical beings, we need to learn the skill of Honoring the Body. See pages 72 and 73 for further information about this skill.

TEACHING TIP

Talking about death   Center the discussion on compassion for the bereaved and respect for the dead. Many students have never attended a funeral or a wake (viewing). Anticipate that they may wonder what to say to the bereaved family. Remind them that their remarks may be very simple: "[Family member's name], I'm very sorry about [deceased's name]. I will pray for [him or her] and for you." If circumstances permit, and even if the student is a member of the bereaved family, he or she might offer to help others by doing errands or chores around the house. Point out to the students that a Rosary may be prayed during the wake or that a prayer service may be held. This service may include hymns, Scripture passages, and an opportunity for people to share stories about the person who has died.

WORKING WITH THE TEXT AND PICTURES

✓ • Read the text and review the picture on this page.

✓ • Discuss the ways in which Jesus healed. *(He healed both body and spirit. He strengthened people by forgiving their sins, comforting them, and giving them hope and trust in God.)*

• Discuss the fine art shown. **How does the art show Jesus' compassion?** *(Answers will vary.)*

• Jesus did not promise physical healing to people of faith. **Why did Jesus ask people about their faith?** *(to show that we must trust in God, who does not abandon us when we are at our weakest)*

✓ • Discuss the healing of the centurion's servant. Emphasize that Jesus showed compassion for someone who was not just an outsider but a sworn enemy: the centurion was part of the Roman occupying forces in Palestine. **What are other interesting elements of the centurion's story?** *(Possible responses: The centurion was not a Jew; Jesus never met or touched the servant; Jesus was concerned not only for the ill person but also for the caregiver.)*

WORKING WITH THE ACTIVITY

Opening the Word

• Ask a volunteer to read aloud *Opening the Word.*

✓ • Allow the students sufficient time to read the additional Scripture passages and respond to the question. *(Possible responses include faith, forgiveness of sins, and humility.)*

✓ • See *Scripture Background* below.

Jesus the **Healer**

Have you ever suffered some physical injury or been seriously ill? If so, you may have felt weak or helpless. You may have been angry because you couldn't do the things you normally enjoy. Perhaps you thought that the situation wasn't fair and that you shouldn't have had to go through it. These are all normal responses to suffering, even if the suffering isn't life threatening. The Church celebrates the Sacrament of the Anointing of the Sick to help us when we suffer or face the possibility of death.

The pain and hurt we experience from sin and its effects can be healed through celebrating the Sacrament of Reconciliation. But when we experience pain and hurt from illness, we also need God's mercy, comfort, and healing. Jesus knew that illness or dying affects the entire person, body and spirit. So when Jesus healed, he healed both body and spirit. He strengthened those who were ill by forgiving their sins as well as by making them physically healthy. He comforted them and gave them hope and trust in God.

Often Jesus asked those he was going to cure to have faith. He did not just mean that faith would cure illness but that we must trust in God no matter what happens. Jesus wants us to remember that God does not abandon us when we are at our weakest. Instead, he is the one we can turn to for support. Illness, like all other aspects of life, can become a means of conversion and can help lead us to God.

4th Sunday of Lent, Cycle A

Then he went and washed and came back able to see. John 9:7

Read *John 9:1–7* as well as *Matthew 8:5–13, Luke 5:12–13,* and *James 5:14–15.* What qualities or attitudes are connected with healing in these Scripture passages?

66 ANOINTING OF THE SICK

SCRIPTURE BACKGROUND ✓

In *John 9:1–7* Jesus' disciples ask him why a local man was born blind. In those days it was thought that blindness was a punishment for either the man's sin or his parents' sin. Jesus clearly states that no one's sin caused the man's blindness. (God does not use physical impairment or illness to punish us when we sin.) The man's blindness is an opportunity for Jesus to reveal himself to us. We are "blind" until we are enlightened by faith. Jesus, the "Light of the World," dispels the darkness so that we can recognize God in all his works. You may wish to point out that this passage is part of the readings for the Fourth Sunday of Lent, Cycle A. Refer to page 108 of this book for more information about the liturgical year.

MULTIPLE LEARNING STYLES

Continuing Jesus' mission as healer Have the students write a skit or dialogue about what might happen if Jesus were to visit a modern-day hospital or doctor's office. Ask them to consider whom Jesus might encounter and what he might say or do. You may wish to have the students work in groups to create the dialogues or skits.

Student Leader Connection

Consider having the Student Leader do the following:

• Read aloud *Opening the Word.*

• Find a comforting poem or psalm and share it with the group.

• Research the hospice movement or a particular hospice, and report the findings to the group.

Hospice Care

The word *hospice* comes from the Latin word *hospitium* meaning "guest house." During the 1960s, the term took on new meaning as British doctors began to specialize in pain-management care specifically for dying patients. The first hospice program in the United States was established in New Haven, Connecticut, in 1974. Today there are more than three thousand hospice programs in the United States, including Puerto Rico and Guam. Most hospice programs include in-home or institutional care and family grief counseling.

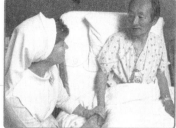

Healing
Action

Scripture tells us that sick people were brought to Jesus and that he laid his healing hands on them. (See *Mark 6:5.*) One story centers on a Roman centurion who sought help from Jesus for his paralyzed servant. (See *Matthew 8:5–13.*) Though the soldier and Jesus were socially and culturally very different, Jesus saw past their differences and healed the centurion's servant. Instead of ignoring the soldier because of his political and social beliefs, Jesus used the occasion to show his generosity and compassion—not just for those who suffer, but for those who care for the suffering.

We are called to have the same compassion when we celebrate the Sacrament of the Anointing of the Sick. The sacrament can be celebrated in many different ways. It can be celebrated for an individual or with a group of people who are ill. We can celebrate it in church, at home, or at a hospital. We can celebrate the sacrament in any of three ways: as part of Mass, together with the Sacraments of Reconciliation and Eucharist, or by itself. And because we sometimes face serious illness more than once, the Sacrament of the Anointing of the Sick can be celebrated as

often as it is needed. In any situation, though, the rite includes the Liturgy of the Word and the *Liturgy of Anointing,* during which the anointing takes place.

As part of the Liturgy of Anointing, those gathered join in a litany for those who are sick. Following this litany, there is a *laying on of hands.* Just as Jesus laid hands on the suffering, so the priest lays his hands on one who is ill. Through this action, the Holy Spirit gives strength. Next, the priest prays over the oil and anoints at least the forehead and hands of the person who is sick. Finally, everyone prays a concluding prayer, usually followed by the Lord's Prayer.

In the Sacrament of the Anointing of the Sick, we pray for physical and spiritual healing. God gives strength, peace, and courage—gifts that offer comfort. Through this sacrament, those who suffer are united more closely with Christ and his suffering. For some, suffering may take on new meaning and help them be a part of Jesus' saving work in the world through his Church. They are witnesses for others through their faithfulness. Anointing of the Sick also joins those who are ill more closely with the Church. They are supported by the prayers of the whole Church and can offer their suffering for the good of the Body of Christ.

WORKING WITH THE TEXT AND PICTURES

- Read the text and review the picture on this page.
- Discuss the Sacrament of the Anointing of the Sick. Note that it may be celebrated as often as needed. ***How may Anointing of the Sick be celebrated?*** *(in a group or individually; in church, at home, or at a hospital or care center; as part of a Mass; with Reconciliation and Eucharist or by itself)*
- Refer to the photograph showing a medical professional holding a patient's hand. ***How does this act reflect Jesus' mission of healing?*** *(It shows compassion and concern beyond administering medications and treatments. Taking time to sit and communicate with a patient and establishing simple physical contact promote a sense of warmth, support, and security that Jesus would have shown.)*
- Explain this sacrament's effect on the lives of those who are suffering. ***Which gifts of the Spirit comfort those who are ill or dying?*** *(Possible answers: strength, peace, courage.)*
- Explain how suffering can be purposeful. ***How can suffering deepen faith?*** *(Suffering has new meaning when it becomes for us a part of Jesus' saving work: we can be witnesses for others by our faith.)*

WORKING WITH THE ACTIVITY
Our Global Community
- Ask a volunteer to read aloud *Our Global Community.*
- Hospice care continues Jesus' mission. ***Why is hospice care a good choice in many situations?*** *(Answers will vary.)*

LINK TO LITURGY

The celebration of the Sacrament of the Anointing of the Sick may take place during Mass. Appropriate music and the priest's white vestments signal the faith and hope associated with the sacrament. The Liturgy of Anointing takes place between the Liturgy of the Word and the Liturgy of the Eucharist. Several of the prayers, including the Eucharistic Prayer, differ from those usually said at Mass. To keep distinct the seasons of the liturgical calendar and to avoid overriding major feasts, the Mass for Anointing of the Sick is permitted only at certain times of the liturgical year. For example, it may not be celebrated during the Sundays of Advent and Lent or during the Easter Triduum.

BACKGROUND

Catholic health care The Catholic Health Association of the United States, founded in 1915, includes more than 2,000 hospitals, nursing centers, assisted living centers, rehabilitation centers, and hospices. This organization addresses the needs of people who are poor and those who cannot care for themselves. The Catholic Health Association works to influence

legislatures, researchers, and the public on health care issues. For more information on the Catholic Health Association of the United States, visit the Web site at *www.chausa.org.*

LINK TO SCRIPTURE

Luke 7:18–23 is a Scripture passage that may be used in the celebration of the Sacrament of the Anointing of the Sick. This passage shows that Jesus' role as physician and healer is part of his role as Messiah. Jesus reveals God's power in our lives by healing. Have the students read this passage and then discuss how the disciples of John the Baptizer recognized that Jesus acted in God's name.

TEACHING TIP

Preparing for a speaker You may wish to ask a representative from the Catholic Health Association or from Hospice in your area to come and speak to the students about the work of these organizations. Help the students prepare in advance a list of questions they would like these professionals to answer.

WORKING WITH THE TEXT AND PICTURES

✓ • Read *Facing Death* on pages 68 and 69, and review the pictures on these pages.

✓ • Use *Vocabulary* below to help the students understand the highlighted terms.

✓ • Discuss how Catholics are helped in facing death. ***Why do we have last rites?*** *(Possible response: Through last rites Christ offers spiritual healing to a dying person.)*

✓ • Discuss the Catholic celebration surrounding a person's death. ***How do we celebrate the life of one who has died?*** *(We have a wake or a viewing, a prayerful gathering of friends and family. We also celebrate a funeral, the rites and ceremonies associated with saying good-bye to one who has died. Though our loss saddens us, we pray that the person is with God eternally.)*

WORKING WITH THE ACTIVITY

Our Christian Journey

• Ask a volunteer to read aloud *Our Christian Journey.*

✓ • Discuss the role that the Sacrament of the Anointing of the Sick once had as a sacrament of the dying. ***Why did people once view this sacrament as a ritual only for those who were dying?*** *(Illness more often led to death than to recovery. The sacrament was all that could be done in many cases.)*

• See *Background* below.

Our Christian Journey

A Sacrament for Strength Before the Second Vatican Council (1962–1965), the Sacrament of the Anointing of the Sick was called ***Extreme Unction,*** which means "last anointing." The sacrament was referred to in this way because it was viewed as a ritual for the dying. It came to be associated with the Sacrament of Reconciliation received when dying. Moreover, in the Middle Ages, when the term ***Extreme Unction*** originated, most people did not live as long as they do today—many did not reach the age of forty-five. Medical treatment was not good. People became ill and died from diseases that are easily prevented or cured today. People expected sickness to lead to death rather than to healing and recovery. For that reason, they wanted to do everything they could to help the person who was ill prepare for death. However, since the Second Vatican Council, the sacrament has come to be understood as more than a preparation for death. It is also about healing and seeking strength from the Holy Spirit for those whose health is made fragile by serious illness or old age.

For further information: Talk with your family and your pastor about their personal experiences with the Sacrament of the Anointing of the Sick. You may also wish to speak with a librarian to find resources that can help you trace the practice of Extreme Unction through history.

Facing **Death**

Although the Sacrament of the Anointing of the Sick may be celebrated by those who are not near death, we sometimes celebrate the sacrament as part of what is called **last rites.** These rites include Reconciliation, Anointing of the Sick, and Eucharist and are meant to prepare a person as he or she ends the earthly life and begins the eternal one. In fact, the Eucharist given to a dying person is called **viaticum,** which means "bread for the journey." These sacraments are the means by which Christ offers spiritual healing to a dying person. Those who celebrate these sacraments often experience great peace as they approach death.

Catholics also have prayers and rites for those who are dying or who have died. Together with the Church community, we express our hope that the dead are now with God eternally. We are sad and we mourn, but our grief is lessened by our faith in Christ, who saved us from everlasting death.

VOCABULARY ✓

The *last rites* are the celebration of Reconciliation, Anointing of the Sick, and Eucharist by a person who is dying. These sacraments help prepare the person to begin eternal life in Christ.

Eucharist received as part of the last rites is called *viaticum,* a Latin word meaning "bread for the journey." Viaticum strengthens one's relationship with Christ during the dying process.

A *funeral* is a series of ceremonies that precede and accompany the burial or cremation of someone who has died. For Catholics these rites include the vigil, the funeral liturgy, and the rite of committal.

BACKGROUND

Catholic teachings on life after death As Catholics we have faith that we will spend eternity with God and with all those who have died in faith. We believe that each spirit receives a particular judgment at death and that a final or general judgment will occur at the end of time. We also believe in heaven, hell, and purgatory.

Student Leader Connection

Consider having the Student Leader do the following:

• Read aloud *Our Christian Journey.*

• Interview a priest and a funeral director and report on the process of planning a Catholic funeral.

• Help moderate the discussion of how Catholics celebrate the life of someone who has died.

As part of our celebration of the life of a person who has died, we join together for a wake, or a prayerful gathering of friends and family, and a **funeral.** A funeral includes the rites and ceremonies associated with saying good-bye to the person who has died. For Catholics, a funeral Mass and prayers at the grave site are said.

The Healing **Church**

Because we belong to the Body of Christ, the Church, we are called to be healers. Through social services, care centers, hospitals, clinics, and other organizations, Catholics offer medical and spiritual support to those who are sick or dying throughout the world. These services are all part of the Church's mission.

(S) You, too, can help in healing others. You can visit those who are suffering and pray with and for them. You can be useful in ways that may seem insignificant but that could be critically important to the person who needs help, such as getting groceries or medicine, cleaning the house, writing letters, and especially just talking with the person.

Through the Sacrament of the Anointing of the Sick, the Spirit strengthens those who suffer spiritually and physically. And through our experience of the sacrament and of those who are suffering, we can learn how to draw strength in times of pain and loss.

Share with your Faith Partner your experiences of healing. FAITH PARTNERSHIP

Catholics Believe

The Anointing of the Sick is not only for those who are dying but for those who are suffering from serious illness or old age.
See Catechism, #1514.

How can we be of assistance to those who are sick, elderly, or dying?
_____
_____
_____

WORKING WITH THE TEXT AND PICTURES

✓ • Read *The Healing Church* on this page.

• Catholics offer medical and spiritual support to those who are ill or dying. ***What are some ways that Catholics participate in Jesus' mission of healing?*** *(Possible answer: through social services, nursing centers, hospitals, clinics, hospices, and other organizations.)*

✓ • Discuss the needs of caregivers. ***How do we support caregivers?*** *(Guide the students to name specific, executable suggestions.)*

✓ • Discuss how the sacrament strengthens those who are suffering spiritually and physically. ***What do we learn from the Sacrament of the Anointing of the Sick?*** *(We gain a better understanding of how we can gain and offer strength in difficult times. We recognize that we are called to offer compassion and support to others.)*

✓ • See *Skill Note* below.

WORKING WITH THE ACTIVITY
Catholics Believe

• Have a volunteer read aloud *Catholics Believe.*

✓ • Allow the students sufficient time to reflect on the question and respond to it. *(We can pray, visit, and run errands; we can listen to the person talk; we can hug him or her; we can bring flowers, cards, or small gifts.)*

• See *Reflecting on Your Faith* below.

• Encourage the students to share with the group their thoughts about the paraphrased Catechism statement and their responses to the question that follows.

REFLECTING ON YOUR FAITH
Consider the people in your life who are frail, lonely, or ill. How can you help them?

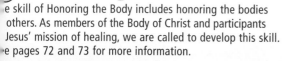

(S) SKILL NOTE ✓
...e skill of Honoring the Body includes honoring the bodies ...others. As members of the Body of Christ and participants ...Jesus' mission of healing, we are called to develop this skill. ...e pages 72 and 73 for more information.

...AITH PARTNERSHIPS
...ggest that the Faith Partners make a list of what they learn ...m each other about healing.

EXTENSION ACTIVITY
Visiting the sick   Help the students prepare for a visit to a hospital. You may wish to invite a nurse or other health care professional to talk with the students about what they might see and how they might feel during such a visit. Ask the students for their own ideas about how to make such a visit pleasant.

BACKGROUND
Understanding funeral symbols   You may wish to provide additional information in conjunction with the Student Leader's report on the process of planning a funeral. Tell the students that the pall, a cloth placed over the coffin, is a reminder of the baptismal garment and also signifies that all are equal in the eyes of God. The water reminds us of the saving water of Baptism. Sprinkling holy water at the rite of final commendation may also signify farewell. The Easter candle reminds us of Christ's undying presence among us, of his victory over sin and death, and of our share in that victory by our initiation in the faith.

WORKING WITH THE TEXT AND PICTURES

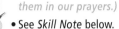 • Read the text on this page, and review the pictures on pages 70 and 71.

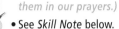 • Discuss the healing power that Anointing of the Sick can have in our lives. *(In this sacrament we receive God's gifts of strength, peace, and courage to face illness and suffering with bravery and patience.)*

• Invite the students to respond to this question: **How can being present at the celebration of this sacrament with those who are ill or facing death help us?** *(Possible response: We can reflect on the meaning of our lives, take better care of ourselves, and have a deeper appreciation of our bodies, which are gifts from God. We might be more compassionate to those who are suffering and include them in our prayers.)*

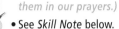 • See *Skill Note* below.

WORKING WITH THE ACTIVITY

Wrap Up

• Have a volunteer read aloud the summary statements.

 • Allow time for the students to consider their remaining questions and write them in their books.

• Discuss any remaining questions the students may have. You may wish to have the students write their questions on separate sheets of paper so that you can collect them and respond during the next session.

Healing and Hope

When we face serious illness or physical suffering, we celebrate the Sacrament of the Anointing of the Sick and experience God's healing grace in our lives. We receive the gifts of strength, peace, and courage to face illness and suffering bravely and patiently. We are reminded of God's presence in our lives and know that we have the prayerful support of the Body of Christ, the Church.

Those who are ill may not be physically healed through the Sacrament of the Anointing of the Sick, although this is possible. But both the person who is ill and those with the person should recognize that God is revealed to us when we are ill as well as when we are healthy. God never abandons or forgets us. He always offers us aid, comfort, and strength.

Celebrating this sacrament helps us reflect on the meaning of our lives. It invites us to have faith when we are struggling physically and are at our weakest point. It brings us to a deeper appreciation of our bodies, which are gifts from God.

Reflect on how anointing can heal us both physically and spiritually. Share your thoughts with your Faith Partner.

WRAP UP

•The Sacrament of the Anointing of the Sick is a Sacrament of Healing.

•In the Sacrament of the Anointing of the Sick, the Holy Spirit strengthens us, heals us in spirit, and can heal us physically.

•Just as Jesus healed people in body and spirit, the Church continues Jesus' work of healing.

•The Sacrament of the Anointing of the Sick is celebrated by those who are seriously ill, fragile from old age or long illness, or facing death.

•The strength and peace of the Holy Spirit give comfort and reveal the presence of God with the person who is suffering.

What questions do you have about this chapter?

_____

_____

_____

70 **ANOINTING OF THE SICK**

FAITH PARTNERSHIPS

Have the Faith Partners discuss anointing as a sign of healing. You may wish to remind the students of what they have already learned about anointing as a sign of the Holy Spirit.

Ⓢ SKILL NOTE

Because our bodies are gifts from God, we must honor them. For more information about this skill, see pages 72 and 73.

MULTIPLE LEARNING STYLES

Art and the experience of illness Art is an excellent medium through which to express feelings and ideas. Distribute drawing materials, and challenge the students to create art that reflects the human experience of illness and healing. When the students have finished their drawings, invite volunteers to explain their work. Display the drawings in a place where everyone can see and reflect on them.

Student Leader Connection

Consider having the Student Leader do the following:

• **Help moderate the discussion about the meaning of this sacrament for our lives.**

• **Read aloud the *Wrap Up* summary statements.**

• **Help moderate the discussion for *Around the Group*.**

• **Pray aloud a prayer written as an example for the *Briefly* activity.**

Heavenly Father,

...member those who suffer in illness.

...f they are in pain, give them comfort.

...they are irritated, give them peace.

...they are depressed, give them hope.

...y are lonely, remind them of your love.

...e ask this through Christ our Lord.

Amen.

Around the Group

Discuss the following question as a group.

What is meant by emotional healing?

After everyone has had a chance to share his or her responses, come up with a group answer upon which everyone can agree.

_____
_____
_____
_____

What personal observations do you have about the group discussion and answer?

_____
_____
_____
_____

Briefly . . .

At the beginning of this chapter, you were asked to explore your attitudes and experience of illness and death. With that reflection in mind, think of someone in need of spiritual or physical healing. Write a prayer for that person in the space below.

_____
_____
_____
_____

WORKING WITH THE ACTIVITIES

Around the Group

✓ • Present the question to the group, and allow time for discussion. You may need to moderate to keep the students focused on the question.

• Encourage the group members to listen to the opinions and perspectives of others.

• Ask the students to consider the emotions that we experience when we are under stress.

✓ • If the group has agreed on an answer, direct the students to write it in their books. If they could not agree, direct them to list in their books the issues that were left unresolved and explain why.

✓ • Encourage the students to note in their books their personal observations about the discussion and any final thoughts they have.

• See *Reflecting on Your Faith* below.

Briefly . . .

• Encourage the students to consider how their understanding of health, illness, death, and healing may have changed since they responded to *What Do You Think?* on page 65.

• Help the students complete the activity by suggesting that they recall some of the hopes we have for people who are ill and use one of these as a starting place for the prayer.

✓ • Allow time for the students to write their resonses in their books. Invite volunteers to pray these prayers aloud or include them in the closing prayer for this chapter.

• See *Reflecting on Your Faith* below.

REFLECTING ON YOUR FAITH

Around the Group: Think about the areas in your life that could use emotional healing. How can you use the students' insights in your life?

Briefly: Who is in need of healing in your life? Pray for this person.

TEACHING TIP

Handling sensitive issues   Keep in mind that some of the students may be facing the serious illness or death of a family member or friend. The emotional distress of a young person in these circumstances may appear in the form of anxiety, depression, withdrawal, hostility, anger, or variations of these feelings. Encourage the students to discuss such difficulties with a trusted adult—perhaps a family member, the parish priest, or a teacher or counselor at school. They may also call an agency such as the local Hospice organization or Catholic Social Services for help or referral. Caution the group to be aware of emotional distress in their friends; stress the importance of being a good listener when a friend needs to talk. You may also wish to keep a list of people and agencies in your area that can help the students through troubled times. Let the students know that such resources are available to them.

WORKING WITH THE SKILL

- Discuss how the skill relates to the chapter. *What does the celebration of the Sacrament of the Anointing of the Sick suggest to you about the importance of each individual and the respect we should have for one another?* (Answers will vary.)

- Ask a volunteer to read aloud *Expressions of Faith. Why does being a member of Christ's Body include taking care of our bodies?* (Answers will vary but might include respect, gratitude, and hopefulness.)

- Ask a volunteer to read *Scripture* aloud.

- See *Scripture Background* below.

- Discuss the Scripture passage. *What do we mean when we say that our bodies are a living sacrifice?* (A sacrifice is dedicated to God, so we are to act in ways that are consistent with the belief that our bodies belong to God.) *What do we mean when we say that we shouldn't conform to this world but we should discern the will of God?* (We are members of the Body of Christ and are reborn in the Spirit, so we live as God calls us to live.)

- Ask a volunteer to read aloud the text for *Think About It.* Give the students enough time to complete the activity.

- Invite the group members to talk about seeking goodness physically. *How do the items you ranked high help you seek goodness?* (Answers will vary.)

- Encourage the students to give three specific examples of things they can do each day to seek goodness in the way they live physically. (Possible answers: exercise, rest, eat healthful foods.)

SKILLS FOR Christian Living

Honoring the Body

Expressions of Faith

We show God how much we love him through our thoughts, words, and actions, but we also show God how much we love him by the way we respect our bodies and those of others. We can live in Christ best by keeping healthy, getting plenty of exercise, and eating the right kinds of foods. Being members of Christ's Body means taking care of the bodies that God has given us.

Scripture

I appeal to you therefore, brothers and sisters, by the mercies of God, to present your bodies as a living sacrifice, holy and acceptable to God, which is your spiritual worship. Do not be conformed to this world, but be transformed by the renewing of your minds, so that you may discern what is the will of God—what is good and acceptable and perfect.
Romans 12:1–2 22nd Sunday of Ordinary Time, Cyc

Think About It

We hear a lot about the importance of being healthy. We know that it means eating a balanced diet and exercising regularly. Honoring our bodies as gifts from God means more than this, though. It includes appreciating the bodies that God has given us and living so that not only our hearts and minds but also our bodies reflect God's love. Just as we seek goodness with our words, thoughts, and actions, we also need to seek goodness in the way we live physically. Rate on a scale of 1 to 10 (1 being the lowest, 10 the highest) how important you think each of the following should be in your daily routine.

_____ Getting a good night's sleep

_____ Watching television

_____ Surfing the Internet

_____ Eating healthful foods

_____ Spending time with your friends

_____ Shopping

_____ Doing homework

_____ Spending time with your family

_____ Praying

_____ Exercising several times a week

_____ Reading

72 ANOINTING OF THE SICK

RESOURCE Center

SCRIPTURE BACKGROUND

Paul's letters to early Christians frequently gave practical advice for daily life in Christ. *Romans 12:1–2* describes how daily life for a Christian is always a religious act of faith and dedication. Honoring our bodies is part of this life in Christ because our bodies are gifts from God. You may wish to point out that this passage is part of the readings for the Twenty-Second Sunday of Ordinary Time, Cycle A. Refer to page 108 of this book for more information about the liturgical year.

EXTENSION ACTIVITY

Exploring body image   Challenge the students to analyze their perceptions of what a healthy, attractive body is. Distribute magazines and invite the students to examine them. Then discuss the illusions that some standards of beauty create. Remind the students that physical beauty, while pleasant to have and observe, is no indicator of a person's inner spirituality and of his or her desire to live virtuously. Emphasize that real beauty lies in our being created in the image and likeness of God, graced by his love and the promise of eternal life.

Student Leader Connection

Consider having the Student Leader do the following:

- **Read aloud *Think About It.***

- **Help moderate the discussion of further examples for the mnemonic device RESPECT.**

- **Organize a small group to plan a prayer service.**

Special Note: Remember to meet briefly with the Student Leader for Chapter 8. You may wish to provide him or her with the Student Leader Prep Page found on page R7.

‎kill Steps-

The skill of Honoring the Body consists of actively showing respect for your body and everyone else's. Memorize the following to help you practice honoring the body.

Rest your body so that you won't get run down.

Exercise regularly to keep your body healthy.

Sexuality is sacred and each person's body should be treated as holy.

Practice good hygiene and stay safe.

Eat properly for health and energy.

Clothe yourself modestly.

Talk about the body with respect, and don't make fun of or use vulgar language when talking about anyone's body.

‎heck It Out-

Place a check mark next to the sentences that apply to you.

○ I appreciate that my body is a gift from God to be treated with respect.

○ I honor not only my own body but also the bodies of others through respectful language and actions.

○ I try to eat properly and dress appropriately.

○ I limit my time watching television and playing video games.

○ I get eight to nine hours of sleep every night.

○ I avoid dangerous activities in which I might hurt myself.

Based on your response, how could you better honor your body?

_____

_____

‎losing Prayer-

Father, in your wisdom you gave us physical, mortal bodies. Help us honor our bodies, whether we are healthy or sick, remembering that they are gifts from you and should be treated with respect. May we live our lives worthy to be considered temples of your Spirit. Amen.

WORKING WITH THE SKILL

- Ask a volunteer to read aloud *Skill Steps*. **What is involved in the skill of Honoring the Body?** *(showing respect for your body and the bodies of others)*

✓ • Introduce the mnemonic device. **How can we show respect?** *(Answers should explain each letter of the mnemonic device in the students' own words.)*

- Ask for seven volunteers, each of whom will give one positive example for each part of the mnemonic device.

✓ • Allow time for the students to complete *Check It Out*. Invite the students to discuss in a general way their response to this skill and how important or unimportant they think it is.

- See *Reflecting on Your Faith* below.

CLOSING PRAYER

✓ • Gather together to pray the closing prayer. You may wish to use the following music from the *Give Your Gifts* series: "Blessed Be the Lord" *(The Songs)*, "Prayer of the Faithful" *(The Basics)*, or "You Are My Shepherd" *(More Songs)* (GIA Publications, Inc.; distributed by Harcourt Religion Publishers).

- If time permits, direct the students to create their own closing reflections or prayers. You may wish to ask a few volunteers to read aloud what they have created or to plan a prayer service.

REFLECTING ON YOUR FAITH
Consider how you show respect for your body and the bodies of others by applying the mnemonic device to your own life.

TEACHING TIP
Research follow-up   You may wish to take time to review ‎ny research the students have been asked to complete. If the ‎tudents need additional time to complete their research, set ‎side a few minutes at the beginning of the next session to ‎llow them to share the information they have gathered.

MULTIPLE LEARNING STYLES
Closing prayer   You may wish to have the students create their closing prayers in the style of a formal prayer or reflection; a poem or song; or a prayer service with readings, psalm response, and music. Remind the students that the tone of their responses can be different from that of the example but should remain respectful.

ASSESSMENT
The Assessment Page for Chapter 7 can be found on page R15.

LINK TO FAMILY
The corresponding Family Resource pages for this skill are 124–126.

Matrimony

KEY CONTENT SUMMARY

Matrimony is one of the Sacraments of Service. Matrimony celebrates the special covenant relationship that is established between the husband and wife and between the couple and God. Marriage should be both love-giving and life-giving. The Sacrament of Matrimony celebrates the role of the family in the life of the Church.

PLANNING THE CHAPTER

OPEN	PACING	CONTENT	OBJECTIVES	MATERIALS
	Suggested Time: Parish **10 min.** School **25 min.** Your Time: ___ min.	pp. 74–75	• Recognize that Matrimony is one of the Sacraments of Service.	• candle, matches (optional) • symbol representing chapter theme (optional) • art supplies (optional)
SEARCH				
	Suggested Time: Parish **25 min.** School **70 min.** Your Time: ___ min.	pp. 76–79	• Identify the two-fold purpose of the Sacrament of Matrimony as both love-giving and life-giving. • Explore the elements and effects of the celebration of the Sacrament of Matrimony.	• Bibles
REFLECT				
	Suggested Time: Parish **10 min.** School **30 min.** Your Time: ___ min.	pp. 80–81	• Reflect on the special role of the family as the domestic Church.	• Bibles (optional) • art supplies (optional)
LIVE				
	Suggested Time: Parish **15 min.** School **35 min.** Your Time: ___ min.	pp. 82–83	• Apply our call to respect the dignity of each person.	• Student Leader Prep Page for Chapter 9 (p. R8) (optional) • music for prayer (optional) • *Living Our Faith Prayer Services* (optional) • copies of Assessment Page for Chapter 8 (p. R16) (optional)

CATECHISM IN CONTEXT

See Catechism of the Catholic Church, #1604.

The most meaningful and natural expressions of love happen in our relationships— between friends, between siblings, between parents and children, and between husbands and wives. It is natural for humans to express love because we are created in the image and likeness of God who *is* love. God calls us to love one another in universal recognition of the fact that, as humans, we function best within a family, an environment of caring and commitment.

The love shared by husbands and wives is so critical to this realization that their vows to each other create not only their own unique relationship but a special covenant with God as well. The Sacrament of Matrimony offers yet another opportunity for us to come closer to Jesus by living faithfully and loving unstintingly. And we use as our example Christ's perfect love for his Church.

ONE-MINUTE RETREAT

READ

"Family is the basic raw material from which community and Church can be formed. Family is the model of Church." —Sister Thea Bowman FSPA

REFLECT

How would I describe the spiritual resources I get from my family?

PRAY

Lord of Covenant, you call me to commit myself to you. Instill within me the desire to live in a sacred relationship with you and my family. Help me support and build on my family, the Church of the home.

LIBRARY LINKS

BOOKS
FOR ADOLESCENTS

"Marriage: Supernatural and Sacramental," by Jim Auer (*Youth Update;* St. Anthony Messenger Press).

Helps the young person form a sacramental vision of his or her own possible marriage.

"No Family Is Perfect," by Leif Kehrwald (*Youth Update;* St. Anthony Messenger Press).

Offers practical ideas for addressing difficult family life issues and making productive changes.

"When Divorce Divides, How Can You Cope?" by Lonni Collins Pratt (*Youth Update;* St. Anthony Messenger Press).

Helps young people know what to expect and suggests how they can deal with the emotional strain brought on when parents divorce.

FOR ADULTS

Marriage and the Spirituality of Intimacy, by Leif Kehrwald (St. Anthony Messenger Press, 1997).

Explores God's presence in partnership, intimacy, conflict, parenting, work, and play.

A Marriage Sourcebook, ed. by J. Robert Baker, Joni Gibley, and Kevin C. Gibley (Liturgy Training Publications, 1994).

A collection of key texts, prayers, and resources.

Through Good Times and Bad: Prayers for a Lifetime Together, by Robert M. Hamma and Kathryn A. Schneider (Sorin Books, 2000).

Prayers and reflections for all times in a marriage.

MULTIMEDIA

"Sacraments of Vocation" (video from the *Mystery of Faith* series) (produced by Fisher Productions; St. Anthony Messenger Press and Franciscan Communications).

Views Matrimony and Holy Orders as expressions of our relationship with God.

To Last a Lifetime (video) (USCC).

Four Catholic couples discuss the challenge of building and maintaining a strong marriage.

FEATURE PREPARATION

STUDENT LEADER CONNECTION

The Student Leader Prep Page for this chapter is located on page R7. You may wish to provide this information to the Student Leader as an introduction and resource for the chapter.

FAITH PARTNERSHIPS

Chapter 8 has the same Faith Partners as Chapter 7. Several opportunities for Faith Partner discussions have been marked throughout the chapter. You may wish to consider other opportunities as you prepare the lesson.

SKILL NOTES

The skill for this chapter is Honoring the Body. You may wish to build on what the students have learned in the previous chapter as you teach this chapter. A few Skill Notes have been called out to help you. The skill lesson for this chapter can be found on pages 82 and 83.

A check mark indicates the chapter's essential questions, statements, activities, and features. If time is limited, such as in a parish group setting, this icon will help you direct the students through the lesson.

Matrimony

unity

love

Marriage

KEY POINTS FROM CHAPTER 7

You may wish to review these points with the students before you begin the new chapter:

- Anointing of the Sick is a Sacrament of Healing.
- Jesus' life and teaching illustrate the important role that healing plays in our faith.
- The Sacrament of the Anointing of the Sick strengthens our bodies and our spirits.
- Honoring the Body is a Skill for Christian Living.

✓ GATHERING

Have each student name a quality that is important in his or her relationships with family and friends.

✓ PRAYER

Invite the students to reflect on the married couples they know. Then pray the opening prayer as a group. If fire regulations permit, you may wish to light a candle at this time.

Heavenly Father, by your plan a man and a woman unite their lives in love. Bless husbands and wives so that they may be patient and forgiving, respectful and loving toward each other all the days of their lives.

74

RESOURCE Center

PRAYER ENVIRONMENT

If you have created a prayer space for the room, you may wish to represent the theme of this chapter by displaying symbols of Matrimony, such as a unity candle, rings, and wedding and family photographs.

MULTIPLE LEARNING STYLES

Praying for married couples   Expand the opening prayer to a more extensive prayer celebration. Invite the students to sing a song appropriate for a wedding and to create and hang a banner showing the names of married couples for whom they wish to pray. The students might also organize a procession in which they carry symbols of marriage and married life. Supply students with chart paper and markers to make a simple banner; you may wish to have them carry in procession the items for the prayer space.

Student Leader Connection

Consider having the Student Leader do the following:

- Pray aloud the opening prayer with the group.
- Help moderate the discussion about media messages concerning love and marriage.
- Bring in an appropriate item or items for the prayer space.

What Do You Think?

What qualities do you think are the most important in a good marriage? Number the qualities listed below on a scale of 1 to 10, with 1 being the most important and 10 the least important.

_____ physical appearance	_____ sense of humor
_____ intelligence	_____ wealth
_____ respect	_____ patience
_____ love	_____ generosity
_____ religion	_____ compassion

What I hope for most if I get married is

_____

_____

Love and
Marriage

Books, movies, television shows, and magazines suggest many ways to find and attract the right person—a "soul mate." However, the focus is frequently more on the search for someone to love and be loved by, and less on how to live happily and meaningfully with that person through many years of marriage.

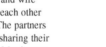

In general, we base our perception of marriage on the relationships of married family members, friends, or neighbors. The lives of people we know can not only offer a realistic view of the positive values of marriage, such as mutual love and respect, but may also show us difficulties that we can learn to resolve or avoid.

In the Sacrament of Matrimony, a husband and wife become one. They are called to love and serve each other as well as their children and extended family. The partners live Christian lives and grow closer to God by sharing their love with others. This is why the Sacrament of Matrimony is called a Sacrament of Service.

WORKING WITH THE ACTIVITY

What Do You Think?

✓ • Allow time for the students to record their thoughts in the space provided.

• See *Reflecting on Your Faith* below.

✓ • *What Do You Think?* is intended as a personal pre-assessment. The students should not be asked to share their responses.

WORKING WITH THE TEXT AND PICTURES

✓ • Read the text on this page, and review the pictures on pages 74 and 75.

✓ • Discuss the word *marriage.* **What does the word** marriage **suggest to you?** *(Answers will vary.)* **What are the positive values of marriage?** *(mutual love, respect, companionship; raising a family)* **What are some of the difficulties to resolve or avoid in marriage?** *(arguing, disrespect, selfishness)*

• Discuss how love and marriage are portrayed in the media. *(Answers will vary but will probably include both positive and negative portrayals.)*

• Refer to the multigenerational family photograph. **What message about marriage and love does the family photograph convey?** *(Marriage and love can last for years and unite several generations as one family.)*

EXTENSION ACTIVITY

Exploring character development Explain to the students that we practice the skills we need in marriage long before we even begin dating. Our experiences of friendship, loyalty, and respect can prepare us for married life. Have the students relate their experiences of friendship, loyalty, and respect in a poem or song lyrics.

TEACHING TIP

Being sensitive to families Keep in mind that the students live in a variety of domestic and family situations. Be sensitive to the fact that the students' experiences of marriage and family life may differ significantly. Avoid judgmental statements and attitudes, and make it clear that every person in this group can someday have a happy, lifelong marriage.

WORKING WITH THE TEXT AND PICTURES

✓ • Read the text and review the picture on this page.

• Discuss how people show that they wish to spend their lives together. *How may a couple show willingness to make a life-long commitment to each other?* *(They become engaged, participate in marriage preparation, and celebrate the Sacrament of Matrimony.)*

✓ • Discuss Matrimony. *What does the Sacrament of Matrimony celebrate?* *(The sacrament celebrates the bond between a man and a woman and between the couple and God.) Why is Matrimony both love-giving and life-giving?* *(God intends marriage for the love and happiness of a husband and wife and for the joy of any children they may have.)*

✓ • See *Skill Note* below.

WORKING WITH THE ACTIVITY

Catholics Believe

• Ask a volunteer to read aloud *Catholics Believe.*

✓ • Give the students time to reflect on and write their responses. *(Answers will vary.)*

• See *Reflecting on Your Faith* below.

• Discuss how a couple shows love for God. *(by loving each other and their children, by praying and celebrating the Eucharist together, by relying on God when they face difficulties and challenges, by communicating well)*

• Encourage the students to share with the group their thoughts about the paraphrased Catechism statement and their responses to the statement that follows.

Life and Love

Ⓢ God gives us a great gift when we meet someone with whom we want to share our lives. And when a man and a woman decide to spend their lives together, they are gifts to each other. They agree to live together, united in heart and mind, body and spirit. By celebrating the Sacrament of Matrimony, a man and a woman express their desire to share all that they are with each other.

The relationship at the center of a marriage brings great love and joy. God intends marriage for the love and happiness of husband and wife and for their joy in the birth of any children they may have.

The Sacrament of Matrimony is a celebration of this love-giving and life-giving relationship. It creates and maintains a bond between a man and a woman as well as between the couple and God. The faithful love that the couple shares is a reflection of God's love for all of us. Through the Sacrament of Matrimony, Christ strengthens the couple with grace to live and, if they have children, to raise them within the bonds of faith and love.

Celebrating Matrimony

Catholics often celebrate the Sacrament of Matrimony within Mass, but there are occasions when the rite is celebrated outside of Mass. Both celebrations invite God's love and grace into the relationship.

The Rite of Marriage follows the Liturgy of the Word. The presider asks about the couple's freedom to marry each other, their intention to be faithful, and their willingness to accept and raise children.

Catholics *Believe*

The love between a husband and a wife reminds us of the eternal love with which God loves all humans. See Catechism, #1604.

List several ways that a couple can show their love for God and for each other.

_____

_____

_____

BACKGROUND

Preparing for marriage The Church recommends that couples participate in a marriage preparation program before they celebrate the Sacrament of Matrimony. In programs such as Pre-Cana, Engaged Encounter, and Sponsor Couples, the engaged couple learns what the Church teaches about Matrimony, listens to married couples talk about married life, discusses various issues together, and receives helpful advice. Marriage preparation programs can help engaged couples decide whether they are ready to make this commitment.

Ⓢ **SKILL NOTE** ✓

Loving someone includes honoring our bodies and those of others. See pages 82 and 83 for further information about the skill of Honoring the Body.

RESOURCE Center

REFLECTING ON YOUR FAITH

How did the group discussion help enlighten you on the ways a married couple can demonstrate love for God and each other? What comments could help you clarify this concept for yourself or for future groups?

Student Leader Connection

Consider having the Student Leader do the following:

• Help moderate a discussion about how people in our lives are gifts from God.

• Read aloud *Catholics Believe.*

• Research and present information on one of the items on the time line from *Our Christian Journey.*

At the heart of the sacrament is the exchange of vows, also called *consent*, or agreement. As they give their complete and free consent to each other before other members of the Body of Christ, the man and woman make a **covenant** before God and his Church. They enter into a sacred and binding promise that establishes their union before God and seeks his grace to keep their vows. The marriage covenant is a sign of the sacred covenant that Christ has with his Church. Through the couple's celebration of the sacrament, God acts in their lives to create a union that is *indissoluble*, a union that cannot be broken.

If it is the custom, the priest blesses the rings and each partner places a ring on the other's finger. The Rite of Marriage ends with the *General Intercessions*, and, at Mass, the Liturgy of the Eucharist follows. The celebration of the Sacrament of Matrimony takes place in a moment of time, but the sacrament is actually lived out over a lifetime.

Living Marriage Vows

A **vocation** is the call to live God's love through single life, marriage, religious life, or priesthood. We know what our vocation is by looking into our hearts, opening ourselves to the guidance of the Holy Spirit through prayer, and seeking the guidance of others. We must take into account our talents and abilities and our willingness to respond to what we believe God asks of us. If we are called to the vocation of marriage, we recognize the signs of love and commitment.

A Holy Couple One of the Church's most popular saints is Thérèse of Lisieux (1873–1897), a holy Carmelite nun also known as the Little Flower. In 1997 she became the third woman to be named a Doctor of the Church. What is not as widely known, however, is that her parents were also very religious. Both her father, Louis Martin, and her mother, Azélie-Marie Guérin, had considered a religious vocation when they were young. Eventually, though, each decided to serve God by raising a family and working in a trade—Louis as a watchmaker and Azélie-Marie as a lacemaker. The couple had nine children. Throughout their lives, Louis and Azélie-Marie stressed the importance of a loving, faithful home. As a result, many of their children, including Thérèse, were inspired to enter religious life and to live in service to their Church family and to God.

For further information: Read a biography of Thérèse. You may also wish to research the family's history on the Internet.

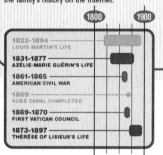

| 1800 | 1900 |

| 1823–1894 LOUIS MARTIN'S LIFE |
| 1831–1877 AZÉLIE-MARIE GUÉRIN'S LIFE |
| 1861–1865 AMERICAN CIVIL WAR |
| 1869 SUEZ CANAL COMPLETED |
| 1869–1870 FIRST VATICAN COUNCIL |
| 1873–1897 THÉRÈSE OF LISIEUX'S LIFE |

WORKING WITH THE TEXT AND PICTURES

- Read the text on pages 77 and 78, and review the picture on this page.

- Use *Vocabulary* below to help the students understand the terms *covenant* and *vocation*.

- Discuss the Rite of Marriage. **What does the presider ask the couple?** *(He asks about the couple's freedom to marry, their intent to be faithful, and their willingness to accept children.)*

- Mention that in the West the Church understands the couple themselves to be celebrating the sacrament. **What is the heart of the sacrament?** *(the exchange of vows)* **What happens when a man and a woman consent in the Rite of Marriage?** *(Before God and the Church, they make a sacred, binding covenant.)*

WORKING WITH THE ACTIVITY

Our Christian Journey

- Ask a volunteer to read aloud *Our Christian Journey.*

- Elicit examples of faith the students have observed in married couples. **How might a married couple demonstrate their faith?** *(Possible answer: in the way they treat each other, raise their children, and deepen their relationship with God.)*

- See *Background* below.

VOCABULARY ✓

A **covenant** is a sacred and binding promise or agreement between humans or between humans and God. The mutual consent of a man and a woman in Christian marriage establishes a covenant with God and with each other.

Each of us has a **vocation**—a call to live God's love through the single life, marriage, religious life, or priesthood.

BACKGROUND

Time line The American Civil War was fought over the issues of slavery, states' rights, and the power of the federal government.

The Suez Canal connects the Mediterranean Sea and the Red Sea. Built by Ferdinand de Lesseps (1805–1894) and controlled by the British from 1882 to 1956, it is now owned and operated by Egypt.

Convoked by Pope Pius IX, the First Vatican Council is most widely remembered for its declaration on papal infallibility.

Saint Thérèse was influenced to become a Carmelite by her desire to serve God and by the example of her two older sisters.

LINK TO LITURGY

The celebration of the Sacrament of Matrimony can include wedding customs that have special meaning for the bride and groom. For example, the couple may light a unity candle or leave a bouquet of flowers at the statue of the Virgin Mary.

Point out that Catholic wedding customs often reflect ethnic and cultural traditions. To show the richness of our heritage, supply the students with information on some of these customs or ask them to research and describe their own families' or cultures' wedding customs. Examples include the Chinese tradition of wearing red, the Mexican tradition of *la riata* (lah ree•AH•tah), and the crowning ceremony of Greek and other Eastern Rite Catholics. Note, too, that in Eastern Churches, the minister of the sacrament is considered to be the priest or bishop.

WORKING WITH THE TEXT AND PICTURES

✓ • Review the text and pictures on this page.

• Refer to the picture of the couple with a new baby and to the picture of the young people celebrating. *What is the purpose of marriage?* *(to be love-giving and life-giving)* *How can family relationships help build our commitment to faith?* *(Answers will vary.)*

✓ • Discuss discerning one's vocation. *How do you discern which vocation is right for you?* *(We pray for the Spirit's guidance, seek the advice of others, and assess our talents and abilities.)*

✓ • Discuss the importance of faithfulness in marriage. *What does faithfulness mean?* *(a loving commitment to each other and sexual fidelity)*

• Discuss annulments. *What is an annulment, or declaration of nullity?* *(If the Church determines that a marriage was invalid from the beginning, it may grant an annulment, a document declaring this fact.)*

• See *Background* below.

✓ • See *Skill Note* below.

WORKING WITH THE ACTIVITY

Focus On

• Ask a volunteer to read aloud *Focus On.*

✓ • Discuss marriage vows. *Why do you think the sacrament includes marriage vows?* *(Answers will vary but should include the fact that marriage is an important commitment with lifelong consequences.)*

• Explore with the students why the celebration of marriage is a public event.

We accept the responsibilities that will come with this way of life, and we accept the person whom we love for all that he or she is—which means accepting both weaknesses and strengths.

One of the most important responsibilities in marriage is *faithfulness.* This means that a husband and wife commit themselves exclusively to each other, both in love and sexual fidelity. A husband and wife are to be faithful to each other as Christ is faithful to his Church.

Of course, there are challenges in every marriage. These may include communication, financial issues, disciplining children, illnesses, and disabilities. God does not abandon a couple when they need him, nor does the Church, which provides marriage counseling and volunteer services to help families with such things as financial counseling and disability assistance. Each day the couple needs to recommit themselves to each other and respond to the grace of the Sacrament of Matrimony.

Not every married person succeeds in living this sacrament for life. If a couple is married in the Catholic Church, their union, because it is a sacrament, cannot be broken except under special circumstances. A couple may choose to obtain a civil divorce to protect their legal rights. But only when the Church determines that the marriage was not valid from the beginning will the Church issue a declaration of nullity, or an *annulment.* Reasons for a declaration of nullity are extremely serious, such as the lack of free consent by either partner at the time of the marriage. Unless a marriage has been annulled, the couple cannot remarry in the Church.

Focus On

Marriage Vows

Marriage vows are not merely promises a man and a woman make to each other; they are promises a man and a woman make to God. In the Catholic Church, marriage is a public celebration; that is, it must take place before two witnesses and a properly authorized minister. Like the other Western Churches, the Latin Rite of the Catholic Church teaches that the partners confer the sacrament upon each other; the Eastern Rites and the Orthodox Churches, however, teach that the presiding priest confers the sacrament on the couple.

BACKGROUND

Annulment and divorce   A civil divorce does not dissolve the marriage bond as understood by the Church. However, in some cases a diocesan marriage tribunal may find that for a serious reason the marriage was invalid from the beginning. Under these circumstances a married couple may obtain an annulment, or decree of nullity. A person married in the Church and then divorced is free to remarry by celebrating the Sacrament of Matrimony only if he or she has received a decree of nullity. If you need more help dealing with questions about divorce and annulment, consult your pastor or local tribunal.

 SKILL NOTE ✓

A husband and a wife show respect for each other through their mutual faithfulness. See pages 82 and 83 for more information about the skill for this chapter.

Student Leader Connection

Consider having the Student Leader do the following:

• Read aloud *Focus On.*

• Introduce *Opening the Word.*

• Help moderate a discussion of how the Sacrament of Matrimony strengthens family life.

RESOURCE Center

Family Life

Because God created us to love and to cooperate with his plan to give life, marriage is intended to be both love-giving and life-giving. This means that, in addition to their commitment to love each other, the couple should be open to the possibility of having children.

Whether they have children or not, though, all married couples live as members of a family, often referred to as the domestic Church. The family is the core of the Church because our faith begins in the home and is continually nourished by our families. As members of a family, we are taught to pray, love, forgive, support, and guide each other in faith. The family as *domestic Church* points to the important role families of all kinds play in the life of the Church.

As part of the sacrament, a husband and wife agree to grow as a family. In return, the love that unites them can become a source of great joy, wisdom, and courage. The lives they lead can truly be lived in service to others because they can share themselves with others.

A happy marriage and family life give us a glimpse of what the kingdom of God is like. The kingdom of God has been described as a banquet and as a wedding feast. (See *Matthew 25:1–10.*)

For us the covenant that is created during the celebration of Matrimony is a celebration for the entire Church. The Body of Christ rejoices at the bond of love that two people share because it is strengthened when a man and a woman vow to share their lives in love.

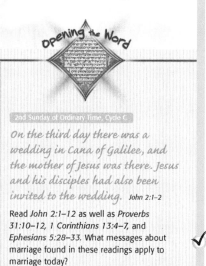

Opening the Word

2nd Sunday of Ordinary Time, Cycle C

On the third day there was a wedding in Cana of Galilee, and the mother of Jesus was there. Jesus and his disciples had also been invited to the wedding. John 2:1–2

Read *John 2:1–12* as well as *Proverbs 31:10–12, 1 Corinthians 13:4–7,* and *Ephesians 5:28–33.* What messages about marriage found in these readings apply to marriage today?

_____

_____

_____

_____

_____

_____

_____

Share your responses and thoughts with your Faith Partner.

WORKING WITH THE TEXT AND PICTURES

✓ • Read the text on this page.

✓ • Use *Vocabulary* below to help the students understand the term *domestic Church.*

✓ • Discuss the background photograph to help the students understand that the core of the Church is the family. **Why is the family called the domestic Church?** *(Our faith begins in the home and is nourished by our families. We are taught to pray, love, forgive, support, and guide each other in faith.)*

• Discuss how the Sacrament of Matrimony is lived every day. **What do you think it takes to maintain a marriage?** *(Possible answers: good communication; physical, spiritual, and emotional care for each other; mutual love and respect.)*

WORKING WITH THE ACTIVITY

Opening the Word

• Ask a volunteer to read aloud *Opening the Word.*

✓ • Allow the students sufficient time to read the additional Scripture passages and respond to the question. *(The messages about marriage indicate the qualities that people who love and respect each other demonstrate.)*

• See *Reflecting on Your Faith* below.

✓ • See *Scripture Background* below.

VOCABULARY ✓

The **domestic Church** is the Church as it exists in the family. The domestic Church is the core of the Body of Christ and the basis upon which the Church is built and strengthened.

FAITH PARTNERSHIPS

Suggest that the Faith Partners create a set of wedding vows based on the messages they find in the Scripture readings. Ask the students to examine the Rite of Marriage and include the wording that the Church uses and requires.

REFLECTING ON YOUR FAITH

Think about what these Scripture passages suggest to you. How are your reactions similar to or different from those of the students?

SCRIPTURE BACKGROUND ✓

John 2:1–2 describes a miracle at a wedding in Cana, signaling the beginning of Jesus' public ministry. Jesus' presence at this wedding heralds the coming of the kingdom of God through his Son. The miracle of turning water into wine connects this passage to other stories of feeding and nourishing found in the Gospels. It also shows God's generosity because wine, wine-making, and grape vines are recurring symbols of God's care for his people. You may wish to point out that this passage is part of the readings for the Second Sunday of Ordinary Time, Cycle C. Refer to page 108 of this book for more information about the liturgical year.

During your discussion you may wish to refer to **Matthew 25:1–10,** another wedding scene suggesting the marriage-like commitment between God and his people. In this parable Christ is the groom, and we are guests invited to the wedding. The metaphor emphasizes the importance of preparedness for the coming of the kingdom of God in its fullness.

WORKING WITH THE TEXT AND PICTURES

✓ • Read the text on this page, and review the picture on pages 80 and 81.

✓ • Discuss the domestic Church. *What virtues would you see in a family that is living as a domestic Church?* (Answers will vary but should be supported with examples.)

• Review the concept of vocation with the students. *What are some of the commitments we will experience in any vocation?* (Possible responses: being honest and faithful, creating healthy friendships, spending time with our families, using talents to help others.)

WORKING WITH THE ACTIVITY

Wrap Up

• Ask a volunteer to read aloud the summary statements.

✓ • Allow time for the students to consider their remaining questions and write them in their books.

• Discuss any remaining questions the students may have. You may wish to have the students write their questions on separate sheets of paper so that you can collect them and respond during the next session.

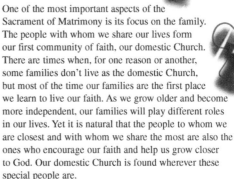

In the Home

One of the most important aspects of the Sacrament of Matrimony is its focus on the family. The people with whom we share our lives form our first community of faith, our domestic Church. There are times when, for one reason or another, some families don't live as the domestic Church, but most of the time our families are the first place we learn to live our faith. As we grow older and become more independent, our families will play different roles in our lives. Yet it is natural that the people to whom we are closest and with whom we share the most are also the ones who encourage our faith and help us grow closer to God. Our domestic Church is found wherever these special people are.

Each day, with every choice and action, we shape who we will become as adults. For now, we are living out the vocation of single life. As such, we develop the virtues and skills that are a part of that vocation. We choose to live honestly, chastely, and faithfully. We create healthy friendships, we share time with our families, and we use our talents to help others. If, as adults, we choose religious life or marriage, we will make many of the same commitments to a religious community or to a spouse. Some will be different, but they will all revolve around the lessons we learned as members of our families.

Reflect on how a family at its best is to be a domestic Church. Share your thoughts with your Faith Partner.

WRAP UP

• The Sacrament of Matrimony is one of the Sacraments of Service.
• The Sacrament of Matrimony celebrates the bond of love between a man and a woman.
• Marriage is both love-giving and life-giving.
• Marriage reminds us of the faithfulness and unity that exist between Christ and his Church.
• The family is meant to be the domestic Church.

What questions do you have about this chapter?

_____
_____
_____

80 **MATRIMONY**

FAITH PARTNERSHIPS

Have the students work with their Faith Partners to talk about how a family at its best is a domestic Church. Encourage the students to think of ways that faith can be lived at home.

EXTENSION ACTIVITY

Becoming a domestic Church   Help the students explore the meaning of the term *domestic Church.* Distribute index cards, scissors, and markers. Have the students create reminders of living faith at home. The students may write words or draw symbols on the index cards, indicating ways to live their faith with family members: celebrating the Eucharist regularly, praying at meals, reading the family Bible, creating an Advent calendar, and keeping Lent by helping those who are suffering or in need. Encourage the students to decorate their cards and cut them into interesting shapes. Suggest that the students post their cards on the refrigerator at home. You may also wish to provide magnets that the students can glue to the back of each card.

RESOURCE Center

Student Leader Connection

Consider having the Student Leader do the following:

• Read aloud the *Wrap Up* summary statements.

• Help moderate the *Around the Group* discussion.

• Discuss with the group the behaviors and qualities that are part of a good friendship or marriage.

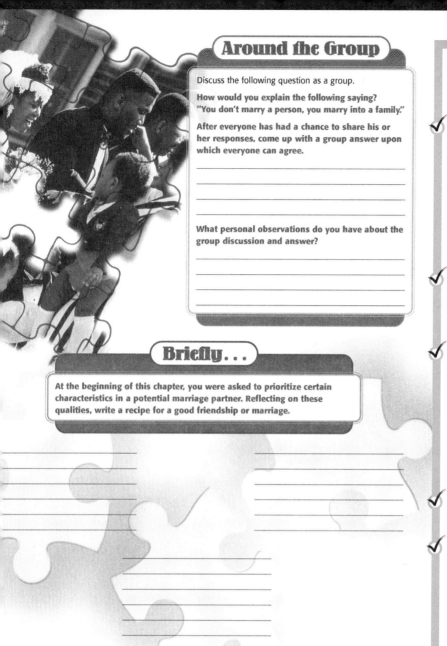

Around the Group

Discuss the following question as a group.

How would you explain the following saying?
"You don't marry a person, you marry into a family."

After everyone has had a chance to share his or her responses, come up with a group answer upon which everyone can agree.

_____
_____
_____

What personal observations do you have about the group discussion and answer?

_____
_____
_____
_____

Briefly . . .

At the beginning of this chapter, you were asked to prioritize certain characteristics in a potential marriage partner. Reflecting on these qualities, write a recipe for a good friendship or marriage.

REFLECT 81

WORKING WITH THE ACTIVITIES

Around the Group

- Present the question to the group, and allow time for discussion. You may need to moderate to keep the students focused on the question.

- Encourage the students to listen to the opinions and perspectives of others.

- Ask the students to consider what it might be like to meet a new set of people who are actually relatives—parents, brothers, and sisters.

- If the group has agreed on an answer, direct the students to write it in their books. If they could not agree, direct them to list in their books the issues that were left unresolved and explain why.

- Encourage the students to note in their books their personal observations about the discussion and any final thoughts they have.

- See *Reflecting on Your Faith* below.

Briefly . . .

- Encourage the students to consider how their opinions may have changed since they responded to *What Do You Think?* on page 75.

- Ask the students to think about behaviors and qualities that are part of a good friendship or marriage.

- Allow the students time to write their recipes for friendship or marriage in their books.

- See *Reflecting on Your Faith* below.

REFLECTING ON YOUR FAITH

Around the Group: How does your family support you in your choice of vocation?

Briefly: What are some of the characteristics that are important to any recipe for a good friendship or a happy marriage?

MULTIPLE LEARNING STYLES

Exploring family life Have the students read *1 Peter 3:8–9.* Arrange the students in two groups. For each quality named in this Scripture passage, have one group create a line of dialogue that might be heard in a family that has this quality. Have the other group of students create a line of dialogue that might be heard in a family that needs to develop this quality. For example, for "unity of spirit" these lines of dialogue might be recorded: "I'll come with you to visit Uncle Jerry in the hospital this afternoon; I can see the movie another time," or "Uncle Jerry can wait—I'm not going to miss a chance to see that movie this afternoon." Make a chart of these comments, and have the students discuss the effects that words and attitudes can have on a spiritual "sense of family."

EXTENSION ACTIVITY

Learning more about vocations Help the students think about vocations. Ask each student to consider how he or she might complete the following statements:

When I grow up I want to be . . .
When I grow up the place I want to live is . . .
One thing I definitely want to accomplish in my life is . . .
I can't imagine living my life without . . .
One thing I hope to avoid in my life is . . .

Then ask the students to suggest vocations that fit their answers to these questions.

WORKING WITH THE SKILL

✓ • Remind the students that the skill for Chapters 7 and 8 is Honoring the Body. Discuss with the students how they have tried to use the skill since the end of Chapter 7.

✓ • Discuss with the students how regarding the family as domestic Church and developing the qualities necessary in a good marriage partner can help them acquire the lifelong habit of honoring the body.

✓ • Direct the students' attention to the photograph of young people having fun. *How does this picture suggest a way to honor the body?* *(Answers will vary but should express that the picture implies that we build our lasting relationships on a foundation of friendship and healthful, unpressured, mutually enjoyable activities. In time we add to such friendships the assurances of trust, respect, and responsibility.)*

• Ask a volunteer to read aloud *Expressions of Faith. What must we remember about God's gift of sexuality to us?* *(That with this gift comes the responsibility of treating each other with kindness and respect.)*

✓ • Read *Scripture* aloud. *What does Paul mean when he describes our bodies as temples of the Holy Spirit?* *(He means that the Holy Spirit lives in and acts within us, so we are to reflect this presence within us, including how we treat our bodies and the bodies of others.)*

✓ • See *Scripture Background* below.

✓ • Ask a volunteer to read aloud *Skill Steps.* Review with the students the mnemonic device RESPECT, which they learned about in Chapter 7.

SKILLS for Christian Living

Honoring the Body

Expressions of Faith-

Just as a loving and committed husband and wife treat each other with respect, so too must we practice the skill of Honoring the Body in our single lives. We must choose attitudes and actions that demonstrate our commitment to the way Jesus wants us to live. We understand that while our interest and affection for others is normal and healthy, we must avoid treating anyone's body selfishly or thoughtlessly. We recognize that our gift of sexuality comes with the responsibility of treating each other with kindness and respect.

Scripture

. . . do you not know that your body is a temple of the Holy Spirit within you, which you have from God, and that you are not your own?
1 Corinthians 6:19 2nd Sunday of Ordinary Time, C

Skill Steps-

The skill of Honoring the Body requires us to RESPECT our bodies. We need to remember to get rest, exercise, use our sexuality as the special gift that it is, practice good hygiene and stay safe, eat properly, clothe ourselves appropriately, talk about our own bodies and the bodies of others with respect, and avoid vulgar language.
Here are some things to remember:

● Our bodies are gifts from God to be appreciated and treated with respect.

● Being members of Christ's Body means taking care of the bodies that God has given us.

● Not only our hearts and minds but also our bodies reflect God's love.

● We show respect for others by honoring their bodies, keeping them from harm or injury.

82 MATRIMONY

EXTENSION ACTIVITY

Design a Web site Ask the students to design a Web site reflecting what they have learned about honoring the body. Encourage them to include information that can help other young people learn to respect their sexuality.

TEACHING TIP

Discussing sexuality Encourage the students to discuss curiosity, concerns, and issues with their parents. Emphasize that a student who experiences any interaction that makes him or her feel uncomfortable regarding his or her body and sexuality should speak to a trusted adult about the encounter.

SCRIPTURE BACKGROUND ✓

1 Corinthians 6:19 is part of Paul's discourse on sexual morality, in which he warns this Christian community away from *fornication*—what we would call sex between unmarried persons. Paul uses the metaphor that each of us is a temple of the Holy Spirit. This image means that having been baptized in

Christ and having received the Holy Spirit, every Christian belongs to Christ. This passage is part of the readings for the Second Sunday of Ordinary Time, Cycle B. Refer to page 108 of this book for more information about the liturgical year.

Student Leader Connection

Consider having the Student Leader do the following:

• **Read *Scripture* aloud.**

• **Help the students recall the mnemonic device RESPECT.**

• **Help moderate the group discussion about responses to** *Skill Builder.*

• **Organize a small group to plan a prayer service.**

Special Note: Remember to meet briefly with the Student Leader for Chapter 9. You may wish to provide him or her with the Student Leader Prep Page found on page R8.

kill Builder-

Do you think that our society and the media support the Christian practice of honoring the body? On the lines below, write down the titles of a movie, a song, and a TV program that you like. Next, rate how each of your choices honors or dishonors the body by giving it a grade of A, B, C, D, or F. When deciding the grade, consider how the body is shown and what kinds of habits or behaviors are shown or described.

Share your thoughts with your Faith Partner.

	Title	Grade
Movie	_____	_____
Song	_____	_____
TV program	_____	_____

utting It into Practice-

For each letter of the word RESPECT and its meaning, suggest one concrete way someone your age could honor his or her body. For example, for the letter *R*, tell how much rest you think someone your age needs each day, including the hours of sleep you think are necessary. Mention any other ideas you have for resting or relaxing, such as quiet hobbies.

losing Prayer-

Loving Father, you have created us to support and love one another as members of our families. Guide us as we decide on a vocation, and teach us how to best live in your service. Be with us as we live our lives, and help us treat ourselves and others with respect.

WORKING WITH THE SKILL

- Ask a volunteer to read aloud *Skill Builder*.
- Encourage volunteers to share their responses with the rest of the group. The students should give reasons for their selections.
- Have the students look at *Putting It into Practice*, and allow them sufficient time to complete the activity.
- See *Reflecting on Your Faith* below.

CLOSING PRAYER

- Gather together to pray the closing prayer. You may wish to use the following music from the *Give Your Gifts* series: "Yes, Lord" *(The Songs)*, "Blessing" *(The Basics)*, or "Heaven Will Sing" *(More Songs)* (GIA Publications, Inc.; distributed by Harcourt Religion Publishers).
- If time permits, direct the students to create their own closing reflections or prayers. You may wish to ask a few volunteers to read aloud what they have created or to plan a prayer service. As an alternative for prayer, you may wish to use "Sacraments: Prayer Service D" from *Living Our Faith Prayer Services* by Robert Piercy and Linda Baltikas (GIA Publications, Inc.; distributed by Harcourt Religion Publishers).

AITH PARTNERSHIPS

nvite the Faith Partners to complete the *Skill Builder* activity by aring their ideas and responses.

REFLECTING ON YOUR FAITH
Which of the parts of the mnemonic device RESPECT do you think you need to work on?

EACHING TIP

esearch follow-up You may wish to take time to review ny research the students have been asked to complete. If the udents need additional time to complete their research, set side a few minutes at the beginning of the next session to low them to share the information they have gathered.

MULTIPLE LEARNING STYLES

Closing prayer You may wish to have the students create their closing prayers in the style of a formal prayer or reflection; a poem or song; or a prayer service with readings, psalm response, and music. Remind the students that the tone of their responses can be different from that of the example but should remain respectful.

ASSESSMENT
The Assessment Page for Chapter 8 can be found on page R16.

LINK TO FAMILY
The corresponding Family Resource pages for this skill are 124–126.

Holy
Orders

9

KEY CONTENT SUMMARY

Holy Orders is one of the Sacraments of Service. Members of the ministerial priesthood guide the laity in the development of their faith. The ordained serve the Church community in the name and person of Jesus. There are three degrees of Holy Orders—deacon, priest, and bishop.

PLANNING THE CHAPTER

	PACING	CONTENT	OBJECTIVES	MATERIALS
OPEN	Suggested Time: Parish **10 min.** School **25 min.** Your Time: ____ min.	pp. 84–85	• Recognize that Holy Orders is a Sacrament of Service.	• candle, matches (optional) • symbol representing chapter theme (optional) • art supplies, notepaper or blank cards (optional)
SEARCH	Suggested Time: Parish **25 min.** School **70 min.** Your Time: ____ min.	pp. 86–89	• Identify and examine the role of ministerial priesthood and the vocation of the ordained. • Explore the elements and effects of the Rite of Holy Orders.	• Bibles • chasuble, stole, chalice, paten (or pictures of them) (optional) • pictures of a crosier and a miter (optional)
REFLECT	Suggested Time: Parish **10 min.** School **30 min.** Your Time: ____ min.	pp. 90–91	• Reflect on how we, as members of the common priesthood, are called to interact with and assist the ministerial priesthood in common service to the community.	• checklist of parish activities (optional) • list of ideas for guest speaker (optional)
LIVE	Suggested Time: Parish **15 min.** School **35 min.** Your Time: ____ min.	pp. 92–93	• Apply the idea that the common and ministerial priesthood share the responsibility of proclaiming the gospel message.	• Student Leader Prep Page for Chapter 10 (p. R8) (optional) • music for prayer (optional) • copies of Assessment Page for Chapter 9 (p. R17) (optional)

CATECHISM IN CONTEXT

See Catechism of the Catholic Church, #1547.

Through the Sacrament of Holy Orders, Jesus confers the grace that allows the ordained—deacons, priests, and bishops—to act in the name of Christ. These representatives of Christ, consecrated in Holy Orders, constitute the ministerial priesthood. They continue Christ's work by preaching the word and celebrating the sacraments.

Others who recognize and follow the call to serve the Body of Christ may elect to do so by joining a religious community, choosing a marriage partner, or remaining single. These people, too, are a part of the priesthood—the common priesthood of all the faithful. Together, we are a "priestly people" committed to the pastoral and liturgical life of the Church and participants in its social and charitable work. We share the responsibilities and the rewards of fulfilling our promise of service to God, to the world and its people, to our friends and families, and to ourselves.

ONE-MINUTE RETREAT

READ

"All I am is the Lord's instrument; my job is to lead others to him."
—Edith Stein

REFLECT

As a baptized member of the "holy priesthood," how do I lead others to Christ?

PRAY

God our Father, you have chosen me to be an instrument of your creative salvation in the name and person of Jesus. May the work of my hands be of service to the community. Bless my life by the power of the Holy Spirit to ever proclaim the gospel message.

LIBRARY LINKS

BOOKS
FOR ADOLESCENTS

"Dare to Consider: Religious Life and Priesthood," by Cathy Bertrand SSND (*Youth Update;* St. Anthony Messenger Press).

Answers the questions young Catholics have about being called to the religious life or priesthood.

Extraordinary Lives: Thirty-Four Priests Tell Their Stories, by Francis P. Friedl and Rex Reynolds (Ave Maria Press, 1998).

First-person accounts of ordained ministry—its blessings and challenges.

"What Being a Priest Is All About," by Greg Friedman OFM (*Youth Update;* St. Anthony Messenger Press).

Fosters vocations and helps young Catholics understand the unique role of the priest in the Catholic tradition.

FOR ADULTS

Downtown Monks: Sketches of God in the City, by Albert Holtz, OSB (Ave Maria Press, 2000).

Tales of ministry from a community of Benedictine monks who live and work in the inner city of Newark, New Jersey.

A Pastor's Challenge: Parish Leadership in an Age of Division, Doubt, and Spiritual Hunger, by George A. Kelly (Our Sunday Visitor, 1994).

A comprehensive overview of modern priesthood.

The Seven Storey Mountain, by Thomas Merton (50th anniversary edition; Harvest Books, 1999).

The classic story of Merton's recognition of his vocation.

MULTIMEDIA

Answering God's Call: The Experience of Priesthood (video) (USCC).

Two very different priests share the challenges of their lives and ministries.

Mystery of Faith (video) (produced by Fisher Productions; St. Anthony Messenger Press and Franciscan Communications).

The segment "Sacraments of Vocation" views Matrimony and Holy Orders as expressions of our relationship with God.

FEATURE PREPARATION

STUDENT LEADER CONNECTION

The Student Leader Prep Page for this chapter is located on page R8. You may wish to provide this information to the Student Leader as an introduction and resource for the chapter.

FAITH PARTNERSHIPS

Chapter 9 begins a new Faith Partnership. Several opportunities for Faith Partner discussions have been marked throughout the chapter. You may wish to consider other opportunities as you prepare the lesson.

SKILL NOTES

The skill for this chapter is Keeping Promises. As you teach the skill lesson on pages 92 and 93, you may wish to refer to the Skill Notes marked throughout the chapter. These notes will help you identify terms and ideas related to the skill.

A check mark indicates the chapter's essential questions, statements, activities, and features. If time is limited, such as in a parish group setting, this icon will help you direct the students through the lesson.

KEY POINTS FROM CHAPTER 8

You may wish to review these points with the students before you begin the new chapter:

- Matrimony is one of the Sacraments of Service.
- Matrimony celebrates the special covenant relationship that is established between the husband and wife, and between the couple and God.
- Marriage should be both love-giving and life-giving.
- The Sacrament of Matrimony celebrates the role of the family in the life of the Church.
- Honoring the Body is a Skill for Christian Living.

Holy Orders

Almighty God, remember your Church. Give our pope and bishops wisdom and courage. Help our priests and deacons serve you in the name of your Son, Jesus Christ. Amen.

84

✓ GATHERING

Ask the students to reflect on these questions silently:

Are you more of a speaker or a listener?

Are you more of a follower or a leader?

Do you prefer to be alone or with others?

Are you comfortable or uncomfortable when you are alone?

Do you interact better with one person or with a group?

✓ PRAYER

Pray the opening prayer, adding the names of the pope, your bishop, and the priest(s) and deacon(s) in your parish. If fire regulations permit, you may wish to light a candle at this time.

RESOURCE Center

PRAYER ENVIRONMENT

If you have created a prayer space for the room, you may wish to display a stole or some other symbol associated with Holy Orders to represent the theme of this chapter.

FAITH PARTNER INTRODUCTION

If you haven't done so already, remind the students that it is time for them to create new Faith Partnerships. After you have assigned new Faith Partners, you may wish to give the students a few moments to complete together a Faith Partner introduction. Ask the Faith Partners to describe for each other someone who is totally committed to a cause or an activity. Then ask them to make a list of the characteristics of such a person to share with the entire group.

Student Leader Connection

Consider having the Student Leader do the following:

- Pray aloud the opening prayer.
- Help moderate a discussion about the people who can best offer advice to adolescents of his or her age.
- Bring in a symbol for the prayer space.

What Do You Think?

Who are some of the people to whom you look for advice, guidance, and support? Identify them by name or by initials.

_____

_____

_____

How do you decide whether or not to ask someone for advice or support? What kind of person does he or she have to be?

_____

_____

_____

_____

Mission to Serve

Each of us looks to the people we trust for advice. Our friends, teachers, family members, and coaches help guide us when we have difficulty making a decision or when we get into trouble. By celebrating the Sacrament of Holy Orders, a Sacrament of Service, the deacons, priests, and bishops of the Church serve God by serving God's people. They are consecrated and given a special power by Christ, for the benefit of his Church, to preside at the sacraments and preach the gospel.

WORKING WITH THE ACTIVITY
What Do You Think?

✓ • Allow time for the students to record their thoughts in the space provided.

• See *Reflecting on Your Faith* below.

✓ • *What Do You Think?* is intended as a personal pre-assessment. The students should not be asked to share their responses.

WORKING WITH THE TEXT AND PICTURES

✓ • Read the text on this page, and review the pictures on pages 84 and 85.

✓ • Discuss with the students the times when people need advice and guidance. **When do people most often need direction in their lives?** *(Possible answer: at times when they are in trouble, struggling with personal problems, or are uncertain about how to live their lives.)*

✓ • Talk about the Church's role in providing guidance. **Why does the Church have priests and bishops?** *(Priests and bishops help us come closer to Jesus through preaching and the sacraments; they help guide us in living as Christians.)*

• Refer to the pictures on pages 84 and 85. **What do these pictures say about the Sacrament of Holy Orders?** *(They indicate that ordained men serve the members of the Body of Christ.)*

REFLECTING ON YOUR FAITH
Whom do you ask for advice, and how do you decide whether or not to ask someone for advice or support?

EXTENSION ACTIVITY
Saying thank you Invite the students to thank those on whom they depend for advice, guidance, and support. Distribute drawing materials and notepaper or blank cards. Have each student create and write a personal note to someone he or she wishes to thank. Encourage the students to send or give the completed cards to the people they have chosen.

BACKGROUND
Fulfilling our mission The word *mission* means "to send forth," and a Christian's mission is quite specific. In *Matthew 28:19–20* Jesus sends the apostles forth to preach the good news, to baptize, and to help people follow his teachings. This is what every Christian is called to do by virtue of his or her Baptism in Christ. When we talk about our mission as followers of Jesus, we are talking about our vocation as Christians. All of us are called to participate in this mission of proclaiming and helping further the kingdom of God. All of us live our Christian vocation according to the talents we have and the circumstances of our lives.

WORKING WITH THE TEXT AND PICTURES

✓ • Read the text and review the pictures on this page.

✓ • Use *Vocabulary* below to help the students understand the term *common priesthood.*

✓ • Refer to the pictures of the candidates at a celebration of Holy Orders. *How might a person recognize the call to become a member of the ministerial priesthood?* *(Answers will vary.)*

• Point out the frieze shown on pages 86 and 87. *What do the male figures and the lambs in the frieze suggest about the ministerial priesthood?* *(Possible answers: The figures suggest the role of the priest as shepherd— one who preaches and leads others to Christ. The figures also suggest Christ as an example of priesthood to the apostles.)*

✓ • Discuss the meaning of *common priesthood.* *How do we live as members of the common priesthood?* *(Possible answer: We live our common priesthood when we live as Christians: teaching others, caring for others, and encouraging others' faith.)*

WORKING WITH THE ACTIVITY

Opening the Word

• Ask a volunteer to read aloud *Opening the Word.*

✓ • Allow time for the students to read the additional Scripture passages and respond to the question. *(Possible answers: spreading the good news about Jesus, casting out demons, distributing food, offering sacrifices.)*

✓ • See *Scripture Background* below.

Our Priesthood in **Christ**

You probably don't realize all the little ways you serve others every day. Think about the times when you have befriended someone in your class who was being picked on or ignored, or when you listened sympathetically to a friend who was worrying about a problem in his or her life. Or perhaps you did a small good deed for someone without being asked. These were times when you served others.

Opening the Word

And he appointed twelve, whom he also named apostles, to be with him, and to be sent out to proclaim the message. Mark 3:14

Read *Mark 3:13–19* as well as *Acts 6:1–6, Hebrews 5:1–10,* and *1 Timothy 3:1–7.* According to Scripture, what are some tasks of leaders of the Church?

_____

_____

_____

Jesus asked all his followers to serve others every day because through living the message of the gospel, we can come to know God's love for us. As we begin to understand and experience his love, we will, with God's grace, share it with others through the gifts of our time, talents, patience, and support.

In the Sacrament of Baptism, we are united with Christ. We are made part of his Body and are promised eternal life with him in his Father's kingdom. Through Baptism we become members of the priesthood of all believers, also called the **common priesthood.** We live our common priesthood when we show people what it means to be a Christian by the way we live. When we teach others, care for them, and encourage their faith, we live as members of the priesthood of all believers.

86 **HOLY ORDERS**

RESOURCE Center

VOCABULARY

The priesthood of all believers, or *common priesthood,* is the whole community of believers who, through their participation in Jesus' gospel message, are members of the "holy priesthood." We come to participate in Christ's priesthood through the Sacraments of Baptism and Confirmation.

SCRIPTURE BACKGROUND ✓

Throughout the Gospels, Jesus calls people to follow him. In *Mark 3:14,* however, Jesus appoints the Twelve, whom he designates *apostles.* This is a significant act, in part because of the symbolic importance of the number *twelve* (the twelve tribes of Israel) and in part because in naming his apostles, Jesus is constituting the people of God by establishing the core of the leadership group for what will become the Church. These twelve share not only in discipleship but also in Jesus' ministry of preaching and healing. The apostles' role among Jesus' disciples is seen as the beginning of the ministerial priesthood.

Student Leader Connection

Consider having the Student Leader do the following:

• **Read aloud selected text.**

• **Help moderate a group discussion about experiences of service.**

• **For the group's reference, make a chart about ways we live our common priesthood.**

Rite **Response**

Religious Vows

Religious vows are special promises made to God, usually by those who have chosen to become members of a religious community. These vows most often include poverty, chastity, and obedience, and may be temporary or permanent.

In Service

The Ordained Priesthood

In addition to the common priesthood, deacons, priests, and bishops are part of what is called the **ministerial priesthood.** The word *ministerial* means to serve God by serving others. Through the sacrament of Holy Orders, men are ordained as priests and bishops to celebrate sacraments, especially the Eucharist. Though deacons cannot preside at Mass, they can celebrate Baptism and Matrimony and preside at funeral rites outside of Mass. Bishops, priests, and deacons preach and teach the word of God and serve, support, and guide the Body of Christ.

When a man is ordained, he receives the grace to serve the Church in the name of Jesus. As part of the ordination, the candidate receives a *sacramental character* to mark the fact that he has become Christ's in a special way. Most priests in the Latin Rite or Western Church promise to live a life of *celibacy,* which means that they do not marry. As celibates, they can give their lives to the service of the Body of Christ.

There are three degrees of priesthood: deacons, priests, and bishops. As such, the Church celebrates three different ordination ceremonies. Each ceremony focuses on the specific calling of those being ordained. Each ceremony includes the laying on of hands and a prayer of consecration.

The ordination of a deacon celebrates the candidate's service to the local parish and to the bishop and priests. During the ceremony the deacon is asked to make a commitment to serve his bishop and to minister to the people. At the end of the ordination, the deacon is presented with his vestments, the stole and the dalmatic, a robe-like vestment.

Some men are ordained transitional deacons while they are preparing for the priesthood. Other men don't wish to become priests and, instead, become permanent deacons. A deacon wears his stole, a narrow band of cloth, over his left shoulder.

Deacons serve the common priesthood by baptizing, witnessing and blessing marriages, and by preaching and teaching the word of God, among other activities. A deacon cannot preside at the Eucharist, Reconciliation, or the Anointing of the Sick.

The deacon is also ordained to do works of charity. He may visit parishioners who are sick, prepare couples for marriage, and help with the parish youth program. Does your parish have a deacon? If so, in what ministries is he involved?

SEARCH 87

WORKING WITH THE TEXT AND PICTURES

- Read the text on this page.
- Use *Vocabulary* below to help the students understand the term *ministerial priesthood.*
- Discuss the ministerial priesthood. **What does it mean to be ordained?** *(A sacramental character marks a man as Christ's, and he receives grace to serve the Church in Jesus' name as a ministerial priest; most priests in the Latin Rite, or Western Church, make a promise of celibacy.)* **What are the three degrees of priesthood?** *(deacons, priests, bishops)*
- Explain the role of a deacon. **How do deacons serve the Church?** *(Deacons baptize, distribute Communion, witness and bless marriages, and preach and teach the word of God.)*
- Discuss examples of service the students have observed. **How have you seen priests and deacons serve the faith community?** *(Answers will vary.)*
- Discuss religious vocations. **Why might someone want to be a priest or a member of a religious community?** *(Answers will vary.)*
- See *Skill Note* below.

WORKING WITH THE ACTIVITY

Rite Response

- Ask a volunteer to read aloud *Rite Response.*
- Discuss the importance of vows. **Why do religious and married people make vows?** *(Vows are statements of commitment to live a certain way of life.)* **How do the vows of poverty, chastity, and obedience help members of a religious community?** *(They help members put God first in their lives.)*

VOCABULARY ✓

Deacons, priests, and bishops belong to the *ministerial priesthood.* Through the Sacrament of Holy Orders, ordained men represent Christ to the faith community. They serve the priesthood of the faithful by building up and guiding the Church in the name of Christ.

(S) SKILL NOTE ✓

The text on this page can be used to discuss the skill of Keeping Promises. See pages 92 and 93 for more information about this skill.

BACKGROUND

Married priests In the Latin Rite of the Catholic Church, most priests make a promise of celibacy. There are small numbers of married priests in the Latin Rite who were previously priests or ministers in other Christian denominations and were already married when they became Catholic. In Eastern Churches in union with the Catholic Church of Rome, priests have long been permitted to marry and to have families if they wish. Married priests of the Eastern Rites must marry before they are ordained and cannot remarry if widowed after ordination. Bishops in the Eastern Rites are chosen from among the celibate priesthood.

WORKING WITH THE TEXT AND PICTURES

✓ • Read the text and review the pictures on this page.

• Discuss how a priest represents Christ as priest (serve), prophet (preach), and king (lead). *(Answers will vary but may include the fact that the priest serves as counselor, administrator, and religious guide; that he preaches the gospel and presides at the sacraments; and that he leads the faith community by example and authority.)*

✓ • Refer to the photograph at the bottom of this page. *What role of the priest is depicted in this picture? Explain.* *(prophet, because he is teaching or proclaiming the gospel)*

✓ • See *Skill Note* below.

WORKING WITH THE ACTIVITY

Our Christian Journey

• Ask a volunteer to read aloud *Our Christian Journey.*

• Discuss what made Saint John Vianney a good confessor. *(He was a good listener and could see into peoples' hearts.)*

✓ • Discuss the characteristics a good advisor should have. *(A good advisor must understand the problem, be genuinely sympathetic, know how to instill confidence, and give wise counsel.)*

• See *Background* below.

OUR CHRISTIAN JOURNEY

A Good Listener Saint John Vianney was noted for his saintliness and for his remarkable ability as a confessor. Ironically, this saint very nearly failed to become a priest. He began studying for the priesthood when he was eighteen, but he could not do the work required and was dismissed from the seminary in 1814. A local priest intervened, tutoring John and arranging for him to be tested and interviewed by seminary officials. John returned to the seminary and was finally ordained, and in 1818 he became the parish priest of a little village called Ars. Through the care and attention he gave to his community, he was able to strengthen and guide the people to a better understanding of their faith. Except for brief interruptions, he spent more than twelve hours a day in the confessional, bringing God's grace and reconciliation to troubled spirits. John Vianney is the patron saint of priests, and his feast day is August 9.

For further information: Research the life of Saint John Vianney in a book about the history of saints. You may also wish to find out whether your diocese includes any churches named after him.

1786-1859
SAINT JOHN VIANNEY'S LIFE

1803
LOUISIANA PURCHASE

1845
IRISH POTATO FAMINE BEGINS

1858
FIRST MESSAGE VIA TRANSATLANTIC CABLE SENT

1869-1870
FIRST VATICAN COUNCIL TAKES PLACE

To Represent Christ

When a priest is ordained, he represents Christ as priest, prophet, and king. During the ceremony the celebrating bishop presents the priest with his vestments, the stole and chasuble (a cape-like garment), and anoints the hands of the new priest. The bishop then presents him with the chalice and paten, inviting him to imitate the mystery of Jesus' saving actions by the way he lives his life. Through a promise of obedience, and the kiss of peace from the bishop at the end of the ordination liturgy, the priest is made a coworker with the bishops of the Church.

Ⓢ

Today, most priests work in parishes, and we most often experience a priest's ministry during Mass. Priests are ordained to preach the gospel, lead the faith community, and preside at the sacraments, especially Eucharist and Reconciliation. The priest also serves as a counselor, administrator, and a religious guide to answer questions we have about our faith.

Discuss with your Faith Partner the things about the priesthood that interest you.

FAITH PARTNERSHIP

88 **HOLY ORDERS**

RESOURCE Center

Ⓢ **SKILL NOTE** ✓

The text about the promise a priest makes at his ordination to serve the Church can help the students understand the skill for this chapter. See pages 92 and 93 for more information.

BACKGROUND

Time line By 1827 thousands of people began coming to John Vianney to confess their sins and receive his guidance.

In 1803 the United States paid France fifteen million dollars for a huge tract of land between the Mississippi River and the Rocky Mountains. This transaction is known as the Louisiana Purchase.

The Irish potato famine caused widespread devastation and starvation in Ireland during the mid-nineteenth century.

The first telegraph cable message between Europe and America was sent in sixteen hours. Previously, a "quick" communication between the two continents required fourteen days or more.

The First Vatican Council declared the doctrine of infallibility, which teaches that the pope cannot err in certain circumstances when he speaks on issues of faith and morals.

FAITH PARTNERSHIPS

Suggest that the Faith Partners discuss what elements of the priestly life might be most difficult, and why.

Student Leader Connection

Consider having the Student Leader do the following:

• **Read aloud *Our Christian Journey.***

• **Research the lives of saints who were ordained, such a Saint John Bosco, Saint Philip Neri, and Saint Peter Cla**

• **Research and present information on one of the items on the time line from *Our Christian Journey.***

Catholics Believe

By means of the ministerial priesthood, Christ builds up and leads the Church. See Catechism, #1547.

Describe the ideal bishop, priest, or deacon.

_____

_____

_____

Shepherds of the Church

As sanctifiers, teachers, and rulers, bishops share in the priesthood of Jesus in a special way. The ordination of a bishop is the fullness of the Sacrament of Holy Orders. Through the celebration of the sacrament, bishops receive the mission that was first given to the apostles—to preach the gospel. During the ceremony the bishop-elect, as he is called, is anointed on the forehead and is presented with the symbols of his office: the Book of Gospels to show that he is to proclaim the word of God;

a ring to show his faithfulness to the Church; the *crosier*, or staff, to show he is our shepherd; and the *miter*, a pointed cap of stiffened cloth, a reminder that followers of Christ are clothed with holiness.

Bishops are called the shepherds of the Church because they, like the apostles before them, have been directed by Christ to watch over his Church. Unlike most deacons and priests, bishops care for a diocese. And together with the other bishops and the pope, they lead the entire Church community.

Because a bishop has many responsibilities and a large territory, we do not often see him. But your bishop's actions affect you in many ways that you probably don't realize. Some of the decisions a bishop makes, together with his administrative staff, include those in areas of religious education, youth ministry, and charitable projects.

Together, deacons, priests, and bishops share in the mission of Christ. They serve, teach, and guide us as members of the Body of Christ. By devoting their lives to God and the Church in this special way, they live out their vocations and enable us to grow closer to God.

WORKING WITH THE TEXT AND PICTURES

✓ • Read the text and review the picture on this page.

• Refer to the picture of the bishop. *How might we experience the presence of the bishop of our diocese?* (Possible answers: We hear his name pronounced at Mass each Sunday, or the priest may read a directive from the bishop at Mass; we may have met the bishop during a Confirmation celebration; we may read messages from the bishop in our parish bulletin or diocesan newspaper.)

✓ • Discuss the role of a bishop. *What does it mean for a bishop to be sanctifier (priest), teacher (prophet), and ruler (king)?* (The bishop is a sanctifier (priest) because he serves the people of his diocese and presides over the sacraments; he is a teacher (priest) because he preaches the gospel; and he is a ruler (king) because he shepherds an entire diocese, watching over the people and leading them to Christ.)

WORKING WITH THE ACTIVITY

Catholics Believe

• Ask a volunteer to read aloud *Catholics Believe*.

✓ • Allow time for the students to respond to the statement. (Possible answers: being in touch with people's needs, being humble, having strong faith, living and teaching Christian values.)

• See *Reflecting on Your Faith* below.

• Encourage the students to share with the group their thoughts about the paraphrased Catechism statement and their responses to the statement that follows.

REFLECTING ON YOUR FAITH

What qualities of an ideal deacon, priest, and bishop do you display?

EXTENSION ACTIVITY

Vestments and sacred vessels Invite the students to learn more about the vestments and sacred vessels a priest uses in presiding at the Eucharist. You may wish to arrange a tour of the parish sacristy or bring some items to show the group, such as a chasuble, a stole, and a paten. These special objects are created by monasteries and by companies that specialize in church furnishings. You might have a priest visit the group to explain the items.

LINK TO SCRIPTURE

The earliest Christians lived in Jewish communities and were familiar with Jewish concepts of sacrifice and priesthood. In the early Church these ideas were transformed to reflect faith in Christ. To be a Christian was to share in the priesthood of Christ and to lead a life of self-sacrifice. Many men and women were involved in ministry in the early Church. In *Romans 12:1–2* Paul discusses the life of sacrifice and alludes to the rejection of materialism, and in *Romans 15:16–21* he explains preaching as a priestly activity. Although the role of priest was important in the early Christian era, the word *priest* is not used in the New Testament to describe the first leaders of Christian communities. Instead, the word *presbyter* appears, in part, it is thought, to make further distinctions between Jewish and Christian communities. Not until the writings of Saint Ignatius of Antioch (d. 115) were the three degrees of priesthood described.

WORKING WITH THE TEXT AND PICTURES

✓ • Read the text on this page, and review the picture on pages 90 and 91.

✓ • Ask the students how we, as members of the common priesthood, work with the members of the ministerial or ordained priesthood. *(Together we work to spread the good news and serve others by using our talents and abilities. We support and pray for one another in our work.)*

✓ • See *Skill Note* below.

WORKING WITH THE ACTIVITY

Wrap Up

• Have a volunteer read aloud the summary statements.

✓ • Allow time for the students to consider their remaining questions and write them in their books.

• Discuss any remaining questions the students may have. You may wish to have the students write their questions on separate sheets of paper so that you can collect them and respond during the next session.

In Service to All

As members of the common priesthood, we work with those in the ministerial priesthood to spread the good news and to serve others. We might give encouragement to a younger brother or sister, or visit an elderly or sick parish member with a parent or grandparent. With the help of teachers and classmates, we might even start a discussion about racism or violence in schools.

When we generously offer our talents and abilities to the Body of Christ, we work with the ministerial priesthood to strengthen the Church. As head of his Body, Christ continues his work in the world through all of us who belong to him. In any vocation to which God calls us—single life, married, or ordained—we can grow in our relationship with God and with one another.

Have you thought about the vocation to which you might be called? Remember to seek the wisdom and counsel of the Spirit as you prepare for the time when you will decide what is right for you, and how you may best serve God and his Church.

Reflect on three specific things you can do to exercise your common priesthood. Share your thoughts with your Faith Partner.

WRAP UP

• Holy Orders is one of the Sacraments of Service.

• The Body of Christ is a community of the priesthood of all believers, also called the common priesthood.

• There are three degrees of ministerial priesthood: deacons, priests, and bishops.

• To be ordained means to be consecrated, set apart by Christ for his Church.

What questions do you have about this chapter?

_____

_____

_____

90 HOLY ORDERS

FAITH PARTNERSHIPS

Have the students work with their Faith Partners to find ways to live their common priesthood.

 SKILL NOTE

Point out to the students that when we are true to our vocations we are keeping important promises to ourselves. See pages 92 and 93 for more information about the skill for this chapter.

EXTENSION ACTIVITY

Getting involved Encourage the students to consider which of their talents and skills might be used in the service of others. Then invite a member of your parish staff to help the students learn about activities and events in which they could participate. You may wish to have the students create a checklist of parish activities. Then have them place next to each item one or two qualities that would help a person contribute successfully to the activity.

Student Leader Connection

Consider having the Student Leader do the following:

• Read aloud the *Wrap Up* summary statements.

• Use a Catholic almanac or a Catholic diocesan newspaper or Web site to learn more about the local bishop and prepare a report for the group.

• Help moderate the discussion for *Around the Group.*

Around the Group

Discuss the following question as a group.

What are the two most important qualities needed as a deacon, priest, or bishop?

After everyone has had a chance to share his or her responses, come up with a group answer upon which everyone can agree.

_____
_____
_____

What personal observations do you have about the group discussion and answer?

_____
_____
_____

Briefly...

At the beginning of this chapter, you were asked to consider the kind of person you would approach for advice and support. What qualities do you share with this person, and in what ways do these qualities help you share the common priesthood with a deacon or priest in your parish or community?

_____
_____
_____

WORKING WITH THE ACTIVITIES

Around the Group

- Present the question to the group, and allow time for discussion. You may need to moderate to keep the students focused on the question.

- Encourage the group members to listen to the opinions and perspectives of others.

- Ask the students to consider which attributes the members of the common priesthood and the members of the ministerial priesthood should share.

- If the group has agreed on an answer, direct the students to write it in their books. If they could not agree, direct them to list in their books the issues that were left unresolved and explain why.

- Encourage the students to note in their books their personal observations about the discussion and any final thoughts they have.

- See *Reflecting on Your Faith* below.

Briefly . . .

- Encourage the students to consider how their opinions may have changed since they responded to *What Do You Think?* on page 85.

- Invite the students to review the duties of the members of the common priesthood as well as those of deacons and priests.

- Allow the students enough time to write their responses in their books.

- See *Reflecting on Your Faith* below.

REFLECTING ON YOUR FAITH

Around the Group: What did the students' response tell you about their experiences of the ordained and ministerial priesthood? How can you help them deepen their understanding and appreciation of the ministerial priesthood?

Briefly: What are some of the connections you can make between the exercise of your common priesthood and the ministerial priesthood of a deacon or priest of your parish?

EXTENSION ACTIVITY

Guest speaker Invite a religious, a deacon, or a priest from your parish to talk with the students about vocations. Ask the speaker to describe how he or she prepared for a religious vocation and what the responsibilities and rewards are. The students might be especially interested in learning how the speaker decided that he or she had such a vocation. You may wish to help the speaker by preparing a three- to five-point list of ideas that he or she can address in talking with the students.

BACKGROUND

The development of seminaries The word *seminary* comes from the Latin word *seminarium,* or "seedbed." Seminaries originated because a decree from the Council of Trent (1563) required bishops to develop diocesan training schools for priests. These individual diocesan seminaries gradually established programs of study for the educational, pastoral, and spiritual formation of candidates for the ordained priesthood. In 1965 the Second Vatican Council issued the Decree on Priestly Formation, directing each national hierarchy to devise a national, rather than a diocesan, course of study for seminary students. At this time it is customary for aspiring priests and deacons to take some of their academic courses at institutions other than the seminary itself. The final year of priestly training is usually spent assisting at a parish or in some other pastoral assignment.

WORKING WITH THE SKILL

✓ • Discuss the promises associated with Holy Orders. *What does the ordination of a priest teach us about the skill of Keeping Promises?* (The priest promises obedience to his bishop and vows to remain celibate. His faithfulness to these promises is an example to guide us in being faithful to our own promises.)

✓ • Ask a volunteer to read aloud *Expressions of Faith. Why is Keeping Promises a skill Christians should have?* (Answers will vary.)

• Ask a volunteer to read *Scripture* aloud. *How would you explain what this Scripture passage means?* (It is critically important to keep one's word.)

✓ • See *Scripture Background* below.

• Have one or two volunteers take turns reading aloud *Think About It. What are some common promises that people make every day?* (Possible answers: promises to meet someone at a certain time, complete a chore, participate in an activity, attend an event, relay a message.)

• See *Reflecting on Your Faith* below.

• Invite the students to talk about their experiences of making and keeping promises. *What are some promises that are easy to keep? What are some that are difficult?* (Answers will vary.)

SKILLS FOR Christian Living

Keeping Promises

Expressions of Faith—

Keeping promises is an important part of living as a follower of Christ, whether we are married, single, or ordained. The ability to keep promises shows that we are people of strong character. It shows that we are trustworthy and responsible.

Scripture

"Let your word be 'Yes, Yes' or 'No, No'; anything more than this comes from the evil one."
Matthew 5:37 6th Sunday of Ordinary Time, Cycle

Think About It—

All of us make promises. We promise our friends that we will keep their secrets. We promise our families that we will be responsible. Some promises are easy to keep. Others shouldn't be made in the first place. And still others challenge us to work tirelessly, calling on the very best that is in us.

A young college basketball player left school after his sophomore year to turn pro. While playing for the NBA, he took correspondence courses during the season and attended classes during the off-season. Just three years later he got his degree. He went to his graduation ceremony in the afternoon and flew back in time to play for his team the same evening. night the team organization allowed any fan who came to the game with a college ID to in for only $10. When reporters asked the ne graduate about his achievement, he replied t he had promised his mother that he would f his degree. On this exciting day, he and his family celebrated the fulfillment of that pro

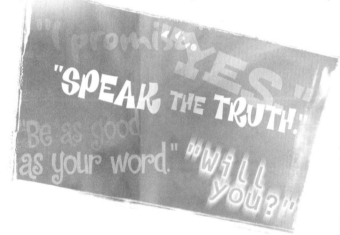

REFLECTING ON YOUR FAITH

How can you relate the athlete's story to an incident in your own experience? How can you best use this story to help the students understand the seriousness of keeping a promise?

SCRIPTURE BACKGROUND

The importance of personal integrity is spelled out for us in *Matthew 5:37.* This passage urges us to keep our word whenever we make a promise, and warns us against swearing an oath when we cannot keep our word or have no intention of keeping our word. Jesus encourages his followers to speak directly and simply on all matters. You may wish to point out that this passage is part of the readings for the Sixth Sunday of Ordinary Time, Cycle A. Refer to page 108 of this book for more information about the liturgical year.

RESOURCE Center

Student Leader Connection

Consider having the Student Leader do the following:

• **Prepare two or three pieces of advice about keeping promises to share with the group.**

• **Help moderate the discussion about experiences of making and keeping promises.**

• **Help moderate the group presentations of examples and advice for keeping promises.**

• **Organize a small group to plan a prayer service.**

Special Note: Remember to meet briefly with the Student Leader for Chapter 10. You may wish to provide him or her with the Student Leader Prep Page found on page R8.

Skill Steps-

Every promise you make will show what kind of person you really are. Here are some *Do*s and *Don't*s of keeping promises.

Do

Consider the motive behind the promise (both your own and that of the person asking for the promise)—*before you make it*. Is the motive a good one?

Consider the cost involved with the promise—*before you make it*. Can you do what it takes?

Say "I made a promise." When keeping a promise conflicts with someone or something else, simply come right out and say that you are under the obligation of a promise. People will understand and respect you for staying faithful to the promise you made.

Sacrifice. You may have to give up other things in order to keep your integrity, keep your word, and fulfill your promise.

Don't

Make promises automatically or quickly. Most of the time it's not necessary to promise—your "yes" or "no" should be good enough.

Make promises lightly. Every promise brings responsibility. Every promise will show the kind of person you are.

Keep a promise if someone is being hurt or endangered by it.

Keep a promise that makes you feel uncomfortable or worried. Tell a trusted adult.

Do something immoral in order to keep a promise (lying, being cruel, and so on).

Check It Out-

Place a check mark next to those statements with which you agree.

○ People count on me because my word is good.

○ I like it when people trust me because they know the truth is important to me.

○ I follow Jesus' example of being willing to make sacrifices to keep my promises.

How good is your word? Circle one of the responses below.

People can count on me.   It depends.

Not so good.   Don't believe a word I say.

What goal can you set for yourself to become better at keeping promises?

_____

Closing Prayer-

We place ourselves before you, Lord our God, with thanks for all you have given us. Guide the leaders of your Church. And give us the strength and courage to fulfill our promises. Amen.

WORKING WITH THE SKILL

- Ask a volunteer to read aloud *Skill Steps*.

- Arrange the students in two groups. Invite one group to think of examples or advice for each point under the *Do* list, and have the other group think of examples or advice for each point under the *Don't* list.

- Have the groups present their ideas. Encourage the students to respond by adding their own examples or advice as well as by commenting on whether or not they agree with what they have heard.

- Discuss the effects our promises have on others. *When were you hurt by a broken promise? How did you recover from a broken promise?* *(Answers will vary.)*

- Allow time for the students to complete *Check It Out*.

- See *Reflecting on Your Faith* below.

CLOSING PRAYER

- Gather together to pray the closing prayer. You may wish to use the following music from the *Give Your Gifts* series: "We Are Called" *(The Songs)*, "Psalm 104: Lord, Send Out Your Spirit" *(The Basics)*, or "Sing to the Glory of God" *(More Songs)* (GIA Publications, Inc.; distributed by Harcourt Religion Publishers).

- If time permits, direct the students to create their own closing reflections or prayers. You may wish to ask a few volunteers to read aloud what they have created or to plan a prayer service.

REFLECTING ON YOUR FAITH

Think about your own experiences of making and keeping promises. What promises do you have a particularly hard time keeping?

TEACHING TIP

Research follow-up You may wish to take time to review any research the students have been asked to complete. If the students need additional time to complete their research, set aside a few minutes at the beginning of the next session to allow them to share the information they have gathered.

MULTIPLE LEARNING STYLES

Closing prayer You may wish to have the students create their closing prayers in the style of a formal prayer or reflection; a poem or song; or a prayer service with readings, psalm response, and music. Remind the students that the tone of their responses can be different from that of the example but should remain respectful.

ASSESSMENT

The Assessment Page for Chapter 9 can be found on page R17.

LINK TO FAMILY

The corresponding Family Resource pages for this skill are 137–141.

Continuing
Our Promise

KEY CONTENT SUMMARY

We are called to live the sacraments every day. The continued celebration of the sacraments, especially Eucharist and Reconciliation, helps us experience God's loving grace in a unique way. We are called to be people of prayer. Christian prayer, personal and communal, can help us develop and strengthen our faith and discern our vocation.

PLANNING THE CHAPTER

	PACING	CONTENT	OBJECTIVES	MATERIALS
OPEN	Suggested Time: Parish **10 min.** School **25 min.** Your Time: ___ min.	pp. 94–95	• Recognize that the sacraments are efficacious signs of our faith, and that we are called to live the sacraments every day.	• candle, matches (optional) • a recording of Gregorian chant (optional) • symbol representing chapter theme (optional)
SEARCH	Suggested Time: Parish **25 min.** School **70 min.** Your Time: ___ min.	pp. 96–99	• Identify and examine how a strong personal and communal faith is vital to living a virtuous life and a Christian vocation. • Explore how prayer and the sacraments, especially the continued celebration of Reconciliation and the Eucharist, help us experience God's loving grace.	• Bibles • sacramentals (optional)
REFLECT	Suggested Time: Parish **10 min.** School **30 min.** Your Time: ___ min.	pp. 100–101	• Reflect on why it is especially important to live out Christ's message in our everyday relationships.	• Bibles (optional) • art supplies (optional)
LIVE	Suggested Time: Parish **15 min.** School **35 min.** Your Time: ___ min.	pp. 102–103	• Apply to our lives ways we can continue to live in the spirit of the sacraments.	• art supplies (optional) • music for prayer (optional) • *Living Our Faith Prayer Services* (optional) • copies of Assessment Page for Chapter 10 (p. R18) (optional)

CATECHISM IN CONTEXT

See *Catechism of the Catholic Church,* #2558. Together, our prayers and the sacraments transform us and make us more Christ-like. Whether our prayer is personal or communal, we praise God and thank him for all he has given us—our families, our faith communities, our world—as well as Jesus and the promise of eternal life. We also ask for God's love, forgiveness, and guidance throughout our lives.

In prayer we lift our minds and hearts to God. According to Scripture the heart is the place of decision and truth; it is the place of the covenant. It is where we answer who we are and whose we are. We maintain our covenant relationship with God through "heartfelt" prayer, which strengthens us to fulfill the promises we have made through the sacraments.

ONE-MINUTE RETREAT

READ

"You walk in this day as God's own messenger; whomever you meet, you meet in God's own way. You are there to be the presence of the Lord God, the presence of Christ, the presence of the Spirit, the presence of the Gospel. . . ."
—Archbishop Anthony Bloom

REFLECT

How can I be the presence of the Lord to others?

PRAY

Promised One, walk with me. Guide my steps as I strive to live out your message in my everyday relationships. As I encounter others, may the sharing of your loving grace mutually encourage each of us to live in the presence of your Spirit.

LIBRARY LINKS

BOOKS
FOR ADOLESCENTS

"Finding Your Own Way to Pray," by Kevin Jones-Prendergast (*Youth Update;* St. Anthony Messenger Press).

A much-needed and down-to-earth examination of prayer styles for teens.

Please Give Me One More Chance, Lord: The Secret of Prayer in a Teen's Life, by Lorraine Peterson (Bethany House Publishers, 1995).

Conversational prayers about common teen experiences.

"Praying on Paper," by Robyn Weaver (*Youth Update;* St. Anthony Messenger Press).

Teens write their thoughts and feelings—a creative way to explore a personal relationship with God.

FOR ADULTS

Character Counts! Youth Ministry Devotions from Extraordinary Christians, by Karl Leuthauser (Group Publishing, Inc.; Harcourt Religion Publishers, 1999).

True stories of men and women who lived their faith without compromise inspire young people to do the same.

Rites of Justice: The Sacraments and Liturgy as Ethical Imperatives, by Megan McKenna (Orbis Books, 1997).

The challenge to live what we celebrate.

Saying Amen: A Mystagogy of Sacrament, by Kathleen Hughes (Liturgy Training Publications, 1999).

Reflections on learning the sacraments by living them out.

MULTIMEDIA

Pray Today (video) (Stepstone Productions; distributed by Harcourt Religion Publishers).

Eight segments addressed to teen audiences help young people develop a better prayer life.

Prayer Services for Teens (CD-ROM) (Twenty-Third Publications).

A searchable collection of 226 prayer services keyed to seasons, the Lectionary, and themes relevant to adolescents.

FEATURE PREPARATION

STUDENT LEADER CONNECTION

The Student Leader Prep Page for this chapter is located on page R8. You may wish to provide this information to the Student Leader as an introduction and resource for the chapter.

FAITH PARTNERSHIPS

Chapter 10 has the same Faith Partners as Chapter 9. Several opportunities for Faith Partner discussions have been marked throughout the chapter. You may wish to consider other opportunities as you prepare the lesson.

SKILL NOTES

The skill for this chapter is Keeping Promises. You may wish to build on what the students have learned in the previous chapter as you teach this chapter. A few Skill Notes have been called out to help you. The skill lesson for this chapter can be found on pages 102 and 103.

A check mark indicates the chapter's essential questions, statements, activities, and features. If time is limited, such as in a parish group setting, this icon will help you direct the students through the lesson.

Continuing Our Promise

Heavenly Father, challenge us to share the message of your love. Dare us to live honestly. Urge us to stand up for our beliefs and to speak out against injustice. Confront us with the truth about ourselves.

94

KEY POINTS FROM CHAPTER 9

You may wish to review these points with the students before you begin the new chapter:

- Holy Orders is one of the Sacraments of Service.
- Members of the ministerial priesthood guide the laity in the development of their faith. The ordained serve the Church community in the name and person of Jesus.
- There are three degrees of Holy Orders—deacon, priest, and bishop.
- Keeping Promises is a Skill for Christian Living.

✓ GATHERING

Engage the students in a brief conversation about their lives today: the things they enjoy doing and the things they are looking forward to experiencing as they grow older.

✓ PRAYER

Play a recording of a traditional or contemporary Gregorian chant, if available, and invite the students to reflect silently for several moments. Then pray the opening prayer aloud. If fire regulations permit, you may wish to light a candle at this time.

RESOURCE Center

PRAYER ENVIRONMENT

If you have created a prayer space for the room, you may wish to represent the theme of this chapter by displaying symbols of all the sacraments.

LINK TO MUSIC

Gregorian chant is the music many people associate with the traditional Latin Mass of the Catholic Church. It originated as a form of *plain song*, or plain chant, and is distinguished by one vocal or melodic line, frequently sung without instrumental accompaniment. Gregorian chant began its ascendancy during the reign of Pope Gregory I (d. 604) and is named in honor of this saint, scholar, and doctor of the Church. Point out to the students that the music we hear and sing at Mass and other services is, like Gregorian chant, a form of prayer.

Student Leader Connection

Consider having the Student Leader do the following:

- **Play a recording of Gregorian chant to accompany the opening prayer.**
- **Pray aloud the opening prayer with the group.**
- **Read aloud *The Good Life?* on page 95.**
- **Help moderate a group discussion on what it means to live a good life.**

What Do You Think?

On the lines below, create a Top Ten list of what you think makes your life worthwhile.

1. _____   6. _____
2. _____   7. _____
3. _____   8. _____
4. _____   9. _____
5. _____   10. _____

What will your life be like in ten years? Describe what you think you will be doing and what you think you will be like.

_____
_____
_____
_____
_____

The Good Life?

Adolescence is a busy and sometimes confusing time. Friendships change. Family relationships change. The decisions we make are more difficult than those we made just a few years ago.

As an adolescent, you may feel pressured to try drugs or sex in order to be part of a group. Perhaps things have been so bad at times that you have even considered suicide. No matter what, you always have the need to feel accepted and loved. How can the sacraments and your faith help you deal with these issues?

For Christians the good life is the life that Christ offers us. It is the virtuous life that helps us grow in faith and love. Through the sacraments God offers us the spiritual nourishment and strength to make good decisions and to live in healthy relationships with others.

OPEN   95

WORKING WITH THE ACTIVITY

What Do You Think?

✓ • Allow time for the students to record their thoughts in the space provided.

• See *Reflecting on Your Faith* below.

✓ • *What Do You Think?* is intended as a personal pre-assessment. The students should not be asked to share their responses.

WORKING WITH THE TEXT AND PICTURES

✓ • Read the text on this page, and review the pictures on pages 94 and 95.

• Ask the students what it means to have a good life. *(Responses will vary.)*

• Discuss with the students the fact that adolescence can be a confusing time. **What threatens a good life?** *(Answers will vary.)* **What are some of the pressures that people your age face?** *(Answers will vary.)*

✓ • Have volunteers suggest some of the ways that adolescents can find support and guidance. **Who or what supports you in your good times and tough times?** *(Possible answers: friends, parents, teachers, heroes, music, activities and interests, faith.)*

• Direct the students' attention to the pictures on pages 94 and 95. Explain how the aesthetics of the great cathedral (Bom Jesus do Monte, Braga, Minho, Portugal) might inspire believers to reflect and pray. Contrast this image with the simplicity of the pictured prayer circle. **What effects might our surroundings have on our prayers?** *(Answers will vary.)*

• Discuss values and ideals that strengthen us in difficult or uncertain times. **Why is a person's integrity a key to a good life?** *(Answers will vary.)*

REFLECTING ON YOUR FAITH

Think about the things that make your life a good life. How has your opinion changed over the years?

MULTIPLE LEARNING STYLES

Talk show discussion   Use a talk show format to discuss what makes for a good life. Ask a volunteer to be the host and others to play the roles of a well-known saint or holy person, a specialist on aging, a dictator interested only in political power, a CEO concerned only with profits, and a Hollywood star focused only on fame. Invite audience participation from the group.

ART BACKGROUND

At the beginning of the eighteenth century, the Archbishop of Braga commissioned the building of the imposing granite and white alabaster staircase that leads from the town of Braga to the Cathedral of Bom Jesus do Monte. Long a place of pilgrimage and one of Portugal's most photographed sites, the church and its terraced gardens are meant to promote reflection on Christ's passion. The neoclassical structure of the present church, the third to be built on the site, is the work of local architect Carlos Amarante.

WORKING WITH THE TEXT AND PICTURES

✓

- Read the text and review the pictures on pages 96 and 97.

- Refer to the collage suggesting the communion of saints. *What does the term communion of saints mean? (We are united with all those Christians who have lived before us; we are part of a community of faith.)*

✓

- Help the students recall what they have learned about how Christ can transform our lives. *What changes can Christ make in our lives through the sacraments? (Our faith in Christ is deepened, and our relationships with ourselves and others become stronger and more positive. Through the sacraments we experience God's grace in rituals that celebrate life, nourishment, reconciliation, healing, and service.)*

✓

- See *Skill Note* below.

WORKING WITH THE ACTIVITY

Catholics Believe

- Ask a volunteer to read aloud *Catholics Believe.*

✓

- Allow time for the students to complete the activity.

- See *Reflecting on Your Faith* below.

- Encourage the students to share with the group their thoughts about the paraphrased Catechism statement and their responses to the direction that follows.

Living the
Sacraments

Participating in the sacraments is important in developing a faith life. Through the sacraments we experience God's saving love in rituals that celebrate life, nourishment, reconciliation, healing, and service. We become aware of our relationship with God—the Father, Son, and Spirit.

(S) But in order to fully appreciate the sacraments, we need to see past the actual rite to recognize how Christ can transform our lives. For example, our celebration of the Sacraments of Christian Initiation doesn't end after we celebrate the rites of Baptism, Eucharist, or Confirmation. Because we become members of Christ's Body, we are called to change the way we think and act. As members of the Church community, we should live as signs of God at work in the world—we should live as sacraments.

Catholics *Believe*

Prayer is a surge of the heart, embracing both sadness and joy.
See Catechism, #2558.

Sketch a picture or write a poem that expresses your feelings about prayer.

Share your thoughts with your Faith Partner. FAITH PARTNERSHIP

FAITH PARTNERSHIPS

You may wish to invite the students to write a prayer that expresses sadness or joy.

(S) SKILL NOTE

Our baptismal promises are an example of the promises we are called upon to keep in our lives. See pages 102 and 103 for more information about the skill for this chapter.

REFLECTING ON YOUR FAITH

Reflect on your experience with prayer. How can you strengthen your prayer life?

Student Leader Connection

Consider having the Student Leader do the following:

- **Help moderate a discussion about the meaning each of the sacraments can have in our lives.**

- **Read aloud *Catholics Believe.***

- **Help moderate the discussion about the importance of the Lord's Prayer.**

RESOURCE Center

Focus On

The Lord's Prayer
The Lord's Prayer we pray during Mass is based on two Gospel passages, *Matthew 6:9–13* and *Luke 11:2–4*. Many people have recognized the importance of this prayer to their individual lives and to the life of the Church. For example, Saint Thomas Aquinas called it the most perfect private prayer.

Through the Sacraments of Initiation we are brought into a community that witnesses to the work of Christ. Through Baptism and Confirmation we are joined to a group of people who care about us. This group wants only what is best for us. Members of the Body of Christ can help us make good decisions that will affect our lives in a positive way.

As part of the Church family, we gather together to be nourished through the Sacrament of the Eucharist. In this sacrament we receive God's love and strength to help us deal with the problems and temptations we face. In fact, each of us can become a sacrament to others by being a sign of love and strength to them. We can look for opportunities to listen to and care for others in a respectful and loving way.

In Reconciliation, one of the Sacraments of Healing, we are forgiven for those times when we have sinned. We, in turn, are better able to forgive others when they hurt us or damage our relationship. We can be peacemakers by trying to resolve arguments or conflicts between friends or family members.

People around us may be suffering because they do not feel accepted and loved. Some may be experiencing physical or emotional abuse. There are many occasions when people need us to reach out to them and be sensitive to what they are feeling. At these times we can bring healing into their lives.

Sometimes a young person can get very sick or be in a serious accident. When this happens, the Sacrament of the Anointing of the Sick—the other Sacrament of Healing—can bring God's grace, love, and forgiveness to him or her. It is especially during these unexpected times that the members of the Body of Christ offer comfort to one another.

The Sacraments of Service are ways in which adults answer God's call to serve others through marriage or ordination. You may eventually make the decision to follow the vocation of marriage or priesthood. Or you may choose religious life or the single life. But for now you should pray for God's guidance and think about what future vocation will allow you to best use your gifts and abilities.

One important way we prepare ourselves for this decision is by developing healthy relationships. Through our friendships and family relationships, we learn about our strengths and weaknesses. We learn to be honest with others and with ourselves. Most of all, we learn respect. We learn to respect people as they are now, and to respect who they can become with God's grace.

As Christians we must care for others and never use people for our own benefit. To do so would go against everything that Jesus taught. He called us to be servants to others. And when we share the gift of ourselves and show others the respect they deserve, we are living lives of service.

SEARCH 97

WORKING WITH THE TEXT AND PICTURES

✓ • Review the text and pictures on this page.

• Discuss how the Sacraments of Christian Initiation change us. **When we are initiated into the Church, how do we change?** *(We become members of the Body of Christ, signs of Christ at work in the world, and part of a community that witnesses to the work of Christ.)*

• Discuss the Sacraments of Healing. **How can we experience Christ's love through the Sacraments of Healing?** *(We receive forgiveness, gain the strength to forgive and be peacemakers, and reach out to others who are hurting.)*

✓ • Discuss vocations that might best allow the students to use their gifts and abilities. **How can you prepare now for your future decision about the vocation to which you are being called?** *(Possible answers: establish healthy relationships, learn my strengths and weaknesses, learn to respect myself and others.)*

WORKING WITH THE ACTIVITY
Focus On

• Have a volunteer read aloud *Focus On*.

✓ • Have the students read silently the two Scripture passages cited in *Focus On*.

✓ • Discuss the importance of the Lord's Prayer. **Can you remember learning the Lord's Prayer? How did you learn it? When do we pray this prayer?** *(Answers will vary.)*

INK TO SOCIAL SCIENCE

emind the students that living as Jesus calls us to live means eveloping a social conscience and working on behalf of those ho are poor and suffering. Encourage the students to learn much as they can about the reality of poverty, hunger, and ckness throughout the world. Have them use the Internet to search famine statistics and the spread of various diseases. ou might also suggest that they identify and study the international aid organizations that work to solve these problems, ch as Catholic Relief Services *(www.catholicrelief.org),* the aryknoll Office for Global Concerns *(www.maryknoll.org),* d Habitat for Humanity International *(www.habitat.org).* You ay also wish to refer the students to *www.thehungersite.com.*

BACKGROUND

The Lord's Prayer When the apostles asked Jesus to teach them to pray, he taught them the prayer we call the Lord's Prayer. This prayer begins by our calling God "Father" as Jesus did. The prayer consists of seven parts. We give glory to God, anticipate the coming of his kingdom, and trust in his will. We present our needs to him by asking him to care for us, to forgive us, to keep us from temptation, and to rescue us from evil. The Lord's Prayer helps us open our hearts to God in love.

WORKING WITH THE TEXT AND PICTURES

✓ • Read *The Prayer in Our Hearts* on pages 98 and 99, and review the pictures on these pages.

✓ • Use *Vocabulary* below to help the students understand the terms *personal prayer* and *communal prayer.*

✓ • Discuss prayer. Include the *what, when, how,* and *why* of prayer. **How can prayer help us find peace and strength?** *(Possible answers: It can give us time to reflect and arrive at good decisions; it allows us to rely on God's wisdom, forgiveness, guidance, and love.)*

✓ • Communal prayer means praying with others. **Why is the liturgy an important communal prayer?** *(The liturgy combines our prayers with those of all the Church, with the Sacrament of the Eucharist, and with our sacrificial offerings in Christ to God the Father.)*

• Focus on the photographs. Explain these as illustrations of actions that constitute prayer. **What parts of your daily life might be considered actions of prayer?** *(Answers will vary.)*

WORKING WITH THE ACTIVITY

Our Christian Journey

• Ask a volunteer to read aloud *Our Christian Journey.*

✓ • Discuss Mother Teresa and the Missionaries of Charity. **What qualities helped Mother Teresa live her vocation?** *(Possible answers: Compassion—she cared about others and wished to help them; faith—she started without resources; courage—she faced poverty, disease, and death; perseverance—she never gave up.)*

• See *Background* below.

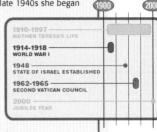

A Woman of Caring

Mother Teresa founded the Missionaries of Charity, a religious order of women dedicated to caring for those who are sick and dying among the poorest people in the world. Mother Teresa was born in Macedonia but spent most of her life in India. When she was just eighteen, she joined a group of Irish sisters and was sent to India to teach in a high school for the daughters of wealthy families. In the late 1940s she began her vocation of caring for those who were poor. She taught children who lived in the slums of Calcutta, cared for those who were sick, and eased the suffering of those who were dying. Eventually, a number of young women joined her in her work, and in 1950 she organized the Missionaries of Charity. Since then the sisters of her order have established hospitals and schools throughout the world. In 1979 Mother Teresa received the Nobel Peace Prize for her work. Believed by many to be a saint, Mother Teresa died in 1997.

For further information: Research the Missionaries of Charity on the Internet or read about the life of Mother Teresa in one of her many biographies.

1900	2000

1910–1997
MOTHER TERESA'S LIFE

1914–1918
WORLD WAR I

1948
STATE OF ISRAEL ESTABLISHED

1962–1965
SECOND VATICAN COUNCIL

2000
JUBILEE YEAR

The Prayer in **Our Hearts**

Like the practice of the sacraments, prayer helps us live as God intended. Through prayer we grow in our faith life and reflect on being sacraments. Prayer is raising our minds and hearts to God. We pray with our thoughts, words, and actions.

When we think of prayer, we usually picture ourselves communicating individually with God. We could be in a church, at the park, or at school. This personal prayer is very important to us as we develop our faith. As members of the Body of Christ, we often join together with others in church or elsewhere for communal prayer. The most important communal prayer is liturgy.

VOCABULARY ✓

Personal prayer is an individual's prayer. We pray in private thanksgiving, lonely anguish, or reflective calm.

Praying with others is *communal prayer.* Praying before and after meals with our families and celebrating the Eucharist together are examples of communal prayer. Prayer as a faith community is a special form of communal prayer.

BACKGROUND

Time line The Missionaries of Charity, with headquarters in India, are comprised of both men and women religious.

Archduke Franz Ferdinand, heir to the Austrian throne, was assassinated by a Serb in 1914. This event was the catalyst for World War I (1914–1918).

Acting for the League of Nations, the British carved out the state of Israel from the Ottoman Empire. Independent since 1948, Israel is the focus of much controversy in the Middle East.

Called by Pope John XXIII, the Second Vatican Council updated Catholic understanding of Church teachings and practice and helped lead the renewal of the liturgical and spiritual life of the Church throughout the world.

The Jubilee Year commemorated two thousand years of Christ's presence in human history. The Church promoted this year as a significant time in which to spread the gospel and work for social justice.

Student Leader Connection

Consider having the Student Leader do the following:

• **Work with one or two other students to create a booklet of prayers to be distributed to the group.**

• **Research and present information on one of the items on the time line from *Our Christian Journey.***

• **Read aloud *Opening the Word.***

RESOURCE Center

From the heights of joy to the depths of grief, we can turn to God in prayer. Before our meals we ask God's blessing on our food and bless God in return for providing for us. We adore him for the awesome God he is. We humbly ask him for the things we need and for help in facing the many challenges and pressures of our lives. We ask God's forgiveness when we sin and when we choose selfishness at the expense of others. We pray for others who are close to us or who may be far away but whose needs are ours in the Body of Christ. We thank God for the many gifts and joys of our lives. We praise God, who is the source and goal of our lives.

Our Life **in Christ**

(S) When we celebrate the sacraments and when we pray, we realize that Christ is present in our lives. He is with us when we find it easy to live virtuous lives, and he is with us when we are struggling to understand how to live as he wants. Christ is with us when our friends believe the worst about us, when our parents don't understand us, and when our teachers and coaches are pushing us to do our best. We can count on him to be there to guide us no matter what we are experiencing.

Throughout our lives, we will experience the breakup of some friendships and the development of new ones. But there is one friend who will never leave us and who will always love us—Jesus. Jesus is our Savior, brother, and friend. Each of us has experienced both good and bad times. Maybe the bad times were caused by a parent who didn't really understand our problem, or by a friend or peer who let us down. Whatever the cause, Jesus is always there to share the good and the bad times. We can talk to him anytime and

anywhere, and he will listen. Because Jesus was once our age, he understands what our needs are. Like us, he was also tempted. He experienced suffering and death. Jesus is the sacrament of all sacraments. With Jesus by our side, we will never be alone or unloved.

Opening the Word

Scripture in the Lord books

"*. . . I am with you always, to the end of the age.*" *Matthew 28:20*

Read *Matthew 28:16–20* as well as *Romans 12:3–8, Ephesians 2:19–22,* and *Colossians 3:12–17.* What does it mean to be a Christian?

_____

_____

_____

_____

WORKING WITH THE TEXT AND PICTURES

✓ • Read *Our Life in Christ* on this page.

• Discuss our relationship with Christ. **When are we aware of Christ with us?** *(Possible answers: when we celebrate the sacraments, when we pray, when we are good, when we struggle to live as Christ wishes us to do, always.)*

✓ • Remind the students that although some relationships end, our relationship with Christ need not end because he always loves us and is always with us. Only we can destroy the relationship.

✓ • See *Skill Note* below.

WORKING WITH THE ACTIVITY
Opening the Word

• Ask a volunteer to read aloud *Opening the Word.*

✓ • Allow sufficient time for the students to read the additional Scripture passages and respond to the question. *(Possible answers: spreading the good news about Jesus, teaching others what Jesus taught, using our talents to cheerfully and compassionately minister to others, participating in the life of our faith community and the Church, acting in the name of Jesus, making wise decisions, and treating others with love and respect.)*

✓ • See *Scripture Background* below.

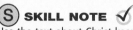

(S) **SKILL NOTE** ✓

Use the text about Christ keeping his promises to us to encourage the students to practice this skill. See pages 102 and 103 for more information.

SCRIPTURE BACKGROUND ✓

Matthew 28:20 reminds us of two things: that Jesus promised to be with us always and that we await the fullness of the kingdom of God at the end of time. The kingdom has been established by Jesus, but he has not yet fully returned. We are called to live faithfully as we wait for our place at the heavenly banquet and for the fulfillment of the kingdom at the end of time. You may wish to point out that this passage is part of the readings for the Feast of the Ascension of the Lord, Cycle A, and for Trinity Sunday, Cycle B. Refer to page 108 of this book for more information about the liturgical year.

MULTIPLE LEARNING STYLES

Praying with sacramentals Show various sacramentals to the students and describe how each can be used in prayer. Then invite the group to pray together using one of the sacramentals. The students may light candles, bless themselves with holy water, and then pray before a crucifix or a statue of Mary. You may wish to review or teach them how to pray the Rosary. See *Prayers and Resources* in both the student edition and the leader's guide for the Hail Mary, the Lord's Prayer, the Doxology, and the Apostles' Creed.

WORKING WITH THE TEXT AND PICTURES

✓ • Read the text on this page, and review the picture on pages 100 and 101.

✓ • Ask the students to identify challenges they face (in addition to those listed on page 100). *What advice do you have for young people facing these challenges?* (Answers will vary.)

• Focus on the photograph. Ask the students to imagine that they are listing items or people to pray about today. Invite volunteers to share their responses with the group. (Answers will vary.)

✓ • See *Skill Note* below.

WORKING WITH THE ACTIVITY

Wrap Up

• Have a volunteer read aloud the summary statements.

✓ • Allow time for the students to consider their remaining questions and write them in their books.

Living Our Faith

Some people say they are Christians, but they mistreat their friends and often deceive their families. Other people don't say very much about what they believe, but they set a good example of faithfulness. How we present ourselves, how we treat those closest to us, and how we behave toward those we barely know tell the world who we really are.

To be united with Christ and to be a member of his Body by virtue of our Baptism should mean something in our daily living. It should mean that Christ directs our actions, informs our ideals, and guides our lives.

No one reaches the height of his or her faith life immediately and becomes close to God all at once. Things that seem insignificant at the moment may be quite important in terms of our faith life and how we develop as people of character. For example, it counts when we overlook an insult. It counts when we share our talents with those who need us. And it counts when we tell the truth at a time when it is hard to do so.

All of us have challenges to face every day. Resisting the temptation to have a beer, turning down cigarettes or drugs, and avoiding sexual activity can be the measure of how well our faith works to help us become people of integrity. That's why the sacraments are so important in our lives. Through them, the Holy Spirit gives us the grace we need to live every day as Christ would.

S Reflect on how we can be Christ-like in our relationships. Share your thoughts with your Faith Partner.

WRAP UP

•We meet Jesus in the sacraments.

•We recognize Jesus as our brother and most loyal friend, the one whose friendship with us never falters and never ends.

•We grow in our faith life through the sacraments and prayer.

•We are called to live the sacraments.

•Jesus taught us to pray the Lord's Prayer, which has been called the perfect prayer for the members of his Body.

What questions do you have about this chapter?

_____

_____

_____

100 CONTINUING OUR PROMISE

FAITH PARTNERSHIPS

Have each Faith Partner describe to the other a person who is Christ-like. Remind the students that their subjects may be people whom they know personally.

 S SKILL NOTE

This text can help the students understand that keeping promises is a sign of the personal integrity that characterizes the committed Christian's pattern of behavior. See pages 102 and 103 for further information.

EXTENSION ACTIVITY

Posters for living faith   Have the students scan Proverbs 10–24 and select one piece of advice for living faithfully every day. Then distribute art supplies and chart paper, and have the students create posters or bumper stickers that encourage members of their faith community to live that advice. Hang the completed posters or bumper stickers where everyone can see them.

RESOURCE Center

Student Leader Connection

Consider having the Student Leader do the following:

• **Read aloud the *Wrap Up* summary statements.**

• **Help moderate the *Around the Group* discussion.**

• **Brainstorm with the group the things that make life worthwhile.**

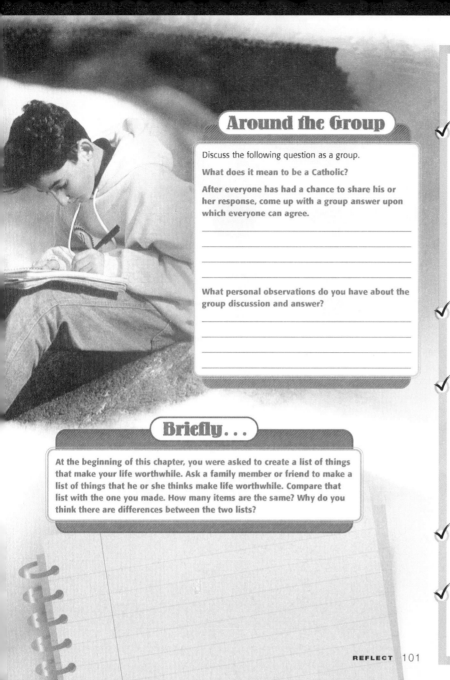

Around the Group

Discuss the following question as a group.

What does it mean to be a Catholic?

After everyone has had a chance to share his or her response, come up with a group answer upon which everyone can agree.

_____
_____
_____
_____

What personal observations do you have about the group discussion and answer?

_____
_____
_____
_____

Briefly . . .

At the beginning of this chapter, you were asked to create a list of things that make your life worthwhile. Ask a family member or friend to make a list of things that he or she thinks make life worthwhile. Compare that list with the one you made. How many items are the same? Why do you think there are differences between the two lists?

REFLECT 101

WORKING WITH THE ACTIVITIES

Around the Group

- Present the question to the group, and allow time for discussion. You may need to moderate to keep the students focused on the question.
- Encourage the group members to listen to the opinions and perspectives of others.
- Help the students answer the question by asking them to recall what they have learned from their study of the sacraments. Invite them to consider how the sacraments have helped them grow closer to Christ and learn to rely on him.
- If the group has agreed on an answer, direct the students to write it in their books. If they could not agree, direct them to list in their books the issues that were left unresolved and explain why.
- Encourage the students to note in their books their personal observations about the discussion and any final thoughts they have.
- See *Reflecting on Your Faith* below.

Briefly . . .

- Encourage the students to consider how their opinions may have changed since they responded to *What Do You Think?* on page 95.
- Ask the students to think about what makes life worthwhile. Encourage them to consider the importance of the sacraments in their lives.
- Allow time for the students to write their responses in their books.
- See *Reflecting on Your Faith* below.

REFLECTING ON YOUR FAITH

Around the Group: Reflect on the students' explanations of what it means to be a Catholic. How have you communicated to the students your understanding of what it means to be a Catholic?

Briefly: Ask a friend or your spouse to list what makes life worthwhile to him or her. How does this list compare with what you think and what the students think? Are there things you would like to reconsider? Why?

TEACHING TIP

Summarizing   Because this is the last *Around the Group* discussion question, review with the students what they have learned about the sacraments in this theme. Encourage the students to recall and summarize earlier *Around the Group* discussions as well as activities and research they have done.

WORKING WITH THE SKILL

✓ • Remind the students that the skill for Chapters 9 and 10 is Keeping Promises. Discuss with the students how they have tried to use the skill since the end of Chapter 9.

✓ • Review with the students how, through the sacraments, God helps us keep promises. *(The sacraments strengthen us to be Christ-like; they influence our character formation and our will to be good and do what is right.)*

✓ • Ask a volunteer to read aloud *Expressions of Faith.* **What promises have we made to God and the Church?** *(our baptismal promises)* **How do we keep these promises?** *(by celebrating the sacraments and seeking to live lives of faith and goodness)*

• Invite the students to read *Scripture* silently.

• Discuss the Scripture passage. **What does this quotation mean?** *(Possible answer: that Jesus asks us to rely on the Holy Spirit, who helps us keep Jesus' teachings.)*

✓ • See *Scripture Background* below.

✓ • Have a volunteer read aloud *Skill Steps.* Review each step with the students. **How does our life in Christ help us keep promises?** *(Possible answer: Because we are followers of Jesus, we can be strengthened to undertake the sacrifices that promises may require of us; the sacraments remind us of the promises we have made to God and the Church.)*

• Ask a volunteer to read aloud *Skill Builder.* **What kinds of promises are involved in our relationships?** *(Possible answer: We may promise to keep secrets, to be truthful, and to help each other in various ways.)*

✓ • Allow the students enough time to complete the activity.

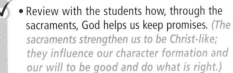

Keeping Promises

Expressions of Faith–

Our life in Christ goes back to the promises made at Baptism. These promises rejected sin and set the direction of our lives as being lived for Christ. Every time we celebrate a sacrament, we are keeping the promises made at our Baptism.

> "But the Advocate, the Holy Spirit, whom the Father will send in my name, will teach you everything, and remind you of all that I have said to you."
> **John 14:26**   6th Sunday of Easter, Cycle C

Skill Steps–

Remember that making and keeping promises is a skill that we use all our lives. We know that we will be judged on how good our word is, and we know that sometimes it isn't easy to keep our word.
  Here are some key points to remember:

● Keeping promises is an important part of living as a follower of Jesus.

● The ability to keep a promise shows that we are trustworthy and responsible.

● Promises can require sacrifices.

● Consider whether a promise should be made and what would be involved in keeping it.

Skill Builder–

To some extent, all of our relationships involve promises.
  What is one of the promises we make to God or that God makes to us in each of the sacraments?

1. Baptism _____
2. Confirmation _____
3. Eucharist _____
4. Reconciliation _____
5. Anointing of the Sick _____
6. Matrimony _____
7. Holy Orders _____

Share your responses and thoughts with your Faith Partner

SCRIPTURE BACKGROUND

In *John 14:26* Jesus promises the apostles that after he leaves them physically he will send the Holy Spirit to be with them. This passage reminds us of Jesus' relationship with his Father, who sends the Spirit, and indicates the Spirit's role in the lives of Christians. The Holy Spirit prompts the followers of Jesus to remember and understand what Jesus taught. The Spirit strengthens the community of believers and helps them grow in faith, hope, and love. You may wish to point out that this passage is part of the readings for the Sixth Sunday of Easter, Cycle C. Refer to page 108 of this book for more information about the liturgical year.

FAITH PARTNERSHIPS

Ask for volunteers among the Faith Partners to share with the group their responses to the *Skill Builder* activity.

Student Leader Connection

Consider having the Student Leader do the following:

• **Read *Scripture* aloud.**

• **Read aloud *Skill Steps* and review each of the points with the group.**

• **Introduce *Putting It into Practice* by reading the instructions aloud.**

• **Organize a small group to plan a prayer service.**

Putting It into Practice—

How well are you making and keeping promises? Have you broken a promise recently? Are you struggling to keep a promise? Are you facing sacrifices that will have to be made? Do you have to re-establish your priorities in order to keep your word?

For each category below, identify a promise that you have made. You can use a word, a symbol, or an initial. Then rate how well you are doing with the promise. Finally, decide what you will have to do next to keep your promise.

Promise Made With	Promise	Rating	What To Do Next
God	_____	_____	_____
Church	_____	_____	_____
Parent	_____	_____	_____
Family Member	_____	_____	_____
Self	_____	_____	_____

Keeping promises is a skill that affects every part of our lives. It affects the relationship we have with our families, how we interact with our friends, and to what extent we live as faithful members of the Body of Christ.

Based on what you have learned about this skill, what do you think are your strengths when it comes to making promises?

_____

_____

What are some things you need to work on?

_____

_____

Closing Prayer—

Lord, we aren't sure what our *futures* hold, but we know you will be there for us. We know we can count on your *love* and *strength* and encouragement. We promise that we will remember to *turn to you* because in guiding us, you *reveal* yourself to us. Help us become the people you want us to be. Draw us *closer* to you. Amen.

WORKING WITH THE SKILL

- Ask a volunteer to read aloud the text for *Putting It into Practice.*

✓ • Give the students sufficient time to complete the activity.

✓ • Talk with the students about this skill. *What have you learned about making and keeping promises or what has been reinforced in your current approach to keeping promises?* (Answers will vary.)

- See *Reflecting on Your Faith* below.

CLOSING PRAYER

✓ • Gather together to pray the closing prayer. You may wish to use the following music from the *Give Your Gifts* series: "I Say Yes, My Lord" *(The Songs),* "Psalm 63: As Morning Breaks" *(The Basics),* or "Hope at the Crossroads" *(More Songs)* (GIA Publications, Inc.; distributed by Harcourt Religion Publishers).

- If time permits, direct the students to create their own closing reflections or prayers. You may wish to ask a few volunteers to read aloud what they have created or to plan a prayer service. As an alternative for prayer, you may wish to use "Sacraments: Prayer Service E" from *Living Our Faith Prayer Services* by Robert Piercy and Linda Baltikas (GIA Publications, Inc.; distributed by Harcourt Religion Publishers).

REFLECTING ON YOUR FAITH
Think about the strengths and weaknesses you have shown in keeping promises. In what ways could you do better?

EXTENSION ACTIVITY
Designing a maze Distribute construction paper and markers to the students. Invite them to design mazes that show some of the problems, challenges, rewards, and achievements that people their age encounter as they make and try to keep their promises. You might have the students work in groups to design larger and more complicated mazes. When the students have completed the activity, ask them to exchange papers with another student or group and try to solve the mazes.

TEACHING TIP
Research follow-up You may wish to take time to review any research the students have been asked to complete.

MULTIPLE LEARNING STYLES
Closing prayer You may wish to have the students create their closing prayers in the style of a formal prayer or reflection; a poem or song; or a prayer service with readings, psalm response, and music. Remind the students that the tone of their responses can be different from that of the example but should remain respectful.

ASSESSMENT
The Assessment Page for Chapter 10 can be found on page R18.

LINK TO FAMILY
The corresponding Family Resource pages for this skill are 137–141.

Prayers and
Resources

The Lord's Prayer

Our Father, who art in heaven,
hallowed be thy name;
thy kingdom come;
thy will be done on earth as it is in heaven.
Give us this day our daily bread;
and forgive us our trespasses
as we forgive those who trespass against us;
and lead us not into temptation,
but deliver us from evil.
Amen.

Hail Mary

Hail, Mary, full of grace,
the Lord is with you!
Blessed are you among women,
and blessed is the fruit of your womb, Jesus.
Holy Mary, Mother of God,
pray for us sinners,
now and at the hour of our death.
Amen.

THE TEN COMMANDMENTS

1. I am the Lord your God. You shall not have strange gods before me.

2. You shall not take the name of the Lord your God in vain.

3. Remember to keep holy the Lord's day.

4. Honor your father and your mother.

5. You shall not kill.

6. You shall not commit adultery.

7. You shall not steal.

8. You shall not bear false witness against your neighbor.

9. You shall not covet your neighbor's wife.

10. You shall not covet your neighbor's goods.

BACKGROUND

The Lord's Prayer   This prayer has its roots in Scripture. In the Gospels of Matthew *(Matthew 6:9–13)* and Luke *(Luke 11:2–4),* Jesus teaches a form of this prayer to his disciples. There are several versions of this prayer in use among Christians of all denominations. Catholics refer to this prayer as the *Our Father,* from its first words. Protestant Christians include in the text of the prayer the additional phrase "for the kingdom, the power, and the glory are yours, now and for ever," which has its roots in Jewish mystical prayer. At Mass, Catholics add these words after the priest prays a prayer known as the *embolism.* The Lord's Prayer is also prayed as part of the Rosary. (For more information on the significance of the Lord's Prayer in Christian spirituality, see the *Catechism of the Catholic Church,* #2759–2865.)

The Hail Mary   The first part of this prayer was used as an antiphon in the Little Office of Our Lady, a form of the Liturgy of the Hours prayed during the Middle Ages. The antiphon combines the Archangel Gabriel's greeting at the annunciation *(Luke 1:26–28)* with Elizabeth's words of praise for Mary's motherhood *(Luke 1:42).* The second part of the prayer (from "Holy Mary" on) was added as devotion to Mary grew.

The Ten Commandments   Also know as the *Decalogue,* or "ten words," the Ten Commandments sum up the duties of the covenant relationship between God and his people. The wording and numbering of the commandments given here is traditional to Catholic and Lutheran communities, originating with Saint Augustine. (Part III, Section Two of the Catechism is devoted to an exploration of the Ten Commandments.)

THE BEATITUDES

Blessed are the poor in spirit,
  for theirs is the kingdom
  of heaven.

Blessed are they who mourn,
  for they will be comforted.

Blessed are the meek,
  for they will inherit the land.

Blessed are they who hunger and
thirst for righteousness,
  for they will be satisfied.

Blessed are the merciful,
  for they will be shown mercy.

Blessed are the clean of heart,
  for they will see God.

Blessed are the peacemakers,
  for they will be called children
  of God.

Blessed are they who are persecuted
for the sake of righteousness,
  for theirs is the kingdom
  of heaven.
(Matthew 5:3–10)

Glory to the Father (Doxology)
Glory to the Father, and to the Son,
and to the Holy Spirit:
as it was in the beginning, is now,
and will be for ever.
Amen.

Gifts of the Holy Spirit
Wisdom
Understanding
Right judgment (Counsel)
Courage (Fortitude)
Knowledge
Reverence (Piety)
Wonder and awe (Fear of the Lord)

Fruits of the Spirit
Charity
Joy
Peace
Patience
Kindness
Goodness
Generosity
Gentleness
Faithfulness
Modesty
Self-control
Chastity

BACKGROUND

The Beatitudes   Christians traditionally give the title Beatitudes to the eight teachings of Jesus presented in *Matthew 5:3–10.* The formula "Blessed is the one who . . ." occurs often in Old Testament wisdom literature; in using this style to describe the values of God's kingdom, Jesus was following a tradition familiar to his Jewish listeners. (For background on the place of the Beatitudes in Christian morality, see the *Catechism of the Catholic Church,* #1716–1729.)

Glory to the Father   This ancient prayer is known as a *doxology,* or "words of praise." The Trinitarian opening originated in the Eastern Church. In the fourth century the last lines were added, and in the fifth century the prayer became common in the Western Church. It is prayed as part of the Rosary and is traditionally used to conclude the praying or chanting of a psalm in the Liturgy of the Hours.

Gifts of the Holy Spirit   These seven qualities are mentioned in the Latin Vulgate translation of *Isaiah 11:1–3* (which substitutes *piety* for one of the two mentions of *fear of the Lord*). In Catholic teaching the gifts are bestowed on every Christian at Baptism and strengthened in Confirmation.

Fruits of the Holy Spirit   These qualities, listed in *Galatians 5:22–23* (the Latin Vulgate adds *modesty, self-control,* and *chastity*), are signs of the Spirit's presence in human life. The Letter to the Galatians contrasts these qualities with the deadly sins, or "works of the flesh."

Act of Contrition
My God,
I am sorry for my sins with all my
heart.
In choosing to do wrong
and failing to do good,
I have sinned against you
whom I should love above all things.
I firmly intend, with your help,
to do penance,
to sin no more,
and to avoid whatever leads me to sin.
Our Savior Jesus Christ
suffered and died for us.
In his name, my God, have mercy.

Works of Mercy
Corporal *(for the body)*
Feed the hungry.
Give drink to the thirsty.
Clothe the naked.
Shelter the homeless.
Visit the sick.
Visit the imprisoned.
Bury the dead.

Spiritual *(for the spirit)*
Warn the sinner.
Teach the ignorant.
Counsel the doubtful.
Comfort the sorrowful.
Bear wrongs patiently.
Forgive injuries.
Pray for the living and the dead.

PRECEPTS OF THE CHURCH

1. Take part in the Mass on Sundays and holy days. Keep these days holy and avoid unnecessary work.

2. Celebrate the Sacrament of Reconciliation at least once a year if there is serious sin.

3. Receive Holy Communion at least once a year during Easter time.

4. Fast and abstain on days of penance.

5. Give your time, gifts, and money to support the Church.

BACKGROUND

Act of Contrition   This form of the prayer of the penitent is part of the revised *Rite of Penance* (1974). The students' parents and grandparents may be more familiar with the traditional Act of Contrition, which begins "O my God, I am heartily sorry. . . ." The word *act* in the title of the prayer refers to a prayer of intention, in which prayer and action are combined.

Works of Mercy   These actions on behalf of those in physical, spiritual, and emotional need are rooted in Scripture and in the Church's practice. They are closely related to action for justice, but where justice obligates us to give others what they need, mercy moves beyond obligation to give freely.

The Precepts of the Church   These "commandments of the Church," as they are sometimes called, have existed in some form since the fourth century. The number and content of the *precepts* (a word that means "teachings") has varied throughout the years, and different lists are honored in different countries. The precepts of the Church, which apply to all Catholics, have never been given the status of law.

RESOURCE Center

The Apostles' Creed

I believe in God, the Father almighty,
   creator of heaven and earth.
I believe in Jesus Christ, his only Son,
   our Lord.
   He was conceived by the power of the
      Holy Spirit
      and born of the Virgin Mary.
   He suffered under Pontius Pilate,
      was crucified, died, and was buried.
   He descended to the dead.
   On the third day, he rose again.

He ascended into heaven,
   and is seated at the right hand
      of the Father.
He will come again to judge the
   living and the dead.
I believe in the Holy Spirit,
   the holy catholic Church,
   the communion of saints,
   the forgiveness of sins,
   the resurrection of the body,
   and life everlasting. Amen.

The Nicene Creed

We believe in one God,
   the Father, the Almighty,
   maker of heaven and earth,
   of all that is, seen and unseen.
We believe in one Lord, Jesus Christ,
   the only Son of God,
   eternally begotten of the Father,
   God from God, Light from Light,
   true God from true God,
   begotten, not made, one in Being
      with the Father.
   Through him all things were made.
   For us men and for our salvation
      he came down from heaven:
   by the power of the Holy Spirit
      he was born of the Virgin Mary,
      and became man.
   For our sake he was crucified under
      Pontius Pilate;
   he suffered, died, and was buried.
   On the third day he rose again
      in fulfillment of the Scriptures;

he ascended into heaven
   and is seated at the right hand
      of the Father.
He will come again in glory to judge
   the living and the dead,
   and his kingdom will have no end.
We believe in the Holy Spirit, the Lord,
   the giver of life,
   who proceeds from the Father and
      the Son.
   With the Father and the Son he is
      worshiped and glorified.
   He has spoken through the Prophets.
We believe in one holy catholic and
   apostolic Church.
We acknowledge one baptism for the
   forgiveness of sins.
We look for the resurrection
   of the dead,
   and the life of the world to come.
Amen.

BACKGROUND

Litany of the Saints   Many of our prayers praise the Father, Son, and Holy Spirit. But the Litany of Saints is an example of a prayer that honors the guiding role of the communion of saints in our lives. The word *litany* comes from the Greek word *litanos,* which means "an entreaty." The Litany of Saints can take many forms. For example, names of patron saints and petitions for the congregation can be added to the litany depending on the occasion.

The Apostles' Creed   This profession of faith received its name from the popular legend that it was composed by the apostles. However, the earliest reference to this creed appears in fourth-century writings, and the earliest text dates from the eighth century. The name is still appropriate because the Apostles' Creed certainly can be said to reflect the teachings of the early Church. Like the Nicene Creed, the Apostles' Creed is trinitarian in structure, and flows from the baptismal formula.

Charlemagne ordered its use throughout his empire. This creed is approved for use in place of the Nicene Creed in children's Masses.

The Nicene Creed   This profession of faith is based on the work of two Church councils, the Council of Nicaea in 325 and the Council of Constantinople in 381. Its language reflects a concern with theological concepts; this creed was developed in response to the Aryan heresy, which denied the divinity of Christ. Originally intended as a test of orthodoxy for bishops, the Nicene Creed was later incorporated into baptismal liturgies.

The Liturgical Year

In the liturgical year the Church celebrates Jesus' life, death, resurrection, and ascension through its seasons and holy days. The liturgical year begins with the First Sunday of Advent.

The readings for the entire Church year are contained in the Lectionary. Readings for Sundays and solemnities of the Lord are placed in a three-year rotation—Cycle A, Cycle B, and Cycle C.

The Season of Advent begins in late November or early December. During Advent we recall the first coming of the Son of God into human history, and we prepare for the coming of Christ—in our hearts, in history, and at the end of time. The liturgical color for Advent is violet.

On Christmas we celebrate the Incarnation, the Son of God becoming one of us. The color for Christmas is white, a symbol of celebration and life in Christ. (Any time white is used, gold may be used.)

Lent is the season of prayer and sacrifice that begins with Ash Wednesday and lasts about forty days. Lent has always been a time of repentance through prayer, fasting, and almsgiving. The liturgical color for Lent is purple, a symbol of penance.

Easter is the high point of the liturgical year because it celebrates Jesus' resurrection from th dead. The week beginning with Palm Sunday is called Holy Week. Lent ends on Holy Thursday evening, when the Easter Triduum begins. The Triduum, or "three holy days," includes the observance of Holy Thursday, Good Friday, and Easter Vigil on Holy Saturday. The liturgical co for the Easter Season is white, a symbol of our in experiencing new life in Christ. The Easter Season lasts about seven weeks (fifty days).

At Pentecost, we celebrate the gift of the Hol Spirit sent to the followers of Jesus gathered in upper room in Jerusalem. The liturgical color fo Pentecost is red, a symbol of the tongues as of on Pentecost and of how Christ and some of hi followers (such as the early Christian martyrs) sacrificed their lives for love of God.

The majority of the liturgical year is called Ordinary Time, a time when the Church comm reflects on what it means to walk in the footste Jesus. The liturgical color for Ordinary Time is green, a symbol of hope and growth.

BACKGROUND

Order of the Mass   As the students' study the list of prayers and resources, you may also wish to review the order of the Mass with them. Point out that there are five major parts of the Mass—the Introductory Rites, the Liturgy of the Word, the Liturgy of the Eucharist, the Communion Rite, and the Concluding Rite. Ask a volunteer to write the following list on the board or on chart paper.

The *Introductory Rites* include the Entrance Song, the Greeting, the Rite of Blessing and Sprinkling (or the Penitential Rite), the Glory to God, and the Opening Prayer.

The *Liturgy of the Word* includes the First Reading, the Responsorial Psalm, the Second Reading, the Gospel Acclamation, the Gospel, the Homily, the Profession of Faith, and the General Intercessions.

The *Liturgy of the Eucharist* includes the Offertory Song, the Preparation of the Bread and Wine, the Invitation to Prayer, the Prayer over the Gifts, the Preface, the Acclamation, the Eucharistic Prayer with Acclamation, and the Great Amen.

The *Communion Rite* includes the Lord's Prayer, the Sign of Peace, the Breaking of the Bread, the Prayers before Communion, the Lamb of God, Holy Communion, the Communion Song, the Silent Reflection or Song of Praise, and the Prayer after Communion.

The *Concluding Rite* includes the Greeting, the Blessing, and the Dismissal.

A absolution — The forgiveness of sin we receive from God through the Church in the Sacrament of Reconciliation.

anoint — To use oil to mark someone as chosen for a special purpose.

C catechumen — An unbaptized person who has publicly stated his or her intention to become a member of the Church.

chrism — Sacred oil, made from olive oil scented with spices, used for anointing in the Sacraments of Baptism, Confirmation, and Holy Orders.

common priesthood — The whole community of believers who, through their participation in Jesus' gospel message, are members of the "holy priesthood."

communal prayer — Prayer that is prayed with others.

conscience — The gift from God that helps us know the difference between right and wrong and choose what is right. Conscience, free will, grace, and reason work together to help us in our decision making.

contrition — The deep sorrow and the resolve to do better that we feel when we have sinned; contrition moves us to turn our lives toward God.

conversion — The process of turning away from sin and evil and turning toward God.

covenant — A sacred and binding promise or agreement joining God and humans in relationship. Jesus' sacrifice established the new and everlasting covenant, open to all who do God's will.

D domestic Church — The Church as it exists within the family.

E Eucharist — The sacrament of Jesus' presence, which we celebrate by receiving his own Body and Blood under the form of bread and wine at Mass. From the Greek word meaning "gratitude," or "thanksgiving."

examination of conscience — A prayerful way of looking at our lives in light of the Ten Commandments, the Beatitudes, the life of Jesus, the teachings of the Church, and reason.

F funeral — The rites and ceremonies accompanying the burial of a deceased person.

G gifts of the Holy Spirit — The seven powerful gifts received in Baptism and strengthened in Confirmation that help us grow in our relationship with God and others. They are wisdom, understanding, counsel (right judgment), courage (fortitude), knowledge, reverence (piety), and wonder and awe (fear of the Lord).

godparent — The sponsor of a child at Baptism; one who promises to help the newly baptized person grow in faith.

grace — God's life in us through the Holy Spirit, freely given; our loving relationship with God; the free and undeserved help God gives us so that we may respond to the call to holiness.

L last rites — The celebration of the Sacraments of Reconciliation, Anointing of the Sick, and Eucharist by a person who is dying.

laying on of hands — A gesture used during the celebration of some sacraments to signify blessing, healing, invocation of the Holy Spirit, or conferral of office.

OCABULARY

the *Catechism of the Catholic Church* reminds us, we do not lieve in formulas or definitions but in the reality expressed in e terms. Yet that expression is vital for understanding and igious literacy. The glossary section of *Living Our Faith* has en designed to help you support the students' growth in igious understanding, so that they and their families can feel mfortable talking about their faith, passing it on, celebrating n the Christian community, and making it a fundamental part their lives. Toward these ends, memorization is only the first p. The students will "grow into" the language of faith on ny levels as they grow to religious maturity. (For more the importance of a shared Catholic vocabulary, see the techism of the Catholic Church, #170–171.)

liturgical year — The annual cycle of Church seasons and feasts that comprise the Church year. The liturgical year, which does not correspond to the traditional calendar, celebrates Christ's life, death, resurrection, and ascension.

Liturgy of the Eucharist — The term for the entire celebration of the Mass as well as for the specific part of the Mass that includes the Preparation of the Gifts, the Eucharistic Prayer, and Communion.

Liturgy of the Word — The first great part of the Mass, lasting from the first reading to the General Intercessions, that celebrates God's word.

M ministerial priesthood — Ordained ministers of the Church who represent the presence of Christ to the faith community.

O original sin — The first humans' choice to disobey God and the condition that became a part of human nature whereby we are deprived of original holiness and justice; only Jesus and Mary, his mother, were free of original sin.

P Paschal mystery — The saving mystery of Jesus' passion, death, resurrection, and ascension.

Passover — An important Jewish holiday of thanksgiving; the day takes its name from the story of the Jewish Exodus from Egypt, during which the Lord spared, or "passed over," the Hebrew people.

penance — Prayers and actions undertaken to help us, in Christ, make up for the harm our sins have caused.

Pentecost — The descent of the Holy Spirit upon the apostles fifty days after Easter. The word *Pentecost* means "the fiftieth day."

personal prayer — Prayer that is prayed by an individual.

R rite — The established procedure for celebrating specific ceremonies in the Church.

S sacrament — A celebration in which Jesus joins with the assembled community in liturgical actions that are efficacious signs and sources of God's grace.

sacramentals — Sacred signs, which bear a resemblance to the sacraments, in that they make us aware of God's presence in our everyday lives. Blessings, holy water, candles, and the rosary are examples of sacramentals.

sacramental character — The spiritual and indelible mark we receive from the Holy Spirit during certain sacraments; it permanently changes our relationship to Christ and the Church.

Seal of the Holy Spirit — The spiritual and indelible character that comes from the Spirit through the anointing with chrism and accompanying words of the bishop.

sign — That which points to or explains something else.

sponsor — The person who presents the candidate for the anointing and promises to help him or her fulfill baptismal promises.

symbol — A sign that has effective emotional or spiritual meaning.

V viaticum — Holy Communion received as part of the last rites at the time of death. The word *viaticum* means "bread for the journey."

vocation — The call to live God's love in our everyday lives through the single life, marriage, the religious life, or the priesthood.

RESOURCE Center

Introduction to Leader Resources

The following resource pages have been created to help you extend and enhance the lessons found in the chapter pages. The resources you use will depend on the extent to which you have included the optional activities in your teaching plan.

Letter to Families

To help include family members in the learning process of their young adolescent, *Living Our Faith* provides a Family Resource titled *Living Our Faith: Nurturing the Spiritual Growth of Your Adolescent,* by Michael Carotta (Harcourt Religion Publishers). (See *Library Links* in Chapter 1 for the full citation.) The Family Resource was written to introduce the adult family members to the Skills for Christian Living that the students will be using and to allow them to recognize and develop these skills in their own lives. By periodically sending home the family letter, you can inform parents and guardians about what their children are studying, while encouraging them to complete the activities in the Family Resource. The letter also includes a complete list of the skills and space for you to highlight which skills will be discussed in the near future.

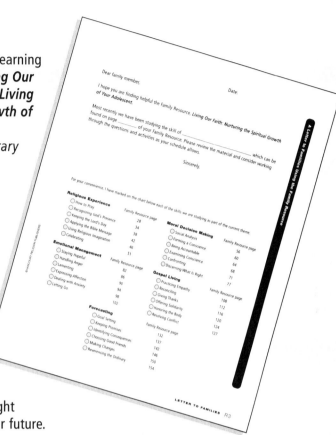

Student Leader Prep Pages

If you have chosen to include the Student Leader feature in your teaching plan, these pages will supply you with ideas for Student Leader activities. These Prep Pages are intended to be photocopied and distributed to the Student Leader for each chapter. You are encouraged to meet with the Student Leader to discuss the options listed and select those activities that best fit your time and resources. Use the open bullet before each entry to check those activities that you have selected. The Student Leader Connection feature in the Resource Center of each chapter will help you keep track of the Student Leader options. Be sure to mark your selections or make any notes here before you begin the lesson.

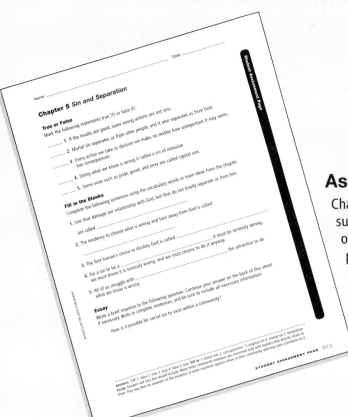

Assessment Pages

Chapter Assessment pages have been supplied to allow for objective testing of each chapter. The answer key is provided at the bottom of each page. Be sure to cover the answer key when you photocopy the pages.

Liturgical Year Supplementary Lessons

As a way to help the students better understand the liturgical year, sixteen activity-based supplementary lessons have been included. Review the activities and select the appropriate lesson(s) for the season. Two lessons have been included for each seasonal theme to provide flexibility and variety over a two-year period.

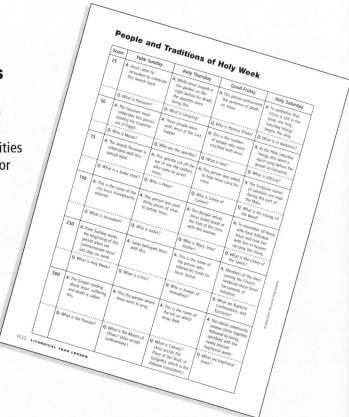

Date: _____

Dear family member,

I hope you are finding helpful the Family Resource, *Living Our Faith: Nurturing the Spiritual Growth of Your Adolescent.*

Most recently we have been studying the skill of _____ which can be found on page _____ of your Family Resource. Please review the material and consider working through the questions and activities as your schedule allows.

Sincerely,

For your convenience, I have marked on the chart below each of the skills we are studying as part of the current theme.

Religious Experience	Family Resource page
○ How to Pray	28
○ Recognizing God's Presence	34
○ Keeping the Lord's Day	38
○ Applying the Bible Message	42
○ Using Religious Imagination	46
○ Celebrating	51

Moral Decision Making	Family Resource page
○ Social Analysis	56
○ Forming a Conscience	60
○ Being Accountable	64
○ Examining Conscience	68
○ Confronting	71
○ Discerning What Is Right	77

Emotional Management	Family Resource page
○ Staying Hopeful	82
○ Handling Anger	86
○ Lamenting	90
○ Expressing Affection	94
○ Dealing with Anxiety	98
○ Letting Go	102

Gospel Living	Family Resource page
○ Practicing Empathy	108
○ Reconciling	112
○ Giving Thanks	116
○ Offering Solidarity	120
○ Honoring the Body	124
○ Resolving Conflict	127

Forecasting	Family Resource page
○ Goal Setting	132
○ Keeping Promises	137
○ Identifying Consequences	142
○ Choosing Good Friends	146
○ Making Changes	150
○ Reverencing the Ordinary	154

Chapter 1 *Symbols and Signs*

This sheet has some ideas to help you prepare for your role as Student Leader for Chapter 1. Discuss the following suggestions with your teacher or catechist, and place a check mark next to the ideas you decide to use.

Pages 4–5

◯ Reflect on the meaning of the prayer before you gather the group to pray. Pray aloud the opening prayer.

◯ Read aloud the text on page 5, and help the group brainstorm examples of self-expression.

◯ Record responses to the discussion.

Pages 6–7

◯ Collect examples of sacramentals and share them with the group.

◯ Read aloud one or more of the additional Scripture passages in *Opening the Word.*

◯ Research and present information on one of the items on the time line from *Our Christian Journey.* How did Theodosius the Great contribute to the growth of Christianity? What people and beliefs influenced Saint Augustine's conversion?

Pages 8–9

◯ Help make a chart to list and describe each sacrament.

◯ Help moderate the group discussion on the symbolism of the Body of Christ.

◯ Read aloud *Ephesians 1:22–23.*

Pages 10–11

◯ Read aloud the *Wrap Up* summary statements.

◯ Record on the board or on chart paper the results of the *Around the Group* discussion.

◯ Collect newspapers and lead the *Extension Activity* to find signs of God's presence in our world.

Pages 12–13

◯ Read aloud *Expressions of Faith.*

◯ Gather examples of religious art to show the group.

◯ Organize a small group to plan a prayer service.

Music for the Chapter

You may wish to play the following songs from the *Give Your Gifts* series: "Joyfully Singing," "He Came Down/ We Are Marching (Siyahumba)," and "Heaven Will Sing." Ask your teacher or catechist for help locating the music.

Notes:

Chapter 2 *Moments of Grace*

This sheet has some ideas to help you prepare for your role as Student Leader for Chapter 2. Discuss the following suggestions with your teacher or catechist, and place a check mark next to the ideas you decide to use.

Pages 14–15

◯ Reflect on the meaning of the prayer before you gather the group to pray. Pray aloud the opening prayer.

◯ Read aloud or review *Getting a Helping Hand.*

◯ Help moderate the discussion about experiences of help and support.

◯ Help moderate the discussion on the characteristics of people who can be counted on to be supportive.

Pages 16–17

◯ Read aloud selected text.

◯ Find a recording of "Amazing Grace" or distribute copies of a parish hymnal.

◯ Record the results of the discussion about the importance of the Paschal mystery.

◯ Read aloud *Opening the Word.*

◯ Research and present information on one of the items on the time line from *Our Christian Journey.* Prepare a brief report on the life of Charles Carroll, one of the signers of the Declaration of Independence. Research the injustices that caused the American colonies to revolt against British rule.

Pages 18–19

◯ Select two or three feasts or liturgical seasons to research, and report the findings to the group.

◯ Record the results of the group discussion on the liturgical year.

◯ Use a television show with which the group is familiar to discuss *Media Message.*

Pages 20–21

◯ Read aloud selected text.

◯ Help moderate the group discussion on ways the sacraments can affect our lives.

◯ Read aloud the *Wrap Up* summary statements.

◯ Help moderate the discussion for *Around the Group.*

Pages 22–23

◯ Read aloud *Matthew 14:22–33.*

◯ Review the skill pages from Chapter 1.

◯ Lead the group in praying the closing prayer.

◯ Organize a small group to plan a prayer service, or lead "Sacraments: Prayer Service A" from *Living Our Faith Prayer Services.*

Music for the Chapter

You may wish to play the following songs from the *Give Your Gifts* series: "Psalm 122: Let Us Go Rejoicing," "Psalm 118: This Is the Day," and "On That Day." Ask your teacher or catechist for help locating the music.

Notes:

Chapter 3 *Baptism*

This sheet has some ideas to help you prepare for your role as Student Leader for Chapter 3. Discuss the following suggestions with your teacher or catechist, and place a check mark next to the ideas you decide to use.

Pages 24–25

◯ Reflect on the meaning of the prayer before you gather the group to pray. Pray aloud the opening prayer.

◯ Read aloud selected text.

◯ Help moderate the discussion about belonging to groups.

Pages 26–27

◯ Read aloud *Opening the Word.*

◯ Record the results of the group discussion about Christian initiation.

◯ Read aloud one or more of the additional Scripture passages.

Pages 28–29

◯ Read aloud *Catholics Believe.*

◯ Help moderate the review of how the Sacrament of Baptism is celebrated.

◯ Collect symbols used in Baptism, and show them to the group.

◯ Help moderate a discussion on how to be faithful to baptismal promises.

Pages 30–31

◯ Read aloud the *Wrap Up* summary statements.

◯ Help moderate the discussion about how to live faith every day.

◯ Help moderate the discussion for *Around the Group.*

◯ Record the results of the group discussion.

Pages 32–33

◯ Read aloud *Expressions of Faith.*

◯ Help moderate a discussion about the meaning of the Scripture quote.

◯ Organize a small group to plan a prayer service.

Music for the Chapter

You may wish to play the following songs from the *Give Your Gifts* series: "Blessed Be the Lord," "All Things New," and "Give Your Gifts." Ask your teacher or catechist for help locating the music.

Notes:

Chapter 4 *Confirmation*

This sheet has some ideas to help you prepare for your role as Student Leader for Chapter 4. Discuss the following suggestions with your teacher or catechist, and place a check mark next to the ideas you decide to use.

Pages 34–35

◯ Reflect on the meaning of the prayer before you gather the group to pray. Pray aloud the opening prayer.

◯ Read aloud selected text.

◯ Help moderate the discussion about the meaning of responsibility.

◯ Research the American Sign Language words for the prayer.

Pages 36–37

◯ Using the format of a game show, help moderate the discussion about being responsible.

◯ Read aloud *Opening the Word.*

◯ Read aloud *Focus On.*

◯ Introduce skits about the gifts of the Holy Spirit.

Pages 38–39

◯ Help moderate the discussion on how Confirmation is celebrated.

◯ Read aloud *Catholics Believe.*

◯ Research and present information on one of the items on the time line from *Our Christian Journey.* What are the Thirteenth, Fourteenth, and Fifteenth Amendments to the United States Constitution? What were some of Thomas Merton's reasons for becoming a Trappist?

Pages 40–41

◯ Read aloud the *Wrap Up* summary statements.

◯ Help moderate the discussion of ways to live faithfully.

◯ Arrange for the display of the completed montage.

Pages 42–43

◯ Read aloud *Expressions of Faith.*

◯ Read aloud *Scripture.*

◯ Organize a small group to plan a prayer service, or lead "Sacraments: Prayer Service B" from *Living Our Faith Prayer Services.*

Music for the Chapter

You may wish to play the following songs from the *Give Your Gifts* series: "Come and Follow Me," "Send Down the Fire," and "With You By My Side." Ask your teacher or catechist for help locating the music.

Notes:

Chapter 5 *Eucharist*

This sheet has some ideas to help you prepare for your role as Student Leader for Chapter 5. Discuss the following suggestions with your teacher or catechist, and place a check mark next to the ideas you decide to use.

Pages 44–45

○ Reflect on the meaning of the prayer before you gather the group to pray. Begin the opening prayer by extending a sign of peace to everyone. Pray aloud the opening prayer.

○ Help moderate the discussion about experiences of thankfulness.

○ Help moderate the discussion about things that make people thankful to God.

Pages 46–47

○ Read aloud *Exodus 12:29–14:30* about Passover.

○ Research and report on the Jewish celebration of Passover.

○ Help moderate the discussion about the Creed.

Pages 48–49

○ Review what happens during the Liturgy of the Eucharist.

○ Read aloud *Our Christian Journey.*

○ Research and present information on one of the items on the time line from *Our Christian Journey.* Research the life of Saint Francis Xavier. Provide additional information on the accomplishments of the Council of Trent.

Pages 50–51

○ Help the group create a graffiti wall about what it means to be Eucharistic people.

○ Read aloud the *Wrap Up* summary statements.

○ Help moderate the discussion for *Around the Group,* or record the results of the discussion.

○ Collect or record any questions the students have, and help find answers to these.

Pages 52–53

○ Help moderate the discussion about the traits of a hopeful person.

○ Show a picture of a yoke, and explain what the Scripture passage means to you.

○ Help the group practice the three-step process of staying hopeful by using an example from real life.

○ Organize a small group to plan a prayer service.

Music for the Chapter

You may wish to play the following songs from the *Give Your Gifts* series: "For Living, For Dying," "Psalm 34: Taste and See," and "Raise Me Up." Ask your teacher or catechist for help locating the music.

Notes:

Chapter 6 *Reconciliation*

This sheet has some ideas to help you prepare for your role as Student Leader for Chapter 6. Discuss the following suggestions with your teacher or catechist, and place a check mark next to the ideas you decide to use.

Pages 54–55

○ Find or create a symbol for the prayer space.

○ Gather the students by inviting them to share their reactions to the day.

○ Play music, turn off the lights, and reflect on the meaning of the prayer before you lead the opening prayer.

○ Read aloud or review selected text.

○ Help moderate a discussion about the harmful effects of sin.

○ Help moderate the discussion about experiences of reconciliation.

Pages 56–57

○ Read aloud *Luke 7:36–50.*

○ Help the group create an examination of conscience.

○ Research and present information on one of the items on the time line for *Our Christian Journey.* Describe the custom of public penance that private penance replaced. Provide background on the life of Saint Columba.

Pages 58–59

○ Direct the activity in *Media Message* about video game violence.

○ Help the group identify examples of conversion.

○ Help moderate a discussion about how people show contrition.

Pages 60–61

○ Help moderate the brainstorming activity about the qualities of a virtuous person.

○ Read aloud the *Wrap Up* summary statements.

○ Help moderate the *Around the Group* discussion.

Pages 62–63

○ Review with the group what they have learned about staying hopeful.

○ Read *Scripture* aloud.

○ Explain *Skill Builder.*

○ Organize a small group to plan a prayer service, or lead "Sacraments: Prayer Service C" from *Living Our Faith Prayer Services.*

Music for the Chapter

You may wish to play the following songs from the *Give Your Gifts* series: "You Are Mine," "Psalm 141: Let My Prayer Rise Up," and "You Are My Shepherd." Ask your teacher or catechist for help locating the music.

Notes:

Chapter 7 *Anointing of the Sick*

This sheet has some ideas to help you prepare for your role as Student Leader for Chapter 7. Discuss the following suggestions with your teacher or catechist, and place a check mark next to the ideas you decide to use.

Pages 64–65

◯ Invite the students to say aloud the names of those who are ill before the group prays the opening prayer.

◯ Read aloud selected text.

◯ Bring in an item for the prayer space.

Pages 66–67

◯ Read aloud *Opening the Word.*

◯ Find a comforting poem or psalm, and share it with the group.

◯ Research the hospice movement or a particular hospice, and report the findings to the group.

Pages 68–69

◯ Read aloud *Our Christian Journey.*

◯ Interview a priest and a funeral director, and report on the process of planning a funeral.

◯ Help moderate the discussion of how Catholics celebrate the life of someone who has died.

Pages 70–71

◯ Help moderate the discussion about the meaning of this sacrament for our lives.

◯ Read aloud the *Wrap Up* summary statements.

◯ Help moderate the discussion for *Around the Group.*

◯ Pray aloud a prayer written as an example for the *Briefly* activity.

Pages 72–73

◯ Read aloud *Think About It.*

◯ Help moderate the discussion of further examples for the mnemonic device RESPECT.

◯ Organize a small group to plan a prayer service.

Music for the Chapter

You may wish to play the following songs from the *Give Your Gifts* series: "Blessed Be the Lord," "Prayer of the Faithful," and "You Are My Shepherd." Ask your teacher or catechist for help locating the music.

Notes:

Chapter 8 *Matrimony*

This sheet has some ideas to help you prepare for your role as Student Leader for Chapter 8. Discuss the following suggestions with your teacher or catechist, and place a check mark next to the ideas you decide to use.

Pages 74–75

◯ Reflect on the meaning of the prayer before you gather the group to pray. Then pray aloud the opening prayer with the group.

◯ Help moderate the discussion about media messages concerning love and marriage.

◯ Bring in an appropriate item or items for the prayer space.

Pages 76–77

◯ Help moderate a discussion about how the people in our lives are gifts from God.

◯ Read aloud *Catholics Believe.*

◯ Research and present information on one of the items on the time line from *Our Christian Journey.* Who were the abolitionists, and what was the Underground Railroad? What were some of the results of the First Vatican Council?

Pages 78–79

◯ Read aloud *Focus On.*

◯ Introduce *Opening the Word.*

◯ Help moderate a discussion of how the Sacrament of Matrimony strengthens family life.

Pages 80–81

◯ Read aloud the *Wrap Up* summary statements.

◯ Help moderate the *Around the Group* discussion.

◯ Discuss with the group the behaviors and qualities that are part of a good friendship or marriage.

Pages 82–83

◯ Read *Scripture* aloud.

◯ Help the students recall the mnemonic device RESPECT.

◯ Help moderate the group discussion about responses to *Skill Builder.*

◯ Organize a small group to plan a prayer service, or lead "Sacraments: Prayer Service D" from *Living Our Faith Prayer Services.*

Music for the Chapter

You may wish to play the following songs from the *Give Your Gifts* series: "Yes, Lord," "Blessing," and "Heaven Will Sing." Ask your teacher or catechist for help locating the music.

Notes:

Chapter 9 *Holy Orders*

This sheet has some ideas to help you prepare for your role as Student Leader for Chapter 9. Discuss the following suggestions with your teacher or catechist, and place a check mark next to the ideas you decide to use.

Pages 84–85

○ Reflect on the meaning of the prayer before you gather the group to pray. Pray the opening prayer aloud.

○ Help moderate a discussion about the people who can best offer advice to adolescents of your age.

○ Bring in a symbol for the prayer space.

Pages 86–87

○ Read aloud selected text.

○ Help moderate a group discussion about experiences of service.

○ For the group's reference, make a chart about ways we live our common priesthood.

Pages 88–89

○ Read aloud Our *Christian Journey*.

○ Research the lives of saints who were ordained, such as Saint John Bosco, Saint Philip Neri, and Saint Peter Claver.

○ Research and present information on one of the items on the time line from *Our Christian Journey.* Investigate Irish Catholic immigration to the United States. (You might explore reasons for immigration, numbers of immigrants, places of settlement, and difficulties with acceptance.) Provide biographical information on Pope Pius IX.

Pages 90–91

○ Read aloud the *Wrap Up* summary statements.

○ Use a Catholic almanac or a Catholic diocesan newspaper or Web site to learn more about the local bishop, and prepare a report for the group.

○ Help moderate the discussion for *Around the Group.*

Pages 92–93

○ Prepare two or three pieces of advice about keeping promises to share with the group.

○ Help moderate the discussion about experiences of making and keeping promises.

○ Help moderate the group presentations of examples and advice for keeping promises.

○ Organize a small group to plan a prayer service.

Music for the Chapter

You may wish to play the following songs from the *Give Your Gifts* series: "We Are Called," "Psalm 104: Lord, Send Out Your Spirit," and "Sing to the Glory of God." Ask your teacher or catechist for help locating the music.

Notes:

Chapter 10 *Continuing Our Promise*

This sheet has some ideas to help you prepare for your role as Student Leader for Chapter 10. Discuss the following suggestions with your teacher or catechist, and place a check mark next to the ideas you decide to use.

Pages 94–95

○ Play a recording of Gregorian chant to accompany the opening prayer.

○ Reflect on the meaning of the prayer before you gather the group to pray. Pray the opening prayer aloud with the group.

○ Read aloud *The Good Life?* on page 95.

○ Help moderate a group discussion on what it means to live a good life.

Pages 96–97

○ Help moderate a discussion about the meaning each of the sacraments can have in our lives.

○ Read aloud *Catholics Believe.*

○ Help moderate the discussion about the importance of the Lord's Prayer.

Pages 98–99

○ Work with one or two other students to create a booklet of prayers to be distributed to the group.

○ Research and present information on one of the items on the time line from *Our Christian Journey.* Research and report on Mother Teresa and her community. Report biographical information on Pope John XXIII.

○ Read aloud *Opening the Word.*

Pages 100–101

○ Read aloud the *Wrap Up* summary statements.

○ Help moderate the *Around the Group* discussion.

○ Brainstorm with the group the things that make life worthwhile.

Pages 102–103

○ Read *Scripture* aloud.

○ Read aloud *Skill Steps* and review each of the points with the group.

○ Introduce *Putting It into Practice* by reading the instructions aloud.

○ Organize a small group to plan a prayer service, or lead "Sacraments: Prayer Service E" from *Living Our Faith Prayer Services.*

Music for the Chapter

You may wish to play the following songs from the *Give Your Gifts* series: "I Say Yes, My Lord," "Psalm 63: As Morning Breaks," and "Hope at the Crossroads." Ask your teacher or catechist for help locating the music.

Notes:

Chapter 1 *Symbols and Signs*

True or False
Mark the following statements true (T) or false (F).

_____ 1. A sign is an object or an event that speaks to us in a personal way and can have more than one meaning.

_____ 2. A symbol touches us by reminding us of what is important to us.

_____ 3. A sacramental is a sign of God's presence in our everyday lives.

_____ 4. Making the Sign of the Cross is a sacrament.

_____ 5. A sacrament is a special way that God enters our lives; we can become one with him through the sacraments.

Fill in the Blanks
Complete the following sentences using the vocabulary words or main ideas from the chapter.

1. Established procedures for celebrating specific ceremonies in the Church are

_____ .

2. When we celebrate the sacraments, God gives himself to us, sharing his

_____ with us.

3. Blessings, holy water, candles, and the rosary are examples of

_____ .

4. Catholics use many _____ and

_____ to celebrate the sacraments.

5. The celebration of the _____ is done by and for the Church.

Essay
Write a brief response to the following question. Continue your answer on the back of this sheet if necessary. Write in complete sentences, and be sure to include all necessary information.

How would you explain to someone that the Church is the Body of Christ?

Answers: **T/F:** 1. false 2. true 3. true 4. false 5. true **Fill in:** 1. rites 2. grace 3. sacramentals 4. signs, symbols 5. sacraments **Essay:** Answers should include some of the following: The writer of the letter to the Ephesians used this image to show how Christ is united to the Church. The Church is the Body of Christ with Jesus at its head.

Chapter 2 *Moments of Grace*

True or False
Mark the following statements true (T) or false (F).

_____ **1.** In the sacraments we are united with Christ.

_____ **2.** We do not continue Christ's saving work in the world.

_____ **3.** The Holy Spirit helped only the apostles.

_____ **4.** We earn grace by being good.

_____ **5.** Lent is the beginning of the liturgical year.

Fill in the Blanks
Complete the following sentences using the vocabulary words or main ideas from the chapter.

1. The saving mystery of Jesus' passion, death, resurrection, and ascension is called the

_____ .

2. In the _____ , we celebrate our life as members of the Body of Christ.

3. The seasons and holy days of the _____ commemorate events in Jesus' life.

4. The high point of the liturgical year is _____ because it commemorates Jesus being raised from the dead.

5. The majority of the liturgical year is called _____ .

Essay
Write a brief response to the following question. Continue your answer on the back of this sheet if necessary. Write in complete sentences, and be sure to include all necessary information.

How can God's grace affect our lives through the sacraments? Give examples.

Answers: T/F: 1. true 2. false 3. false 4. false 5. false **Fill in:** 1. Paschal mystery 2. sacraments 3. liturgical year 4. Easter 5. Ordinary Time **Essay:** Responses should include some of the following: The sacraments confer the grace of which they are a sign because Christ is at work in them. By celebrating the Paschal mystery, we enter more deeply into a relationship with Christ. The grace of the sacraments helps us respond to God with love and to love ourselves and others. For example, we make the right moral choices, we overcome the challenges we face everyday, we value virtue and goodness, and we live responsibly and wisely.

Chapter 3 *Baptism*

True or False
Mark the following statements true (T) or false (F).

_____ 1. The Sacraments of Christian Initiation are Baptism, Reconciliation, and Eucharist.

_____ 2. A person can join the Church at any age.

_____ 3. A baptized person's white garment symbolizes Christ as the Light of the World.

_____ 4. Water and the words of Baptism are the essential signs of the Sacrament of Baptism.

_____ 5. In Baptism water is a sign of death to one's old life and rebirth to a new life in Christ.

Fill in the Blanks
Complete the following sentences using the vocabulary words or main ideas from the chapter.

1. A person who is preparing to be baptized is called a

_____.

2. Along with our parents and the assembly, our _____ participate in the celebration of our Baptism and help us grow in faith throughout our lives.

3. The mark of the Holy Spirit that we receive in Baptism is called a

_____.

4. In the waters of Baptism we are cleansed of _____.

5. In Baptism the celebrant _____ us with

_____, a sacred oil made from olive oil scented with spices.

Essay
Write a brief response to the following question. Continue your answer on the back of this sheet if necessary. Write in complete sentences, and be sure to include all necessary information.

What does it mean to be true to our baptismal promises? Give at least one example.

Chapter 4 *Confirmation*

True or False

Mark the following statements true (T) or false (F).

_____ 1. The Sacrament of Confirmation is not one of the Sacraments of Christian Initiation.

_____ 2. The gift of fear of the Lord means that we should be afraid of God.

_____ 3. Wisdom and courage are gifts of the Holy Spirit.

_____ 4. The gesture of laying on of hands means that we become members of the Church for the first time.

_____ 5. Because we have godparents, we do not need a sponsor for Confirmation.

Fill in the Blanks

Complete the following sentences using the vocabulary words or main ideas from the chapter.

1. Through the Sacraments of Baptism and Confirmation we receive seven

_____ to help us live as Christians.

2. The Holy Spirit came upon the apostles on _____.

3. A _____ promises to help the candidate live his or her faith.

4. A gesture used to call down the Holy Spirit upon the person celebrating the sacrament is called

_____.

5. The spiritual and indelible mark that comes from the Sacrament of Confirmation is called the

_____.

Essay

Write a brief response to the following question. Continue your answer on the back of this sheet if necessary. Write in complete sentences, and be sure to include all necessary information.

What does it mean to bear witness to Christ in our everyday lives?

Answers: T/F: 1. false 2. false 3. true 4. false 5. false **Fill in:** 1. gifts of the Holy Spirit 2. Pentecost 3. sponsor 4. laying on of hands 5. seal of the Holy Spirit **Essay:** Responses should include some of the following: Bearing witness to Christ means celebrating our faith in Christ, spreading the gospel message to others, living our faith every day, being active members of the Church according to our age and our abilities, and, in many other ways, showing the love that Christ has for all of us.

Chapter 5 *Eucharist*

True or False

Mark the following statements true (T) or false (F).

_____ **1.** The Gospel writers compared Jesus' sacrifice with the sacrificial goat the Jews slaughtered on Passover.

_____ **2.** We celebrate the Eucharist to give thanks to God through a community meal.

_____ **3.** The Profession of Faith and General Intercessions are part of the Liturgy of the Eucharist.

_____ **4.** The Eucharistic Prayer is prayed aloud by the gathered assembly.

_____ **5.** When we gather for Eucharist, we celebrate our membership in the Body of Christ.

Fill in the Blanks

Complete the following sentences using the vocabulary words or main ideas from the chapter.

1. The Jewish feast celebrating the deliverance of the Israelites from slavery in Egypt is called

_____ .

2. In Greek the word _____ means "thanksgiving."

3. During the _____ we listen to the word of God in readings from Scripture.

4. During the _____ we bring our offerings, including bread and wine, to the altar.

5. Our celebration of the Eucharist is a _____ because Jesus lived and died to save us.

Essay

Write a brief response to the following question. Continue your answer on the back of this sheet if necessary. Write in complete sentences, and be sure to include all necessary information.

What are some of the results (effects) of celebrating the Eucharist?

Answers: **T/F:** 1. false 2. true 3. false 4. false 5. true **Fill in:** 1. Passover 2. Eucharist 3. Liturgy of the Word 4. Liturgy of the Eucharist 5. sacrifice **Essay:** Answers should include some of the following: Our venial sins are forgiven; we are nourished with the Spirit's love, joy, and hope; we anticipate the eternal happiness that will be ours; we become more sensitive to those who are suffering and want to help them; and we are moved to pray and work for the union of Christian Churches.

Chapter 6 *Reconciliation*

True or False
Mark the following statements true (T) or false (F).

_____ 1. To reconcile means to be separated from others by sin.

_____ 2. In the Sacrament of Reconciliation, we celebrate God's forgiveness and learn to heal our relationships.

_____ 3. A sin of omission is deliberately choosing to do something you know is wrong.

_____ 4. Venial sin breaks the bond with Christ and his Church completely.

_____ 5. In the Sacrament of Reconciliation, we confess our sins to a priest.

Fill in the Blanks
Complete the following sentences using the vocabulary words or main ideas from the chapter.

1. Changing our hearts and turning back to God is called

_____.

2. When we celebrate the Sacrament of Reconciliation, the priest prays a prayer of

_____ and gives us a

_____ to help us, in Christ, make up for the harm our sins have caused.

3. Recognizing the harm our sins have caused, we experience

_____, or sorrow, for what we have done or failed to do.

4. God gave each of us a _____ to help us tell right from wrong and to choose what is right.

5. We think about our lives and recognize our strengths and weaknesses during the

_____.

Essay
Write a brief response to the following question. Continue your answer on the back of this sheet if necessary. Write in complete sentences, and be sure to include all necessary information.

Why is reconciling with ourselves, others, the Church, and God part of being a virtuous person?

Answers: T/F: 1. false 2. true 3. false 4. false 5. true **Fill in:** 1. conversion 2. absolution, penance 3. contrition 4. conscience 5. examination of conscience **Essay:** Answers should include some of the following: Reconciliation means making things right and strengthening our relationships with God and others. Reconciling helps us avoid sin, live honestly, and make right choices for ourselves. We can live virtuously because God is a priority in our lives and because we care about how we treat others.

Name: _____   Date: _____

Chapter 7 *Anointing of the Sick*

True or False

Mark the following statements true (T) or false (F).

_____ 1. Jesus refused to heal the centurion's servant because the centurion wasn't Jewish.

_____ 2. The Sacrament of the Anointing of the Sick can be celebrated only once in a person's life.

_____ 3. The celebration of the sacrament includes both a laying on of hands and an anointing.

_____ 4. In the Sacrament of the Anointing of the Sick we receive spiritual healing and may receive physical healing as well.

_____ 5. God does not abandon us when we are at our weakest.

Fill in the Blanks

Complete the following sentences using the vocabulary words or main ideas from the chapter.

1. The _____ are meant to prepare a person as he or she ends the earthly life and begins the eternal one.

2. A _____ includes the rites and ceremonies for saying good-bye to someone who has died.

3. The Eucharist given to a dying person is called _____.

4. As members of the Body of Christ, we are called to participate in Jesus' mission of

_____.

5. Jesus healed people both in body and _____.

Essay

Write a brief response to the following question. Continue your answer on the back of this sheet if necessary. Write in complete sentences, and be sure to include all necessary information.

How does celebrating the Sacrament of the Anointing of the Sick help us when we are ill or facing death?

Answers: **T/F:** 1. false 2. false 3. true 4. true 5. true **Fill in:** 1. last rites 2. funeral 3. viaticum 4. healing 5. spirit/soul **Essay:** Answers should include some of the following: By celebrating this sacrament we experience spiritual healing and perhaps physical healing as well. We receive the strength, courage, healing, and comfort of the Holy Spirit; we may reflect on the meaning of our lives and have a deeper appreciation for our bodies.

Student Assessment Page

Chapter 8 *Matrimony*

True or False

Mark the following statements true (T) or false (F).

_____ 1. A happy marriage and family life give us a glimpse of what the kingdom of God is like.

_____ 2. Catholics often celebrate the Sacrament of Matrimony within Mass.

_____ 3. Catholics are permitted to divorce once in their lives.

_____ 4. At the heart of the sacrament is the exchange of vows.

_____ 5. A husband and wife are to be faithful to each other as Christ is faithful to his Church.

Fill in the Blanks

Complete the following sentences using the vocabulary words or main ideas from the chapter.

1. The faith that family members share with one another makes them the

_____.

2. Faithfulness is the _____ that a husband and wife make exclusively to each other, both in love and sexual fidelity.

3. When a man and a woman marry, they make a _____ before God and his Church.

4. The call to live God's love through single life, marriage, religious life, or priesthood is our

_____.

5. God intends for Matrimony to be a celebration of a _____

and _____ relationship.

Essay

Write a brief response to the following question. Continue your answer on the back of this sheet if necessary. Write in complete sentences, and be sure to include all necessary information.

Why is the family called the domestic Church?

Answers: T/F: 1. true 2. true 3. false 4. true 5. true **Fill in:** 1. domestic Church 2. commitment 3. covenant 4. vocation 5. love-giving, life-giving **Essay:** Answers should include some of the following: The family is the domestic Church because it is the core of the Church. Our faith begins in the home and is continually nourished by those closest to us. As members of a family, we are taught to pray, love, forgive, support, and guide each other in faith.

Chapter 9 *Holy Orders*

True or False

Mark the following statements true (T) or false (F).

_____ 1. All Christians are members of the ministerial priesthood because they are baptized.

_____ 2. Deacons can say Mass but are not permitted to baptize.

_____ 3. There are three degrees of ministerial priesthood: deacons, priests, and bishops.

_____ 4. When a priest is ordained, he becomes one of the apostles.

_____ 5. A bishop-elect is given a crosier, or staff, to show he is our shepherd.

Fill in the Blanks

Complete the following sentences using the vocabulary words or main ideas from the chapter.

1. Through Baptism we become members of the _____ priesthood.

2. Deacons, priests, and bishops are part of the _____ priesthood.

3. Most priests in the Latin Rite, or Western Church, promise to live lives of

_____ .

4. Bishops are Church leaders who have the mission to preach the

_____ to the people in their dioceses.

5. Most priests work in _____, where they help us live our faith.

Essay

Write a brief response to the following question. Continue your answer on the back of this sheet if necessary. Write in complete sentences, and be sure to include all necessary information.

What are some of the ways that members of the ministerial priesthood serve the Church?

Answers: **T/F:** 1. false 2. false 3. true 4. false 5. true **Fill in:** 1. common 2. ministerial 3. celibacy 4. gospel 5. parishes **Essay:** Answers should include some of the following: Members of the ministerial priesthood preside at the sacraments and preach and teach the word of God. Deacons are also ordained to do works of charity, such as visiting parishioners who are sick, preparing couples for marriage, and helping with youth programs. Most priests work in parishes, leading the faith community and serving as counselors, administrators, and religious guides. Bishops are sanctifiers, teachers, and rulers. They are the shepherds of the Church because they teach, lead, and help the Church become more holy.

Chapter 10 *Continuing Our Promise*

True or False

Mark the following statements true (T) or false (F).

_____ 1. Accepting the role of prophet requires us to use our talents to promote good or ill.

_____ 2. Through the sacraments we experience God's saving love.

_____ 3. There is nothing we can do today to prepare for our future vocations.

_____ 4. The Sacrament of Reconciliation strengthens us to forgive others and to be peacemakers.

_____ 5. The most important communal prayer is liturgy.

Fill in the Blanks

Complete the following sentences using the vocabulary words or main ideas from the chapter.

1. Saint Thomas Aquinas called the _____ "the most perfect of prayers."

2. Through the _____ the Holy Spirit gives us the grace to live as Christ would.

3. Individual communication with God is called _____.

4. Joining to pray with others is called _____.

5. Raising our minds and hearts to God is _____.

Essay

Write a brief response to the following question. Continue your answer on the back of this sheet if necessary. Write in complete sentences, and be sure to include all necessary information.

   Why are the sacraments important to our lives as Catholics?

Answers: **T/F:** 1. false 2. true 3. false 4. true 5. true **Fill in:** 1. Lord's Prayer 2. sacraments 3. personal prayer 4. communal prayer 5. prayer **Essay:** Answers should include some of the following: The sacraments help us keep our baptismal promises, live our lives in Christ, and become persons of integrity; they also help us grow ever closer to God, deepen our faith, and strengthen us to deal with problems and temptations.

Feast Days of Mary

Gathering   Begin the lesson by asking the students to consider the loving influence of their mothers, grandmothers, sisters, aunts, or other special women they know.

Opening Prayer   Together pray aloud the Hail Mary.

Activity   **Introduction**   This activity, which helps the students learn more about the feast days of Mary, is a memory matching game. The object of the game is to match a card containing the name of a Marian feast with the card that gives an explanation of that feast.

Directions   Divide the group into pairs, and give each pair a copy of the handout. Allow the students time to study the list. Answer any questions the students may have. When the group is ready to begin, direct each pair to cut apart the cards on their handout. Then ask them to separate the cards that list the names of the feasts from the cards that list their descriptions. Deal each set of cards into separate groups. Place them randomly into a 3 × 3 grid with the type-side down. The students should take turns trying to match the cards from the two groups. If a match is not made, the student should replace the two cards, type-side down, in their original places. If a match is made, the student keeps the matched cards and continues choosing until he or she guesses incorrectly. (When the game is over, you may wish to provide another copy of the handout for the students to check their matches.)

Option   To make the game progress more quickly, organize the students into two large groups rather than into pairs. You may also wish to direct the students to highlight clue words on each card.

Closing Reflection   Discuss with the students how the activity has helped them understand Mary's role in their faith lives. Ask the students to recall the women they chose at the beginning of the lesson. Invite each student to do something special this week to show how important that person is to him or her.

Closing Prayer   Complete the session by having the group read together *Luke 1:46–55*— the Magnificat.

Feast Days of Mary

January 1 **Solemnity of Mary, Mother of God**	This feast honors Mary as the mother of Jesus, who was both God and man. The scriptural basis for this feast day is found in the opening chapters of Matthew and Luke.
February 11 **Our Lady of Lourdes**	In France in 1858, Mary appeared to Bernadette Soubirous as a young woman, dressed in a white gown with a blue cinch, carrying a rosary.
March 25 **Annunciation of the Blessed Virgin Mary**	The Angel Gabriel announced to Mary that God had chosen her to be the mother of the Son of God.
May 31 **Visitation of the Blessed Virgin Mary**	After learning she would bear God's Son, Mary visited Elizabeth. Elizabeth was filled with the Holy Spirit and said, "Blessed are you among women, and blessed is the fruit of your womb."
August 15 **Assumption of the Blessed Virgin Mary**	At the end of her life, Mary was assumed (lifted) into heaven body and soul. Mary is the first person to freely and completely share in Christ's resurrection.
September 8 **Birth of the Blessed Virgin Mary**	This feast celebrates Mary's birthday. Her parents were Saint Anne and Saint Joachim.
October 7 **Our Lady of the Rosary**	This feast was established to honor Mary through the recitation of the Rosary. In 1893 Pope Leo XIII urged all Catholics throughout the world to recite the Rosary, especially during the month of October.
December 8 **Immaculate Conception of the Blessed Virgin Mary**	This feast honors the day God created Mary full of his grace. Mary was preserved from sin from the first moment of her life.
December 12 **Our Lady of Guadalupe**	Mary appeared to Juan Diego in Mexico. She told him that she is the mother of all God's people.

Liturgical Year Lesson

Feast Days of the Saints

Gathering   Ask the students to discuss some of the characteristics of people they would consider holy.

Opening Prayer   Sing or listen to "Peace Prayer" (John Foley SJ, *Glory and Praise,* OCP) or pray together the Prayer of Saint Francis by reciting one line at a time and having the students repeat it.

Prayer of Saint Francis

Lord, make me an instrument of your peace.
Where there is hatred, let me sow love;
where there is injury, pardon;
where there is doubt, faith;
where there is despair, hope;
where there is darkness, light;
where there is sadness, joy;

O Divine Master, grant that I may not so much seek
to be consoled, as to console;
to be understood, as to understand;
to be loved, as to love.
For it is in giving that we receive;
it is in pardoning that we are pardoned;
and it is in dying that we are born to eternal life.

Activity   **Introduction**   This activity tests the students' knowledge of the saints. To prepare, make a copy of the activity page. Cut out the strips on the handout, and place them in a basket or bowl. Divide the group into teams. Direct the teams to create names for themselves; then write the names on the board or on chart paper. Under each team name write the word *saint*.

Directions   To begin the activity, ask a member from the first team to select a strip of paper from the basket and (without reading the answer) read the clue to the second team. If the second team names the correct saint, award them a point by crossing out one letter from the word *saint* under their name. If the team cannot name the saint referred to, the reader then moves on to the next group. This continues until the saint is correctly identified or until each team gets a chance to guess. If no team answers correctly, the reader gives the correct answer and the clue is returned to the basket. Each team takes a turn reading a selection. Play progresses until all of one team's letters are crossed out.

Option   If time allows, direct the students to research additional information on the saints presented in the activity and report their findings to the group.

Closing Reflection   Discuss how the students might incorporate into their lives a virtuous attribute from someone they respect as being holy.

Closing Prayer   Using the names of the saints on the handout, lead the students in a Litany of the Saints. Students should respond "Pray for us" after each name is read.

For additional activities see *www.harcourtreligion.com*

Feast Days of the Saints

This man, who was one of Jesus' apostles, was a brother to Saint Peter. *(Saint Andrew, November 30)*

This saint was the mother of the Blessed Virgin Mary. *(Saint Anne, July 26)*

This saint is often called on to help find something that is lost. *(Saint Anthony of Padua, June 13)*

This young man and his friends are known as the African Martyrs. *(Saint Charles Lwanga and companions, June 3)*

This saint was the mother of John the Baptist. *(Saint Elizabeth, November 5)*

This saint established the first parochial school in the United States. *(Saint Elizabeth Ann Seton, January 4)*

This angel announced to Mary that she was to be the Mother of God's Son. *(Saint Gabriel the Archangel, September 29)*

This saint translated the Bible into Latin, the language of his people at the time. *(Saint Jerome, September 30)*

This man is credited with the Book of Revelation as well as one of the Gospels. *(Saint John the Evangelist, December 27)*

This man is the patron saint of parish priests. *(Saint John Vianney, August 4)*

This man was Jesus' cousin and baptized many people in the Jordan river. *(Saint John the Baptist, June 24)*

This saint is known as the foster father of Jesus. *(Saint Joseph, March 19)*

This man wrote the Acts of the Apostles as well as one of the Gospels. *(Saint Luke, October 18)*

This sixteenth-century Dominican brother ministered to black slaves in Lima, Peru. *(Saint Martin de Porres, November 3)*

This saint offered his life in place of another man's during the Holocaust. *(Saint Maximilian Kolbe, August 14)*

This saint's son was Saint Augustine. *(Saint Monica, May 4)*

This saint was also called by the name Saul. *(Saint Paul, June 29)*

These two young North African women were imprisoned, tortured, and killed for their Christian beliefs. *(Saints Perpetua and Felicity, March 7)*

This saint cried after he denied knowing Jesus three times. *(Saint Peter, June 29)*

This archangel is also called the "healer of God." *(Saint Raphael the Archangel, September 29)*

This saint is considered the first martyr for our Christian faith. *(Saint Stephen, December 26)*

This woman is the patron saint of Spain. *(Saint Teresa of Ávila, October 15)*

This nun from France was called "Little Flower." *(Saint Thérèse of Lisieux, October 1)*

Because of his great love for study, this man is the patron saint of students. *(Saint Thomas Aquinas, January 28)*

This saint was beheaded because he refused to recognize the king as the leader of the Church in England. *(Saint Thomas More, June 22)*

Jesus' Family Tree

Gathering Explain to the students that the Old Testament tells the stories of many people who were waiting for the arrival of the messiah. These people were part of Jesus' ancestry. We remember these people at Advent because they help us recall God's love for us and for all humanity.

Opening Prayer Sing or listen to "O Come, O Come, Emmanuel." Read *Luke 3:23–38.* In the silence of prayer, offer intercessions for family members.

Activity **Introduction** This activity enables the students to study the people of Scripture and their connection to Jesus. Using heavy paper or cardboard, design and cut out a game wheel and spinner. Divide the wheel into seven spaces, numbering the spaces from 1 to 5. Include a space for "Lose Turn" and "Lose All Points." Attach the spinner to the wheel with a fastener.

Directions Divide the group into teams. Appoint a student to be scorekeeper. Select one entry from the handout. On the board or on chart paper, place one dash for each letter in the entry, leaving spaces between words if necessary. Have team one spin the wheel to determine the number of points their turn will be worth. Then direct the team to choose a letter of the alphabet. If the letter is part of the answer, place that letter on the appropriate dash (or dashes if the letter appears more than once). Their score is equivalent to the number of points on the spinner multiplied by the number of times their letter appears. The team can then try guessing the name or spin again. If a team guesses incorrectly, the spinner passes to the next team. Encourage the students in each group to take turns spinning and guessing. Add to the students' knowledge by reading the information on each person from the handout.

Option To provide additional background on the people identified, ask a volunteer to read aloud the Scripture references given.

Closing Reflection Remind the students that our families influence who we are and who we will become. Ask that during this Advent Season, they try to treat their families with the same love and kindness Jesus had for his family.

Closing Prayer Loving God, bless each member of our families. Keep them safe from harm. Help us love each other as the members of the Holy Family loved each other. We give you thanks for our families and for coming to earth to be our Savior and our brother. Amen.

For additional activities see www.harcourtreligion.com

Jesus' Family Tree

Adam and Eve
The names we give the first humans in the Bible. Jesus is spoken of as the new Adam in Scripture. *(1 Corinthians 15:45)*

Abraham and Isaac
Abraham believed God wanted him to offer Isaac as a human sacrifice. Jesus offered his life to God the Father for us. *(Genesis 22:1–13; John 19:30)*

Joseph and his brothers
The twelve brothers were the leaders of the twelve tribes of Israel. Jesus belonged to the tribe of Judah. *(Genesis 49:1–28; Hebrews 7:14)*

Jesse, the father of David
God choose the youngest son of Jesse to be king of Israel. *(1 Samuel 16:1–13)*

Samuel, one called by God
God called Samuel. Samuel responded, "Here I am, Lord." *(1 Samuel 3:1–18)*

Ruth, daughter-in-law of Naomi
After her husband's death, Ruth chose to stay with her mother-in-law and be faithful to the one true God she worshiped. *(Ruth 1:15–18)*

Isaiah the prophet
Isaiah foretold that the messiah would suffer and die for his people. He also stated that "A shoot shall come out from the stump of Jesse, and a branch shall grow out of his roots." *(Isaiah 11:1)*

Daniel in the lions' den
God saved Daniel from death because of Daniel's great faith. Those who believe that Jesus is the Messiah are saved from the power of sin and everlasting death. *(Daniel 6:10–23; Acts 7:56–60)*

Joseph the carpenter
Joseph was betrothed to Mary and would become the foster father of Jesus. *(Matthew:1:19–25)*

Mary, the mother of Jesus
Mary, though a virgin, said "yes" to becoming the Mother of God. *(Luke 1:30–31; Matthew 13:55)*

People of the Christmas Season

Gathering Begin the session by discussing with the students some of the traditions that are part of the Christmas Season. Ask them to explain how they think each tradition began.

Opening Prayer A prayer that honors Mary and Jesus is the Angelus. It was traditionally prayed at 6 A.M., noon, and 6 P.M. This prayer reminds us how God showed his love for us by sending his Son to earth. Copy this prayer from the handout, and distribute it to the students. Then pray the prayer together.

Activity **Introduction** The Christmas story is built on a mix of Scripture stories and oral traditions. This activity will be used to review and offer additional facts about the people in the Bible who are part of the Christmas story.

Directions Copy the handout and cut out the clues. Using colored paper, design and cut out five gift-shaped slips of paper. Label one gift box 5, one 10, one 15, one 25, and one 50. Place the clues in one basket and the slips of gift-shaped paper in another. Divide the group into teams. A person from the first team will draw out a slip of paper from the basket containing the clues. He or she will then draw pictures on the board or on chart paper to try to get the team to guess the answer. The team will have thirty seconds to guess. If the team fails to guess correctly, the student reads the name for the group and places the slip back in the basket. If the team guesses correctly, the person giving the clues then draws out a gift slip from the second basket. In order for the group to receive the number of points indicated on the gift slip, the student must be able to tell those gathered what part this person played in the Christmas story. The gift slip should then be returned to the basket.

Option Have the students read *Matthew 1:1–2:18* and *Luke 1:1–2:38* and list the details of the Christmas story found in these books of the Bible. Discuss what information has been added through oral tradition.

Closing Reflection Gather the students around the Christmas crèche or nativity scene. Have one of the students read aloud *Luke 2:1–7.* Sing or listen to "Away in a Manger." Instruct the group to share with their family members some of the information they learned.

Closing Prayer God of Mary and Joseph, bless us whenever we gaze on this nativity scene. Through all the days of the Christmas Season may these figures tell the story of how we found the Christ Child in this place. Guide our steps in the way of peace. Grant this through Christ our Lord. Amen.

People of the Christmas Season

The Angelus

Leader:	The angel spoke God's message to Mary,
All:	and she conceived of the Holy Spirit.
All:	Hail, Mary, full of grace, . . .
Leader:	"I am the lowly servant of the Lord:
All:	Let it be done to me according to your word.
All:	Hail, Mary, full of grace, . . .
Leader:	Pray for us, holy Mother of God,
All:	that we may become worthy of the promises of Christ.
Leader:	Let us pray.
All:	Lord, fill our hearts with your grace: once, through the message of an angel you revealed to us the incarnation of your Son; now, through his suffering and death lead us to the glory of his resurrection. We ask this through Christ our Lord. Amen.

People in the Christmas story—clues

Blessed Virgin Mary	Holy Spirit
Joseph	Angel Gabriel
John the Baptist	the baby
wise men from the East	Elizabeth
Zachariah	Emmanuel
shepherds	King Herod
Messiah	

Listed below is information that students might give in response to each name:

Blessed Virgin Mary—mother of Jesus

Holy Spirit—"Mary was found to be with child by the Holy Spirit" *(Matthew 1:18).*

Joseph—foster father of Jesus

Angel Gabriel—announced to Mary that she was to be the Mother of the Son of God

John the Baptist—cousin of Jesus

the baby—the Son of God came to earth as a baby

wise men from the East—three persons who came seeking the king of the Jews

Elizabeth—mother of John the Baptist

Zachariah—father of John the Baptist

Emmanuel—another name for Jesus; word meaning "God is with us"

shepherds—the first people to be told of the birth of the Messiah

King Herod—ordered all the male children in and around Bethlehem under the age of two to be killed

Messiah—another name for Jesus; savior expected by the Israelites; Hebrew word for "anointed"

Lenten Traditions

Gathering   During the Lenten Season the Church asks its people to do penance. Discuss some of the ways people do this.

Opening Prayer   Read *Ephesians 5:8–14*. Pray together an Act of Contrition or recite the following prayer, and have the students repeat it after you one line at a time.

Act of Contrition

My God,
I am sorry for my sins with all my
   heart.
in choosing to do wrong
and failing to do good,
I have sinned against you
whom I should love above all things.
I firmly intend, with your help,

to do penance,
to sin no more,
and to avoid whatever leads me
   to sin.
Our Savior Jesus Christ
suffered and died for us.
In his name, my God, have mercy.

Activity   **Introduction**   This activity, which is based on tic-tac-toe, is designed to help the students learn about some Lenten Season traditions.

Directions   Draw a large tic-tac-toe grid on the board or on chart paper. Divide the group into two teams. One team will be designated as the *X*s; the other group will be the *O*s. Begin by asking a person on team one a statement from the first list. The student decides if the statement is true or false. If the student answers correctly, he or she places the group's letter on the grid. If the student answers incorrectly, no letter is placed on the grid. Next, the second team is asked the first statement from the second list. Discuss each statement as needed. Because the statements build on one another, they should be asked in the sequence presented.

Option   You may also wish to divide the group into pairs, with one student playing the *X*s and the second student playing the *O*s. Make copies of the handout, and cut them apart. Give the top half to one member of each group and the lower half to the other member.

Closing Reflection   Find out from a parish bulletin when the Sacrament of Reconciliation will be held and plan on attending and celebrating this sacrament as a group.

Closing Prayer   God is willing to forgive us and asks us to forgive each other. As a sign of their faith, invite the students to extend a sign of peace to one another. Conclude by singing or listening to a song of forgiveness, such as "Pardon Your People" (Carey Landry, *Glory and Praise [Comprehensive]*, OCP).

Liturgical Year Lesson

For additional activities see www.harcourtreligion.com

Lenten Traditions

Team 1

1. Advent is the forty-day season before Easter. (False; the name for the forty-day season before Easter is *Lent.*)

2. Lent consists of three Sundays and forty weekdays. (False; there are six Sundays in Lent.)

3. The wearing of ashes is a public way of showing we are sorry for our sins. (True.)

4. The development of Lent as a forty-day period of fasting was based on the forty years that Moses and the Israelites spent in the desert. (False; the forty days of fasting was based on Jesus' own fast in the desert.)

5. To fast means to eat only one full meal, two lighter meals, and nothing between meals. (True.)

6. The age for abstaining is 14 years of age and older. (True.)

7. The process of preparation and ceremonies for joining the Catholic Church is called the *Rite of Christian Initiation of Adults.* (True.)

8. Parishes often offer communal reception of the Sacrament of Reconciliation during the Lenten Season. (True.)

9. The word that describes the transformation of the entire person—mind, heart, and will—toward God is called *contrition.* (False; the word is *conversion.*)

10. The Gloria and Alleluia are sung during Masses celebrated in the Lenten Season. (False; they are not sung at any of the Masses during the Lenten Season.)

Team 2

1. Lent is the Church season that extends from Ash Wednesday to the beginning of the celebration of the Lord's Supper on Holy Thursday. (True.)

2. We receive ashes on Good Friday. (False; we receive ashes on Ash Wednesday.)

3. During the days of Lent, the only thing we are asked to do is to give up something. (False; Lent is a time of prayer, fasting, and almsgiving. It can also be seen as a time for doing something extra.)

4. Catholics are obliged to fast on all days during the Lenten Season. (False; only Ash Wednesday and Good Friday are days of obligatory fasting.)

5. The Catholic Church community is obliged to abstain from meat only on Ash Wednesday during Lent. (False; Catholics are also asked to abstain on all the Fridays of Lent and on Good Friday.)

6. Like abstaining, the age for fasting is 14 years of age and older. (False; fasting is required between the ages of 18 and 59.)

7. Those who are preparing during the Lenten Season to be initiated into the Church are referred to as the *elect.* (True.)

8. During Lent the Church calls us to do penance for our sins. (True.)

9. The journey of conversion that we travel during the Lenten Season is a journey we have to travel alone. (False; our community of faith, the parish, is on this journey with us.)

10. Praying more often or attending Mass more frequently are two ways to grow in faith during the Lenten Season. (True.)

People and Traditions of Holy Week

Gathering Listen to the song "Were You There?" Explain to the students the rhythm and melody of the song is purposely slow and sad-sounding. Discuss with the students the songwriter's purpose for this.

Opening Prayer Read *John 18:1–19:42.* Assign various students the roles of narrator; Jesus; the soldiers; the first, second, and third persons who question Peter; Peter; the high priest; the temple guard; Pilate; the chief priest; and the crowd.

Activity **Introduction** This activity tests the students' knowledge of Holy Week. The students must provide the questions to the answers that are provided. To prepare for the activity, write the following headings on the board: Palm Sunday, Holy Thursday, Good Friday, and Holy Saturday. Make a copy of the handout, cut the answers apart, and attach each answer, type-side down, to the board in the order that they appear on the handout. Number the back of each answer with the appropriate score.

Directions Divide the group into teams of four or five. In front of the board, place as many chairs as there are groups. Have one member from each group come forward and sit in the chair assigned to his or her team. Explain that you will read the answer aloud and the students should answer in the form of a question. Only the students in the chairs in front of the board will be allowed to respond to the answer. The student representing team one chooses the first category. The student who first raises his or her hand guesses first. Stop reading as soon as a player raises his or her hand, even if you are in the middle of the answer. If the person provides the correct question, his or her team is awarded the appropriate points for that answer. If the person does not provide the correct question, finish reading the answer and wait for another student to raise his or her hand. Each student in the front chairs may make only one guess. If no one in the front chairs knows the correct question, open it up to the other members of the teams (reminding them that they need to be recognized before they respond). After each question, every group sends a different person to the front chairs. Remove the answers from the board as they are guessed. The new representative from the group who gave the last correct question chooses the next category. Continue until the board is cleared.

Option Place the Gospel references below on the board. Allow the groups to read these verses to find the proper questions.

Matthew 21:1–10; 26:14—27:66   *Mark 11:1–11; 14:10—15:47*
Luke 19:28–40; 22:1—23:56   *John 13:1–38; 18:1—19:42*

Closing Reflection Allow the students time to reflect silently on what it would take to be more like Jesus. Encourage the students to attend Holy Week services and celebrations with their families.

Closing Prayer Listen to or sing a song of faith, such as "I Put My Life in Your Hands/Pongo Mi Vida" (David Haas, *Gather,* GIA Publications, Inc.).

People and Traditions of Holy Week

Score	Palm Sunday	Holy Thursday	Good Friday	Holy Saturday
25	**A:** Jesus came to Jerusalem to celebrate this Jewish feast.	**A:** While Jesus prayed in the garden on the night before his death, the apostles were doing this.	**A:** This person pronounced the sentence of death on Jesus.	**A:** To symbolize that Christ is still in the tomb, the Holy Saturday liturgy begins this way.
	Q: What is Passover?	**Q:** What is sleeping?	**Q:** Who is Pontius Pilate?	**Q:** What is in darkness?
50	**A:** The Passover meal celebrates this person leading the Israelites out of Egypt.	**A:** These people were with Jesus at the Last Supper.	**A:** This is the number of people who were crucified with Jesus.	**A:** At the Holy Saturday liturgy, this word is again sung before the gospel acclamation.
	Q: Who is Moses?	**Q:** Who are the apostles?	**Q:** What is two?	**Q:** What is *alleluia?*
75	**A:** The Jewish Passover is celebrated with this special meal.	**A:** This apostle cut off the ear of one the soldiers who came to arrest Jesus.	**A:** This person was asked to help Jesus carry his cross.	**A:** The Scripture stories of salvation are read during this part of the Mass.
	Q: What is a Seder meal?	**Q:** Who is Peter?	**Q:** Who is Simon of Cyrene?	**Q:** What is the Liturgy of the Word?
100	**A:** This is the name of the city Jesus triumphantly entered.	**A:** This person was paid thirty pieces of silver to betray Jesus.	**A:** The disciple whom Jesus loved stood at the foot of the cross with this woman.	**A:** To remember all those who have followed Jesus and now live with him in heaven, we pray this litany.
	Q: What is Jerusalem?	**Q:** Who is Judas?	**Q:** Who is Mary, Jesus' mother?	**Q:** What is the Litany of the Saints?
250	**A:** Palm Sunday marks the beginning of this period when we commemorate Jesus' last days on earth.	**A:** Judas betrayed Jesus with this.	**A:** This is the name of the person who offered his tomb for Jesus' burial.	**A:** Members of the elect joining the Church celebrate these three Sacraments of Initiation.
	Q: What is Holy Week?	**Q:** What is a kiss?	**Q:** Who is Joseph of Arimathea?	**Q:** What are Baptism, Confirmation, and Eucharist?
500	**A:** The Gospel reading about Jesus' suffering and death is called this.	**A:** This the garden where Jesus went to pray.	**A:** This is the name of the hill on which Jesus died.	**A:** The whole community renews these together, followed by being sprinkled with the newly blessed baptismal water.
	Q: What is the Passion?	**Q:** What is the Mount of Olives? (Also accept Gethsemane.)	**Q:** What is Calvary? (Also accept the Place of the Skull, or Golgotha, which is the Hebrew translation.)	**Q:** What are baptismal vows?

Easter People

Gathering Ask the students what they think Jesus' being raised from the dead meant to his apostles, Jesus' mother, and the Romans. What does it mean to each of the students?

Opening Prayer Read aloud *Psalm 150.* Direct the students to respond "Praise the Lord!" after each verse.

Activity **Introduction** This activity will help the students better understand the Easter Season. Divide the group into three teams. Explain that each team will have three lifelines, or places they can go for help. They can ask a member of their group, ask for a consensus from their team, and ask that half of the possible answers be eliminated. Be sure that students understand that when someone from their team uses a lifeline, it cannot be used by anyone else on their team. Points are never lost, but questions that are incorrectly answered are given no points. All teams continue with the activity regardless of incorrect answers. Ask for a volunteer to keep track of team scores, as well as what lifelines each team has used.

Directions Begin by asking a person on each team one of the hundred-point questions. After each of the teams has had a chance to answer, go on to the five-hundred-point questions. Continue in the same manner with the rest of the questions. Discuss the correct answers with the students as they are given. (Note that the answers marked with an asterisk are those that should remain if the student asks for two of the incorrect answers to be eliminated.) If a student guesses incorrectly, he or she gives up his spot to another team member.

Option To help save time, mark a Bible with sticky notes at the following chapters dealing with the resurrection, so that the students can find the correct pages quickly: *Matthew 28; Mark 16; Luke 24; John 20, 21.*

Closing Reflection Remind the students that the words "He has risen!" were whispered among Jesus' believers on that first Easter Sunday two thousand years ago. What started as a whisper has now become a shout that has been heard around the world. Ask the students how they will allow this news to change their lives.

Closing Prayer Invite the students to pray quietly for the Spirit to help guide them to live as Easter people, sharing the good news of Jesus' resurrection with others.

For additional activities see www.harcourtreligion.com

Easter People

100-point questions

1. Easter is always on this day of the week.
   *a. Sunday
   b. Wednesday
   c. Friday
   *d. Saturday

2. These were the first people to visit Jesus' tomb on the day after the Sabbath.
   *a. the apostles
   b. the shepherds
   c. the soldiers
   *d. the women

3. In the Gospel of John, Peter walks on this to try to get to Jesus.
   a. hot coals
   *b. hot sand
   *c. water
   d. snow

500-point questions

4. In the Gospel of John, this is the apostle who didn't believe Jesus had been raised from the dead.
   *a. Peter
   b. John
   c. Andrew
   *d. Thomas

5. The angel in the Gospel of Matthew gives this reason for the absence of Jesus' body.
   a. "The body has been stolen."
   *b. "He has been raised."
   *c. "He really never died."
   d. "You're at the wrong grave."

6. In the Gospel of Matthew, Jesus first appeared to these people.
   *a. the women who had come to the tomb
   b. the soldiers who were guarding the tomb
   *c. the apostles
   d. some fishermen

1,000-point questions

7. In the Gospel of Luke, the disciples who recognized Jesus in the breaking of the bread were traveling to this city.
   *a. Jerusalem
   b. Bethlehem
   c. Galilee
   *d. Emmaus

8. The name *Thomas* means this (*John 20:24*).
   *a. rock
   *b. twin
   c. liar
   d. trusted-one

9. How many times did Jesus ask Peter this question: "Simon, son of John, do you love me?"
   *a. once
   b. twice
   *c. three times
   d. four times

2,500-point questions

10. Easter is always celebrated on the first Sunday after the full moon that occurs closest to this event.
    a. the groundhog seeing his shadow
    *b. the first day of spring
    c. the melting of the last snow
    *d. the planting of the first seeds

11. In *Matthew 28:2* this is given as the reason for how the stone to the tomb was moved.
    *a. an earthquake
    b. a flood
    c. the soldiers moved it
    *d. an angel moved it

12. In the Gospel of John, Mary Magdalene mistakes Jesus for this person.
    a. an apostle
    b. an angel
    *c. a soldier
    *d. a gardener

5,000-point questions

13. In the early Church all Baptisms were held on this day.
    a. Holy Thursday
    b. Good Friday
    *c. Holy Saturday
    *d. Easter Sunday

14. In the shorter ending of the Gospel of Mark, after a man in a white robe tells the women that Jesus has risen, the women did this.
    *a. They told everyone.
    *b. They told no one.
    c. They told the apostles.
    d. They laughed at the man.

15. In the longer ending of the Gospel of Mark, Jesus appeared to this woman.
    *a. Mary Magdalene
    b. Mary, the mother of Jesus
    *c. Martha
    d. Salome

10,000-point questions

16. In the Gospel of Luke, he was the first apostle to see the empty tomb.
    *a. Peter
    b. Matthew
    c. Thomas
    *d. Philip

17. In the Gospel of John, he was the first apostle to see the empty tomb.
    *a. Peter
    *b. the disciple that Jesus loved
    c. Thomas
    d. Philip

18. This is the last celebration of the Triduum.
    a. Holy Thursday liturgy
    b. Good Friday liturgy
    *c. Holy Saturday liturgy
    *d. Easter Sunday liturgy

50,000-point questions

19. The word *Easter* means this.
    *a. dawning
    *b. rising
    c. new life
    d. freedom

20. In the Gospel of John, this is the number of fish caught when Jesus tells the apostles where to fish.
    *a. 3
    *b. 77
    c. 153
    d. 2,000

21. The Easter Season ends on this day.
    a. the ascension
    b. Trinity Sunday
    *c. Pentecost
    *d. Feast of Christ the King

Correct answers are as follows:
1. a 2. d 3. c 4. d 5. b 6. a
7. d 8. b 9. c 10. b 11. d
12. d 13. c 14. b 15. a 16. a
17. b 18. d 19. a 20. c 21. c

People, Places, and Things of Pentecost

Gathering Begin by asking the students to share what they know about the Holy Spirit, the third Person of the Trinity. Read aloud the story of Pentecost in *Acts 2:1–12.* Discuss how the coming of the Holy Spirit changed the lives of those in the upper room.

Opening Prayer Pray together the Apostles' Creed (found on page 107 of the student text).

Activity **Introduction** The aim of this activity is to review and learn more about Pentecost. Before the session, make one copy of the handout for every two people in the group. Create one set of cards for every pair by cutting apart each copy.

Directions Instruct the students to pair off and place their set of cards, type-side down, between them. Explain to the students that each card contains information about a place or thing that has something to do with Pentecost. The name of the person or place is noted at the bottom of the card. One person in the pair is to begin by picking the top card and, guided by the text at the top of the card, state whether the answer is a person, place, or thing. He or she then reads the first sentence after the introductory statement. The second person has ten seconds to guess who the person is or what the place or thing might be. If the guess is correct, he or she is awarded four points. If the guess is incorrect, or if the person has no guess, the person reading the statements moves on to the next statement. Each statement read lessens by one the points awarded. Once the answer is correctly guessed, the roles change and the second person reads clues to the first person. After the correct guess has been made, invite the students to read any remaining clues.

Option When everyone in the group has completed the activity, discuss how the people, places, and things mentioned are associated with Pentecost.

Closing Reflection Discuss with the students how the Holy Spirit continues to change lives today. One of the ways to get in touch with the Holy Spirit is to sing or recite a short prayer over and over to invite the Holy Spirit to come into our lives.

Closing Prayer Through the power of the Holy Spirit, the apostles found the courage to go into the streets and tell others about Jesus Christ. Pray: Holy Spirit, give us strength to be witnesses for Christ in our words and actions.

Liturgical Year Lesson

For additional activities see www.harcourtreligion.com

People, Places, and Things of Pentecost

I am a person.
I am an apostle.
My nickname is *Rock*.
I am also called Simon.
I was recognized as a leader by Jesus.
I am Peter.

I am a person.
I am called the thirteenth apostle.
I was elected to take Judas's place.
I followed Jesus from the day of his baptism.
I am a saint.
I am Matthias.

I am a place.
Jesus died outside my walls.
Jesus often visited me.
The temple is built within me.
I am a city.
I am Jerusalem.

I am a thing.
I am the celebration of the Holy Spirit descending
    on the apostles.
The presider at liturgy will wear red when
    celebrating me.
I am celebrated as the birthday of the Church.
A dove and flames are decorations that
    celebrate me.
I am Pentecost.

We are a group of people.
We are not Jewish.
Paul was our spokesperson.
Most of us lived outside the city of Jerusalem.
Many of us became Christians.
We are the Gentiles.

I am a thing.
I am a book in the Bible.
I tell the first story of Pentecost.
I was written by the same author as the Gospel
    according to Luke.
I am the first book after the Gospels in the Bible.
I am the Acts of the Apostles.

I am a person.
You cannot touch me.
I am a Person of God.
I am sometimes symbolized by a dove.
I was promised by Jesus.
I am the Holy Spirit.

I am a person.
I am considered the first disciple of Christ.
I am the patron of the United States.
I was in the upper room at the time of Pentecost.
Jesus was my son.
I am Mary, the mother of Jesus.

I am a place.
I am the second story of a house.
I have a door that can be locked.
I was a gathering place for people who were
    scared.
I can hold many people.
I am the upper room.

We are a group of people.
The apostles were part of our group.
We were known for the way we showed love for
    each other.
There were three thousand of us added on the day
    of Pentecost.
We devoted ourselves to the breaking of bread
    and prayers.
We are the early Christians.

I am a person.
I wrote one of the Gospels.
Many people believe I was a doctor.
I wrote the Acts of the Apostles.
I wrote the story of the angel telling Mary
    about becoming the Mother of God's Son.
I am Luke.

We are a group of people.
We accepted the call to follow Jesus.
There were twelve of us.
Eleven of us were martyred because of our belief
    in Jesus.
We were together in the upper room.
We are the apostles.

Symbols of Mary

Liturgical Year Lesson

Gathering To begin the lesson, ask the students to think of an object or symbol that represents their relationship with a trusted woman, such as their mother.

Opening Prayer If the students have memorized the *Memorare,* pray it together. If they are not familiar with this prayer, pray one line at a time and have the students repeat it after you.

The Memorare

Remember, O Most gracious Virgin Mary, that never was it known that anyone who fled to your protection, implored your help, or sought your intercession was left unaided.

Inspired by this confidence, I fly to you, O Virgin of virgins, my mother. To you I come; before you I stand, sinful and sorrowful.

O Mother of the Word Incarnate, despise not my petitions, but in your mercy, hear and answer me. Amen.

Activity **Introduction** This activity, a memory matching game, helps the students learn more about the symbols associated with Mary. The object of the game is to match a card containing the name of a Marian feast with the card that shows a symbol connected to that feast.

Directions Divide the group into pairs, and give each pair one copy of the handout. Allow the students time to study the feast dates and symbols. Discuss the information as needed. When the group is ready to begin, direct each pair to cut apart the cards on their handout. Then ask them to separate the cards that list the names of the feasts from the cards that show their symbols. Deal each set of cards into separate groups. Place them randomly into a 3 × 3 grid with the type-side down. The students should take turns trying to match the cards from the two groups. If a match is not made, the student should replace the two cards, type-side down, in their original places. If a match is made, the student keeps the matched cards and continues choosing until he or she guesses incorrectly. (When the game is over, you may wish to provide another copy of the handout for the students to check their matches.)

Closing Reflection Discuss with the students how the activity has helped them better understand Mary's role in their faith. Ask the students to recall the woman they chose at the beginning of the lesson. Direct them to create a card for her that includes the symbol of that special relationship and a personal message.

Closing Prayer We turn to you for protection, holy Mother of God.
Listen to our prayers and help us in our needs.
Save us from every danger, glorious and blessed Virgin.

For additional activities see *www.harcourtreligion.com*

Symbols of Mary

January 1
Solemnity of Mary, Mother of God
"The angel said to her, 'The Holy Spirit will come upon you, . . . therefore the child to be born will be holy; he will be called Son of God'" *(Luke 1:35)*

March 25
Annunciation of the Blessed Virgin Mary
"In the sixth month the angel Gabriel was sent by God . . . The virgin's name was Mary" *(Luke 1:26–27).*

July 16
Our Lady of Mount Carmel
This feast day is in memory of the giving of the brown scapular to Saint Simon Stork. "Whoever dies wearing this scapular shall not suffer eternal fire" (Our Lady's scapular promise).

August 22
The Queenship of the Blessed Virgin Mary
"A great portent appeared in heaven: a woman clothed with the sun, with the moon under her feet, and on her head a crown of twelve stars" *(Revelation 12:1).*

September 15
Our Lady of Sorrows
"When Jesus saw his mother and the disciple whom he loved standing beside her, he said to his mother, 'Woman, here is your son.' Then he said to the disciple, 'Here is your mother'" *(John 19:26–27).*

October 7
Our Lady of the Rosary
"Pray the Rosary every day in honor of Our Lady of the Rosary to obtain peace in the world" (Our Lady of Fatima, July 13, 1917).

The day after the Sacred Heart of Jesus
Immaculate Heart of Mary
Simeon met Joseph and Mary as they presented the child Jesus at the temple. He said to Mary, ". . . and a sword will pierce your own soul too" *(Luke 2:35).*

December 8
The Immaculate Conception of the Blessed Virgin Mary
The image of Mary on this medal represents her appearance to Saint Catherine Labouré in 1830.

December 12
Our Lady of Guadalupe
The image of Mary, which appeared on Juan Diego's cloak, was the sign his bishop had asked for as proof of Mary's appearance.

Symbols of the Saints

Gathering Ask the students to discuss some of the characteristics of people they would consider holy.

Opening Prayer Sing or listen to "Prayer for Peace" (David Haas, *Gather,* GIA Publication, Inc., and *Walking By Faith,* GIA and Harcourt Religion Publishers) or pray together the Prayer of Saint Patrick by reciting one line at a time and having the students repeat it.

Prayer of Saint Patrick

Christ with me,
Christ before me,
Christ behind me,
Christ in me,
Christ beneath me,
Christ above me,
Christ on my right,
Christ on my left,
Christ in breadth,
Christ in length,
Christ in height,

Christ in the mouth of everyone who
    speaks to me,
Christ in the heart of everyone who
    thinks of me,
Christ in every eye that sees me,
Christ in every ear that hears me.
I arise today
Through a mighty strength, the
    invocation of the Trinity,
Through belief in the Threeness,
Through confession of the Oneness,
Of the Creator of Creation.

Activity **Introduction** This activity tests the students' knowledge of the saints. To prepare, make a copy of the activity page. Cut out the strips on the handout, and place them in a basket or bowl. Divide the group into teams. Direct the teams to create names for themselves; then write the names on the board or on chart paper. Under each team name write the word *saint.*

Directions To begin the activity, ask a member from the first team to select a strip of paper from the basket and (without reading the answer) read the clue to the second team. If the second team names the correct saint, award them a point by crossing out one letter from the word *saint* under their name. If the team cannot name the saint referred to, the reader then moves on to the next group. This continues until the saint is correctly identified or until each team gets a chance to guess. If no team answers correctly, the reader gives the correct answer and the clue is returned to the basket. Each team takes a turn reading a selection. Play progresses until all of one team's letters are crossed out.

Closing Reflection Discuss how the students might incorporate into their lives a virtuous attribute from someone they respect as being holy.

Closing Prayer Using the names of the saints on the handout, lead the students in a Litany of the Saints. The students should respond after each name read with "Pray for us."

For additional activities see *www.harcourtreligion.com*

Symbols of the Saints

This apostle's symbol is in the shape of an *X*, indicating the way he was crucified. *(Saint Andrew, November 30)*

Two candles in the shape of an *X* placed around the throat symbolize this saint. *(Saint Blaise, February 3)*

This saint is often pictured holding loaves of bread because he used his talents for cooking to serve God's people. *(Saint Benedict the Black, April 4)*

Because she was a dairy farmer before she became a nun, she is often shown milking a cow. *(Saint Bridget, February 1)*

Pictures of this saint often show her with a dove on her shoulder—a sign to her father that she was to remain unmarried. *(Saint Catherine of Siena, April 29)*

The harp is the symbol for this patron saint of musicians. *(Saint Cecilia, November 22)*

This rich Hungarian saint is often shown carrying bread and roses. *(Saint Elizabeth of Hungary, November 17)*

Because of his love of nature, this saint is often pictured with a bird on his shoulder and other animals around his feet. *(Saint Francis of Assisi, October 4)*

The head of an eagle is the symbol for this evangelist. *(Saint John, December 27)*

This saint, the foster father of Jesus, is sometimes shown with a carpenter's tool in his hands. *(Saint Joseph, March 19)*

The winged ox is the symbol for this evangelist. *(Saint Luke, October 18)*

A winged lion is the symbol for this evangelist. *(Saint Mark, April 25)*

A winged man is the symbol for this evangelist. *(Saint Matthew, September 21)*

This woman who waited on Jesus is the patron saint of housewives and cooks. *(Saint Martha, July 29)*

A three-legged stool is the symbol for this saint, who sat at the feet of Jesus while her sister prepared the meal. *(Saint Mary of Bethany, July 29)*

This archangel is shown holding a shield because he is known as a strong warrior against evil. *(Saint Michael the Archangel, September 29)*

This saint is remembered by the delivering of food, money, and toys to those in need. He is considered the patron saint of children. *(Saint Nicholas, December 6)*

This saint used a shamrock to describe how there can be three Persons in one God. *(Saint Patrick, March 17)*

Hanging on a cross upside down symbolizes the way this saint died. *(Saint Peter, June 29)*

While in prison this saint sent letters with hearts on them to his family. He is remembered on his feast day with the sending of messages to those we love and care about. *(Saint Valentine, February 14)*

Advent Symbols

Liturgical Year Lesson

Gathering   Ask the students to share a time when they have had to wait for something they really wanted.

Opening Prayer   Help us, loving God, to be patient with our lives, to be patient with ourselves, and to be tolerant of others as we wait for you to come again in peace. Amen.

Activity   **Introduction**   Advent is about waiting. Many of the Israelites had waited a long time for the messiah. All these people played a part in the story of Jesus' ancestry. Each Advent we remember these people because they help us remember God's love for us and for all humanity. This activity enables the students to study these people and the symbols connected with them. Explain that often these symbols are part of a Jesse tree—a decoration seen during the Advent Season to explain Jesus' ancestry. Using heavy paper or cardboard, design and cut out a game wheel and spinner. Divide the wheel into seven spaces, numbering the spaces from 1 to 5. Include a space for "Lose Turn" and "Lose All Points." Attach the spinner to the wheel with a fastener.

Directions   Divide the group into teams. Appoint a student to be scorekeeper. Select one entry from the handout. On the board or on chart paper, place one dash for each letter in the entry, leaving spaces between words if necessary. Have team one spin the wheel to determine the number of points their turn will be worth. Then direct the team to choose a letter of the alphabet. If the letter is part of the answer, place that letter on the appropriate dash (or dashes if the letter appears more than once). Their score is equivalent to the number of points on the spinner multiplied by the number of times their letter appears. The team can then try guessing the name or spin again. If a team guesses incorrectly, the spinner passes to the next team. Encourage students in each group to take turns spinning and guessing.

Closing Reflection   Direct each student to draw one of the Jesse tree symbols to take home. Each symbol represents a person through the ages who had faith that God would keep his promise to send a messiah who would free us all from the power of sin and everlasting death. Encourage the students to hang the symbol where it will remind them to put their faith in God.

Closing Prayer   Pray together the Acts of Faith and Hope, or pray one line at a time and have the students repeat each after you.

Act of Faith   O God, we firmly believe that you are one God in three divine Persons— Father, Son, and Holy Spirit; we believe that your divine Son became man and died for our sins, and that he will come to judge the living and the dead. We believe these and all the truths that the holy Catholic Church teaches, because you have revealed them, and you can neither deceive nor be deceived.

Act of Hope   O God, relying on your almighty power and your endless mercy and promises, we hope to gain pardon for our sins, the help of your grace, and life everlasting, through the saving actions of Jesus Christ, our Lord and Redeemer.

For additional activities see *www.harcourtreligion.com*

Advent Symbols

The snake and Adam and Eve *(Genesis 3:1–7)*

Noah and the ark *(Genesis 6:9–22)*

God's covenant to Noah sealed with a rainbow *(Genesis 9:1–14)*

Jacob dreams of a ladder to heaven. *(Genesis 28:10–22)*

Moses is given the stone tablets. *(Deuteronomy 5:1–21)*

The tree of Jesse *(Isaiah 11:1–2)*

King David wears the crown of the king. *(1 Samuel 16:13)*

Jonah in the whale *(Jonah 1—2)*

Joseph's hammer *(Matthew 13:54–55)*

The heart of Mary *(Luke 1:30–31)*

Liturgical Year Lesson

Symbols of the Christmas Season

Gathering Begin the session by discussing with the students why gift giving has become one of the symbols of the Christmas Season.

Opening Prayer Write the name of each student in the group on a slip of paper, and place the strips in a bowl or basket. Explain to the students that Christmas celebrates the gift of Jesus given to us by God the Father. We, too, are gifts to each other. Have each student draw a name out of the basket. Give the students time to think about the person whose name they have drawn. What unique gift or talent does that person bring to the group? Copy the prayer on the handout, and distribute it to the students. Then pray the prayer together.

Activity **Introduction** The Christmas story is built on a mix of Scripture stories and oral traditions. This activity will be used to review and offer additional facts about symbols that are part of the Christmas Season.

Directions Copy the handout and cut out the clues. Using colored paper, design and cut out five gift-shaped slips of paper. Label one gift box 5, one 10, one 15, one 25, and one 50. Place the clues in one basket and the slips of gift-shaped paper in another. Divide the group into teams. A person from the first team will draw out a slip of paper from the basket containing the clues. He or she will then draw pictures on the board or on chart paper to try to get the team to guess the answer. The team will have thirty seconds to guess. If the team fails to guess correctly, the student reads the name for the group and places the slip back in the basket. If the team guesses correctly, the person giving the clues then draws out a gift slip from the second basket. In order for the group to receive the number of points indicated on the gift slip, the student must be able to tell those gathered what the symbol has to do with the Christmas story. The gift slip should then be returned to the basket.

Closing Reflection Ask the students to remember whose name they drew during the Opening Prayer activity. Remind them that we should recognize one another's talents and treat each person as though he or she is a gift given to us by God.

Closing Prayer Sing or listen to "Joy to the World."

For additional activities see *www.harcourtreligion.com*

Symbols of the Christmas Season

People Are Gifts

Lord, we gather today as people filled with hope and gratitude. Be with us as we share our gifts with those gathered. May this sharing bring us closer to you and to each other. May we see each other as a special and unique gift and as a sign of your love. We call to mind the special gift that each person here brings to our group. (Allow enough time so that each person is named and affirmed.)

Gracious God, we praise and thank you for the many gifts and blessings that you have given us. Today, we especially praise and thank you for your gift of Jesus. Be with us always so that we continue to be people who love and appreciate each other. Fill our hearts with the joy of loving you. Amen.

Symbols

stable	star in the East
donkey	lamb
angels	two turtledoves
three crowns	a shepherd's staff
manger	three gifts
temple	

Listed below is the information that the students might give in response to each symbol:

stable—There was no room in the inn, so Jesus was born in the room that housed the animals.

star in the East—The star led the wise men to the place where the baby Jesus could be found.

donkey—Mary rode a donkey to Bethlehem; a donkey is often pictured in the stable scene.

lamb—Jesus, the sacrificial lamb, offered himself for humanity; the lamb is often pictured in the stable scene.

angels—An angel announced to Mary that she would be the Mother of the Son of God; the angels announced to the shepherds that the Messiah was born.

two turtledoves—This was the offering of a couple who was poor. The doves were offered by Mary and Joseph in the temple in thanksgiving for Jesus' birth.

three crowns—The crowns represent the three kings (magi or wise men) who came to visit the baby. These people are spoken of as the wise men in Matthew's Gospel.

a shepherd's staff—The shepherds in the field were the first to be told of the Messiah's birth.

manger—The baby Jesus was laid in a manger after his birth.

three gifts—The wise men came bearing gifts of gold, frankincense, and myrrh.

temple—The baby Jesus was presented in the temple where he was greeted by Simeon and Anna.

Lenten Symbols

Gathering Begin the session by discussing Lenten symbols that the students may have in their homes. Some of these may be present all year; others may be displayed just during the six weeks of Lent. Possible answers include crucifixes, palm branches, or rice bowls. Discuss the reason for the presence of these symbols.

Opening Prayer Read aloud *Daniel 9:3–10.* Then pray the following petitions, and have the students respond to each of the petitions.

Leader: For the times we have not shared our lives with God in prayer.
All: Lord, have mercy.
Leader: For the times we have not shared generously with others.
All: Lord, have mercy.
Leader: For the times we did not appreciate our own talents by giving into laziness, jealousy, envy, and dishonesty.
All: Lord, have mercy.

Activity **Introduction** This activity, which is based on tic-tac-toe, is designed to help the students learn about some Lenten Season traditions.

Directions Draw a large tic-tac-toe grid on the board or on chart paper. Divide the group into two teams. One team will be designated as the *X*s; the other group will be the *O*s. Begin by asking a person on team one a statement from the first list. The student decides if the statement is true or false. If the student answers correctly, he or she places the group's letter on the grid. If the student answers incorrectly, no letter is placed on the grid. Next, the second team is asked the first statement from the second list. Discuss each statement as needed. Because statements build on one another, they should be asked in the sequence presented.

Closing Reflection Discuss the role of these symbols in the students faith lives. Have each student create a Lenten symbol that can be used as a reminder to pray more and give of his or her money, time, and talents during this Lenten Season.

Closing Prayer Have the students repeat or sing the refrain to "All Glory, Laud, and Honor" (*Gather [Comprehensive]*, GIA Publications, Inc.) as someone reads the verses of the song. (*Refrain:* All glory, laud, and honor to you, Redeemer King! To whom the lips of children made sweet hosannas ring.)

For additional activities see *www.harcourtreligion.com*

Lenten Symbols

Team 1

1. The word *Lent* means "springtime." (True.)
2. The ashes we receive on Ash Wednesday are placed on our foreheads in the shape of a heart to remind us that Jesus loves us. (False; the ashes are placed on our forehead in the shape of a cross to remind us that Jesus died for us.)
3. Jesus offered the Samaritan woman something to eat. (False; Jesus offered her "living water" [John 4:10].)
4. Meat cannot be eaten on Ash Wednesday, all the Fridays during Lent, and Good Friday. This is called *abstinence.* (True.)
5. Limiting yourself to bread and water is one way to fast. (True.)
6. The devil tempted Jesus with an offer to turn stones into cookies. (False; the devil, knowing Jesus was hungry after fasting for forty days, tempted Jesus with turning stones into bread.)
7. A cross and a crucifix look the same. (False; a crucifix carries the representation of Christ on the cross.)
8. The color purple symbolizes repentance and conversion. (True.)
9. Jesus' head was crowned with thorns because the soldiers believed he was the king of the Jews. (False; the soldiers were mocking Jesus and the people who had said this.)
10. Praying more during the Lenten Season is a sign that we want to be closer to God. (True.)
11. Almsgiving is sharing money and possessions with those in need. (True.)

- -

Team 2

1. We receive ashes on Ash Wednesday as a public sign of sorrow for sin. (True.)
2. During the Lenten Season, the Gospel story about the Samaritan woman is read. The site of this event is Jacob's well. (True; see *John 4:12.*)
3. Fasting and abstaining during Lent teaches self-discipline. (True.)
4. Giving up our daily candy bar or can of soda throughout the Season of Lent is a way to fast. (True.)
5. Rocks are sometimes placed in the church during the Lenten Season to remind us that we all are sinners and need to repent. (True; in the story of the adulterous woman, Jesus said, "Let anyone among you who is without sin be the first to throw a stone at her" [John 8:7].)
6. The cross is a symbol of Jesus' love for us. (True.)
7. The liturgical color for the Lenten Season is green. (False; the liturgical color for Lent is purple.)
8. In most parishes the priest wears pink vestments at the Masses on the First Sunday of Lent. (False; pink is usually worn on the Fourth Sunday of Lent.)
9. Increasing our charitable acts during Lent has no purpose. (False; it shows our concern for others.)
10. We are given palms during Lent to remind us to give alms. (False; the palms are a reminder of Jesus' entry into Jerusalem. The people waved palm branches and shouted, "Hosanna! Blessed is the one who comes in the name of the Lord—the King of Israel!")
11. Pretzels or hot-crossed buns are symbols of Lent because they resemble arms crossed in prayer. (True.)

Holy Week Symbols

Gathering   Ask volunteers to name and explain a symbol used during Holy Week services and celebrations.

Opening Prayer   Ask students to respond "Lord, have mercy on us" to each of the following petitions:

Leader: You went to Jerusalem to suffer and to enter into your glory. Bring your people to a fuller understanding of your love for us.

Leader: On the cross you forgave the repentant thief. Forgive us our sins.

Leader: You were nailed to the cross and pierced by the soldier's lance. By your wounds help us endure our sufferings.

Leader: You made of the cross a tree of strength; strengthen us to live our baptismal vows.

Leader: Let us pray as Christ taught us: (Together, pray the Lord's Prayer.)

Activity   **Introduction** This activity tests the students' knowledge of Holy Week. The students must provide the questions to the answers that are provided. To prepare for the activity, write the following headings on the board: Palm Sunday, Holy Thursday, Good Friday, and Holy Saturday. Make a copy of the handout, cut the answers apart, and attach each answer, type-side down, to the board in the order that they appear on the handout. Number the back of each answer with the appropriate score.

Directions Divide the group into teams of four or five. In front of the board, place as many chairs as there are groups. Have one member from each group come forward and sit in the chair assigned to his or her team. Explain that you will read the answer aloud and the students should answer in the form of a question. Only the students in the chairs in front of the board will be allowed to respond to the answer. The student representing team one chooses the first category. The student who first raises his or her hand guesses first. Stop reading as soon as a player raises his or her hand, even if you are in the middle of the answer. If the person provides the correct question, his or her team is awarded the appropriate points for that answer. If the person does not provide the correct question, finish reading the answer and wait for another student to raise his or her hand. Each student in the front chairs may make only one guess. If no one in the front chairs knows the correct question, open it up to the other members of the teams (reminding them that they need to be recognized before they respond). After each question, every group sends a different person to the front chairs. Remove the answers from the board as they are guessed. The new representative from the group who gave the last correct question chooses the next category. Continue until the board is cleared.

Closing Reflection   Allow the students time to reflect silently on what it would take to be more like Jesus. Encourage the students to attend Holy Week services and celebrations with their families.

Closing Prayer   Using the prepared Stations of the Cross books available in most parishes during the Lenten Season, have the group pray together the Stations of the Cross.

Liturgical Year Lesson

For additional activities see www.harcourtreligion.com

Holy Week Symbols

Score	Palm Sunday	Holy Thursday	Good Friday	Holy Saturday
25	A: The people waved these as Jesus entered Jerusalem.	A: This is the price Judas was paid for identifying Jesus.	A: Jesus' head was crowned with this.	A: Of water, ashes, or a crucifix, this is the item the priest blesses as a reminder of our initiation into the life of Christ.
	Q: What are palm branches?	Q: What is thirty pieces of silver?	Q: What is a crown of thorns?	Q: What is water?
50	A: Palms left over from Palm Sunday are burned. The ashes are used on this day.	A: This object was blessed by Jesus and became his body.	A: These were placed in Jesus' hands and feet to hang him on the cross.	A: At the very beginning of the Holy Saturday liturgy, this is lit.
	Q: What is Ash Wednesday?	Q: What is bread?	Q: What are nails?	Q: What is the Easter fire?
75	A: This was the animal that Jesus rode into Jerusalem.	A: This is the name of the cup used at Mass that holds the Blood of Christ.	A: This is the instrument of Jesus' death that we venerate during the Good Friday service.	A: During the service of light, this is lit from the Easter fire.
	Q: What is a donkey? (Also accept colt.)	Q: What is a chalice?	Q: What is a cross?	Q: What is the Easter candle? (Also accept Paschal candle.)
100	A: In addition to palms, these were spread on the road in front of Jesus.	A: The celebration of Eucharist on Holy Thursday reminds us of this.	A: These depictions show fourteen events from the last hours of Christ's life.	A: The five grains of incense inserted into the Easter candle represent these.
	Q: What are people's cloaks?	Q: What is the Lord's Supper? (Also accept the Last Supper.)	Q: What are stations of the cross?	Q: What are the five wounds of Christ?
250	A: This is the word that the people repeated over and over as Jesus entered Jerusalem. It means "Save us!"	A: When he washed these, Jesus showed us not only how to love but how to serve others.	A: This daily Catholic ritual is not celebrated on Good Friday.	A: These two Greek letters are often inscribed on the Easter candle.
	Q: What is hosanna?	Q: What are the apostles' feet?	Q: What is the Mass?	Q: What are the alpha and the omega?
500	A: We repeat the people's calls of "Hosanna!" each time we pray or sing this prayer at Mass.	A: This is the way the altar is left at the end of the Mass on Holy Thursday.	A: These letters appear on the top of most crucifixes and stand for the Latin words for "Jesus of Nazareth, King of the Jews."	A: Those who are being baptized are given these to put on to show their new life in Christ.
	Q: What is "Holy, Holy, Holy, Lord"?	Q: What is bare? (Also accept stripped.)	Q: What is INRI?	Q: What are white robes?

Easter Symbols

Gathering Discuss with the students their vision of what happens when a person dies. What happens to the body? What happens to the spirit? What does the Church profess about death and the afterlife? What objects do we use to help us remember someone's life?

Opening Prayer Listen to or sing, "Jesus Christ Is Risen Today." Have the students silently meditate on the following question: What stone must I roll away from the door of my heart for me to say, and mean, "Alleluia, he is risen!"?

Activity **Introduction** This activity will help the students better understand the Easter Season. Divide the group into three teams. Explain that each team will have three lifelines, or places they can go for help. They can ask a member of their group, ask for a consensus from their team, and ask that half of the possible answers be eliminated. Be sure that the students understand that when someone from their team uses a lifeline, it cannot be used by anyone else on their team. Points are never lost, but questions that are incorrectly answered are given no points. All teams continue with the activity regardless of incorrect answers. Ask for a volunteer to keep track of group scores, as well as what lifelines each group has used.

Directions Begin by asking a person on each team one of the hundred-point questions. After each of the teams has had a chance to answer, go on to the five-hundred-point questions. Continue in the same manner with the rest of the questions. Discuss the correct answers with the students as they are given. (Note that the answers marked with an asterisk are those that should remain if the student asks for two of the incorrect answers to be eliminated.) If a student guesses incorrectly, he or she gives up his spot to another team member.

Closing Reflection Discuss the students' experience of the activity. Encourage them to work to live a life that is a witness to the love that God has for his people.

Closing Prayer The Exsultet is an ancient prayer cantered by the presider at the Easter Vigil. Pray part of this prayer with the group by having the students repeat each line after you.

Exsultet

Rejoice, heavenly powers! Sing, choirs
   of angels!
Exult, all creation, around God's
   throne!
Jesus Christ, our King, is risen!
Sound the trumpet of salvation!

Rejoice, O earth, in shining splendor,
Radiant in the brightness of your King!
Christ has conquered! Glory fills you!
Darkness vanishes for ever!
For Christ has ransomed us with
   his blood

And paid for us the price of Adam's sin
To our eternal Father!

This is our Passover feast,
When Christ, the true Lamb, is slain,
whose blood consecrates the homes
   of all believers.

This is the night when Jesus Christ
broke the chains of death
and arose triumphant from the grave.

Night truly blessed when heaven is
   wedded to earth
And man is reconciled with God.

Liturgical Year Lesson

For additional activities see *www.harcourtreligion.com*

Easter Symbols

100-point questions

1. This Easter symbol is used at every Baptism.
   a. a rabbit
   b. a butterfly
   *c. the Easter candle
   *d. Easter lilies

2. This flower is most often associated with Easter.
   a. rose
   *b. tulip
   * c. lily
   d. petunia

3. Easter day celebrates this event.
   a. Jesus' triumphant entry into Jerusalem
   *b. Jesus' being raised from the dead
   * c. Jesus' dying on the cross
   d. the celebration of the Lord's Supper

500-point questions

4. When the women went to the tomb on Easter morning, this was rolled back.
   a. the lid of the coffin
   *b. the stone
   c. the red carpet
   *d. wrappings around the body

5. Because Jesus died on the cross for us, this animal is sometimes seen as an Easter symbol.
   a. bird
   *b. lamb
   c. donkey
   *d. calf

6. Easter eggs are associated with Easter because they symbolize this in many cultures.
   a. food
   *b. freshness
   c. the color yellow
   *d. new life

1,000-point questions

7. Easter candy reminds us that this is over.
   *a. our time of Lenten fasting
   b. winter
   c. dieting
   *d. sharing with others

8. Chicks are symbols of Easter because their breaking forth from their shells represents this.
   *a. Moses coming down from the mountain
   b. Noah on the ark
   *c. Jesus coming forth from the tomb
   d. bears coming forth from their caves

9. Jesus' tomb was made out of this material.
   *a. wood
   b. cloth
   c. metal
   *d. stone

2,500-point questions

10. This is the liturgical color for the Easter Season.
    *a. white
    *b. green
    c. purple
    d. red

11. The Easter candle is first lit at this liturgy.
    a. Holy Thursday
    b. Good Friday
    * c. Holy Saturday
    *d. Easter Sunday

12. Because it celebrates our salvation, this is the most important Christian feast day.
    *a. Christmas
    *b. Easter
    c. ascension
    d. Pentecost

5,000-point questions

13. The Easter candle symbolizes this.
    a. heat
    *b. new life
    * c. Jesus, Light of the World
    d. Mary, Mother of God

14. The women brought this to the tomb to anoint Jesus' body.
    a. holy water
    *b. oils
    c. palms
    *d. spices

15. The word *alleluia* means this.
    *a. God saves.
    b. So be it.
    * c. Praise God.
    d. Hosanna.

10,000-point questions

16. Holy Saturday is also called the Easter Vigil. The word *vigil* means this.
    a. original
    *b. keeping watch
    c. virgin
    *d. morning

17. This is God's answer to the promises of salvation history.
    a. Jonah's three days in the whale
    *b. the rainbow
    c. the four seasons
    *d. Jesus being raised from the dead

18. New clothes for Easter are a symbol of this.
    a. those who are poor and need our help
    b. new birth
    * c. a new season
    *d. the new robes worn by those who are baptized during the Easter Vigil

50,000-point questions

19. This prayer prayed at the Easter Vigil is an ancient song that proclaims the resurrection of Jesus.
    *a. Exsultet
    b. Lord's Prayer
    * c. Gloria
    d. litany

20. Jesus' suffering, dying, and resurrection is called this.
    *a. the passion
    *b. the Paschal mystery
    c. Easter Vigil
    d. Christmas

21. Jesus' death made up for the disobedience of the first humans. That is why Jesus is sometimes called this.
    *a. the new Adam
    b. the new Moses
    c. the new Creation
    *d. the new promise

Correct answers are as follows:
1. c   2. c   3. b   4. b   5. b   6. d
7. a   8. c   9. d   10. a   11. c
12. b   13. c   14. d   15. c   16. b
17. d   18. d   19. a   20. b   21. a

Pentecost Symbols

Gathering Discuss with the students the feelings of anticipation that people share when they are waiting for someone special to enter a room or hall. Discuss whether they think these were the feelings that the apostles were sharing while gathered in the upper room.

Opening Prayer Pray together the Prayer to the Holy Spirit by reciting one line at a time and having the students repeat after you.

Prayer to the Holy Spirit

Come, Holy Spirit, fill the hearts of your faithful,
And kindle in them the fire of your love.
Send forth your Spirit and they shall be created.
And you will renew the face of the earth.

Lord, by the light of the Holy Spirit you have taught the hearts of your faithful.
In the same Spirit
help us relish what is right
and always rejoice in your consolation.

We ask this through Christ our Lord.
Amen.

Activity **Introduction** Read the entire story of Pentecost in *Acts 2:1–12.* Discuss the changes that happened to the apostles as a result of the Holy Spirit's power within them. The aim of this activity is to review and learn more about Pentecost. Before the session, make one copy of the handout for every two people in the group. Create one set of cards for every pair by cutting apart each copy.

Directions Instruct the students to pair off and place their set of cards, type-side down, between them. Explain to the students that each card contains information about a thing that has something to do with Pentecost. The name of the thing is noted at the bottom of the card. One person in the pair is to begin by picking the top card and announcing "I am a thing." He or she then reads the first sentence after the introductory statement. The second person has ten seconds to guess what the thing might be. If the guess is correct, he or she is awarded four points. If the guess is incorrect, or if the person has no guess, the person reading the statements moves on to the next statement. Each statement read lessens by one the points awarded. Once the answer is correctly guessed, the roles change and the second person reads clues to the first person. After the correct guess has been made, invite the students to read any remaining clues.

Closing Reflection Through the power of the Holy Spirit, the apostles found the courage to go into the streets and tell others about Jesus Christ. Ask the Holy Spirit in prayer to give you strength to be a witness for Christ in your words and actions.

Closing Prayer Discuss how the Holy Spirit continues to work in our Church today. One of the ways to get in touch with the Holy Spirit is to sing or recite a mantra over and over to invite the Holy Spirit to come into our lives. Help the students experience this by singing or listening to the song "Veni Sancte Spiritus" (*Gather [Comprehensive],* GIA Publications, Inc.)

For additional activities see www.harcourtreligion.com

Pentecost Symbols

I am a thing.
I am a number.
I am the number of days that passed between
    Jesus' resurrection and Pentecost.
I am more than a month, but less than
    two months.
I am five times ten.
I am the number fifty.

I am a thing.
I am a color.
I am seen at liturgies honoring the Holy Spirit or
    martyrs.
Sometimes people are said to see me when they
    are angry.
There is a sea named after me.
I am the color red.

I am a thing.
You can hear me but not see me.
You can feel me.
I sometimes symbolize the presence of the
    Holy Spirit.
I can be gentle or strong.
I am the wind.

I am a thing.
I occurred ten days before the Holy Spirit came.
I occurred forty days after the resurrection.
On this day Jesus returned to his Father in
    heaven.
I am a holy day.
I am the Ascension.

I am a thing.
I sometimes symbolize the presence of the
    Holy Spirit.
I am hot.
I am shaped like a tongue.
I am orange and red.
I am fire.

I am a thing.
I am a word that means "change of heart."
I am a word that means "turning around."
Saint Paul knew all about me.
This happened to many people who heard
    about Jesus.
I am conversion.

I am a thing.
I am a language.
The apostles would have used me to speak
    to each other.
Jesus knew and used me.
Some people don't understand me.
I am the Aramaic language.

I am a thing.
I am something everyone wants to hear.
The apostles spread me all over the known world.
The New Testament is sometimes called this.
I tell others of Jesus' words and works.
I am the good news. (Accept gospel also.)

I am a thing.
I am white or gray.
I lifted Jesus into heaven to return to his father.
During the day, I led Moses and the Israelites in
    the desert.
I am fluffy.
I am a cloud.

I am a thing.
I started on Pentecost.
I am present in all parts of the world.
I am guided by the power of the Holy Spirit.
My leader on earth is the pope.
I am the Church.